RENZO PIANO BUILDING WORKSHOP

Phaidon Press Limited

140 Kensington Church Street

London W8 4BN

First published 1993

© 1993 Phaidon Press Limited

ISBN 0 7148 2809 2

A CIP catalogue record for this book is
available from the British Library

Frontispiece illustration: San Nicola
Stadium, Bari, Italy

Printed in Hong Kong

RENZO PIANO BUILDING WORKSHOP

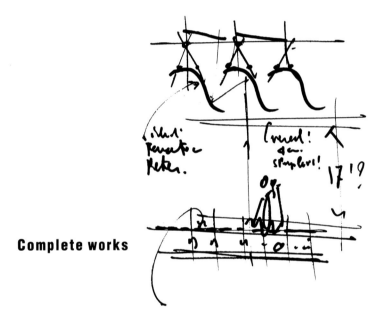

Complete works **Volume one**

Peter Buchanan

Contents

6

Preface

As the name suggests, the Renzo Piano Building Workshop is no conventional architectural practice. It is committed to hands-on experiment and engagement with all aspects of the making of architecture, the intensity of this immersion in process being essential to the qualities sought in the built end-product. This process is highly collaborative. The Building Workshop is dominated by Renzo Piano, so that the way it operates and the resultant architecture are very much the product of his predilections and personality. Yet it is also utterly dependent on the contributions of exceptionally talented in-house collaborators and outside consultants. Without their contributions, the works would be literally inconceivable – so much so that in retrospect it might be unclear who contributed what to a design that often has the clear imprint of the collaborators as well as Piano himself.

Particularly important for their contribution to all the work shown here is the contribution of the core team that first gathered around Piano during the construction (with Richard Rogers) of the Pompidou Centre. These are Shunji Ishida, now in the Genoa workshop, Noriaki Okabe and Bernard Plattner who ran the Paris workshop together during the period to which this volume is dedicated, and two engineers from Ove Arup & Partners, London – the late Peter Rice, the brilliant structural engineer, and Tom Barker, the services engineer. Also important as engineer of some of the early works is Flavio Marano, who now manages the Genoa workshop. Collaborators who later became and continue to be important are Paul Vincent (now in charge of several schemes in the Paris office), Mark Carroll, R Venanzio Truffelli, Giorgio Bianchi, Giorgio Grandi, Maurizio Varratta and Donald L Hart. More recent collaborators who are becoming increasingly important include Emanuela Baglietto, Antoine Chaaya, Loïc Couton, Olaf de Nooyer, Kenny Fraser, Maìre Henry, Akira Ikegami, Tetsuya Kimura, Claudio Manfreddo, Maria Salerno, Ronnie Self, Taichi Tomuro and Hiroshi Yamaguchi. Since 1985, a special role has been played by Alain Vincent as administrative co-ordinator and, more recently, by Alberto Giordano as team and general co-ordinator.

When the Renzo Piano Building Workshop adopted this name in 1981, Piano had already been a principal in three previous practices: Studio Piano (1964–70), Piano & Rogers (1971–78) and Piano & Rice Associates (1978–81). From all of these he learnt crucial lessons that are now consolidated in the work of the Building Workshop. This volume, and those succeeding it, are dedicated to the architecture of the Building Workshop. But to better understand this architecture, this first volume also shows key works from the earlier practices and explains how current work evolved from them. Also described are the early formative influences on Piano. Before this, though, an introductory essay discusses the exceptional timeliness and relevance of the work.

By any standards the Renzo Piano Building Workshop is a very successful enterprise. It has bases in three cities: Genoa (where it also has a satellite, the laboratory–workshop outside the city at Vesima), Paris and Osaka. Current work is similarly far flung with ongoing projects in various parts of Italy, France, Germany, Switzerland, the Netherlands, the USA, Japan and even the Pacific island of New Caledonia. Projects under construction include those as huge and complex as the 1.7 kilometre-long, state-of-the-art Kansai International Airport Terminal in Japan (p20) and the conversion of that historic monument and prime icon of Modernism, the 0.5 kilometre-long Fiat Lingotto Factory in Turin, into a multi-functional trade and cultural centre that also includes a hotel, science faculty and shopping centre. Both these commissions were won in international competitions. More recent international competitions won by the Building Workshop include those for a cultural centre near Nouméa, New Caledonia, and for a huge tract between the Potsdamerplatz in what was East Berlin and the National Library in what was West Berlin.

But the reasons for admiring and paying attention to the architecture of Renzo Piano

A Natural Architecture
Time and place, technology and nature in the work of the Renzo Piano Building Workshop

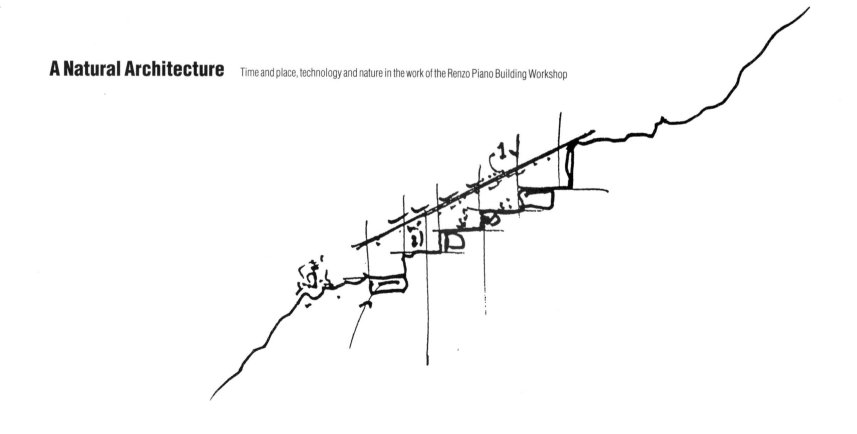

1

Previous page Vesima Laboratory–workshop, 1990–91: the building shows the interweaving of inside and outside, architecture and site, and technology with tradition and nature that characterises the work of the Renzo Piano Building Workshop.
1 Fiat Lingotto Factory, Turin: currently being converted into a multi-functional cultural and trade centre.
2, 3 J M Tjibaru Cultural Centre, Nouméa, New Caledonia, 1991: model of the outer 'case' that mediates between the building and its heavily wooded site, **2**, and section with 'case' to the left, **3**.

and the Building Workshop far transcend those for taking an interest in other successful architectural practices. Piano remains aloof from the pure pursuit of that unholy trinity of fashion, fame and fortune that has undone so many of today's star architects whose work is, as a result, shallow and of only short-term significance. The Building Workshop offers much more than the predictable professionalism that large corporate practices, at best, provide. It has not lapsed, like so many successful architects faced with the pressures of productivity and market image, into any safe formula or readily recognisable style, which inevitably inhibits any full response to programme and place. Instead, the work remains extraordinarily diverse, a product of both unflagging inventiveness and a precision of response to the particulars of each project. The Kansai International Airport Terminal, with its steel structure and stainless steel cladding, is very different to the Padre Pio Pilgrimage Church for San Giovanni Rotondo, Foggia, in southern Italy, which is now under design development, with huge arches of local stone and timber props supporting a copper-clad timber roof. And very different from these large projects, as well as from each other, are

the terracotta-clad and, in townscape terms, pivotal, tower extension of the Institute for Research and Co-ordination of Acoustics and Music (IRCAM) in Paris (p202) and the unassertive transparency of the laboratory–workshop that clings close to its steep slope at Vesima, outside Genoa.

Within the diversity suggested by the above examples, and seen in the projects shown in this and future volumes, there are also striking and perhaps even more significant consistencies. Not least of these is the thoroughness with which these designs are shaped by the place, programme and times. These alone account for many of the differences between not just the Kansai terminal in Japan and the Padre Pio church, the IRCAM Extension and the Vesima Laboratory–workshop but also between the Pompidou Centre in Paris (p52) and the Menil Collection in Houston, USA (p140), both of which serve the study of artworks. What these differences, and the comparison of the Menil and the Pompidou, show is how much Piano's architecture with the Building Workshop, as opposed to that with the previous practices, is shaped not just by function and technology but also by the place and its traditions, and by an urge to settle into and integrate with the sur-

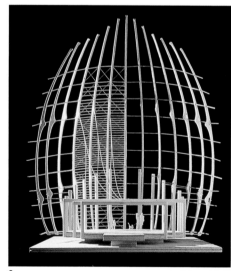

2

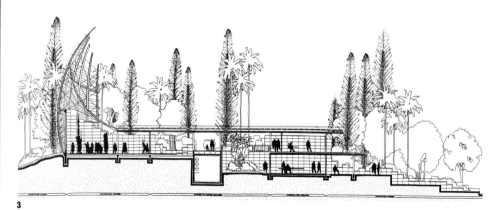

3

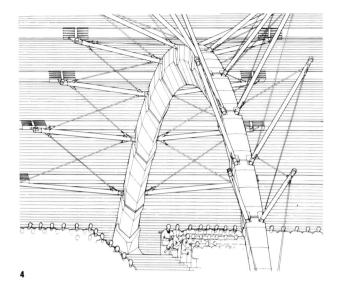

4 Padre Pio Pilgrimage Church, San Giovanni Rotondo, Foggia, 1991: one of the huge stone arches.

5 IRCAM Extension, Paris, 1987–90: its cladding of terracotta units in metal frames links it both to the adjacent brick buildings and to the Pompidou Centre.

6 The Vesima Laboratory–workshop, 1990–91: it clings to its steep slope above the sea.

roundings and nature. Combined with other constant intentions, such as finding new potentials in materials and pushing forward the frontiers of technology as well as of being involved in the very physical nature of proto-typing and construction, these show an urge to engage and participate with the world and in our times as fully as possible. It is this quality, perhaps more than anything else, that singles out and is the significance of the work of Building Workshop, and which also makes it so different to that of most other architects. The latter too often tend to be trapped in what Piano sometimes refers to as 'the golden cage of style' and in fairly set and superficial ways of work-ing 'efficiently and economically', all of which have culminated in the simultaneous fragmentation and homogenisation of the built environment and the resultant dessication of experience.

There are other consistent elements in the architecture of the Building Workshop that we will discuss as we proceed. But another striking and significant consistency is people's response to it. Many who are familiar with the work feel sure, even if they are unable to explain fully why, there is something particularly right and relevant about this architecture for our times, a certainty that goes beyond being impressed by the Building Workshop's success.

To understand what these people intuitively respond to and trust, reading or listening to the pronouncements of Piano himself helps only a little. As is regularly remarked upon, he is an excellent communicator – as he needs to be. Without such a skill it would be difficult to lead the Building Workshop with its bases in three countries, consultants in others and far-flung clients and building sites. Piano conveys in a clear and inspiring way not just ideas, but often subtle feelings as well, to a wide variety of colleagues and consultants, clients and con-tractors. Adept at handling the media, in inter-views he speaks both fascinatingly and very quotably about his architecture, the intentions behind it, his working methods and so on. Yet ultimately, and the more you listen the more this is apparent (though it is also true of most architects), all that he says never adds up to a fully articulated and completely coherent posi-tion on, or approach to, architecture. Or, per-haps more to the point, you never feel that he has quite touched on the core impulses that explain and lie behind his work. And sooner or later he usually lapses, on auto-pilot almost, into some oft-repeated litany: architecture

11

5

6

1 IBM Travelling Pavilion, 1982–84: Renzo Piano and Shunji Ishida shaping components at full size in the workshop.
2 Vesima Laboratory–workshop, 1990–91: night view emphasises the extreme transparency of the building and shows how it steps with the terraced hillside.

is a contaminated art on which everything impinges; it is not about drawing but about the making of things; it requires a balance between science and craft, head and hand, experiment and memory; it is not necessary for technology to be incompatible with nature or history. In similar vein he also iterates the inspiration of modernity, of transparency and lightness … always lightness, a quality with which Piano seems almost obsessed.

The general import of this litany and the visions it conjures are laudable and often poetic. What is more (and with architects this should never be taken for granted), what Piano advocates is actually exemplified in the architecture of the Building Workshop. But this does nothing to curb the feeling that there must be much more behind the architecture than is told in these slogans and aphorisms, some larger vision that connects, guides and inspires the ideas and qualities he adumbrates. And of course there is: the work is too complex and complete and, behind the diversity, too consistent for there not to be. But the impulses that underlie Piano's work come not from a formulated intellectual position, nor even one he seems fully conscious of. Indeed Piano displays a considerable distrust of the intellect, particu-

larly of its quickly deduced and exclusive certainties. Instead he is guided by instinct and intuition, which tend to be as fluid as the intellect can be fixed, and by an acutely honed sensibility that discerns not just nuances of material and form but also the forces at work in complex situations. These, rather than any theoretical position or specialist knowledge, about technology for instance, are his greatest strengths as an architect.

The lack of a fully formulated position might be expected to lead to mistrust and misunderstandings, in that the work might be seen as capricious and even contradictory in its extraordinary heterogeneity. Instead, most people respond instinctively to it. They react not just to its mixture of inventiveness, refinement and so on, but perhaps also by subconsciously recognising that instinct can range free and wide to be in touch with more complex and shifting realities than can be accommodated by any intellectual position that is almost axiomatically rigid and narrow. Guided by similar instincts and intuition, and helped by familiarity with the buildings and observation of Piano at work, this essay is an attempt to elucidate the largely unconscious vision that seems to underpin Piano's work and

2

3   **4**

Examples of 'pieces' of both exquisite elegance and striking biomorphic form.

3 'Gerberettes' are conspicuous on the corner of the Pompidou Centre, Paris, 1971–78, by Piano & Rogers.

4 The light-diffusing 'leaves' and trusses that extend as a colonnade around the Menil Collection gallery, Houston, USA, 1981–86.

5 Shapely laminated wood and cast aluminium struts and crystalline polycarbonate pyramids that formed the exoskeletal structure of the IBM Travelling Pavilion, 1982–84.

6 Dinosaur skeleton-like main truss and props of the Kansai International Airport Terminal, Osaka, Japan, 1988–.

so shed light on why to many it seems so right and relevant. Starting on the safe ground of drawing out threads common to all the buildings, this investigation becomes progressively more speculative. If sometimes the interpretation seems exaggerated or fanciful, even ridiculously idealised, it should at least offer insight from the educative and ennobling perspective of what might be only a benevolent myth. After all, we are probably best motivated to come to terms with and learn from something when it is seen from the most inspiring perspective.

From any overview of the output of the Building Workshop, and even more so if the projects of the Piano-led practices that preceded it are considered too, the most immediate and striking impression is of just how various are its works, not only in scale, location and programme but in their forms, materials and construction methods too. The architecture conforms to no distinctive personal idiom: there is no equivalent of the market image that most architects feel obliged to adopt to ensure fame and fortune; design is free to respond in all sorts of ways to whatever problems and potentials present themselves. Of the obvious common themes running through the works, the best known because of

Piano's continuing association with the Pompidou Centre, is the use of advanced technology. And yet, unlike so-called High-Tech with which Piano (thanks to the Pompidou Centre) is still sometimes mistakenly associated, the buildings freely mix technologies and materials of very different levels of sophistication. In some, such as the recent laboratory–workshop at Vesima outside Genoa, which the Building Workshop shares with UNESCO (published in volume two), those high-technology elements that there are make far less of an impression than the wood and pink stucco. What is striking here, as in all other works by the Building Workshop, is not just the mix of technologies and materials but also the uncontrived and authoritative way in which the most advanced of these are brought together with the most prosaic.

Piano and the Building Workshop are concerned not just with technology, but with all aspects of construction and craftsmanship. These concerns generally come together in most intense focus in the design and shaping of components and junctions. Often of exquisite elegance, these 'pieces' as Piano calls them, such as the 'gerberettes' of the Pompidou and the light-diffusing 'leaf' and truss of the Menil

13

5

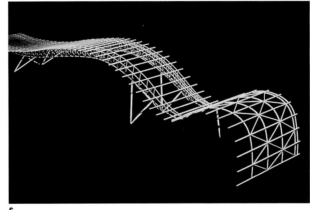

6

roof, are frequently of striking biomorphic form. The laminated wood and cast aluminium struts of the IBM (p110) and Ladybird travelling pavilions (p132), and the dinosaur skeleton-like trusses of Kansai are further examples. All have the sensuous shape and suggestion of tactility (even if thwarted by the components being too big and out of reach) that are further hallmarks of the Building Workshop's architecture. And these components and most of the resultant buildings have a distinctive poise and sense of lightness that is very important to Piano. This quality is obvious in the early experiments of Studio Piano and can be seen in the way the 'leaves' of the Menil seem to float in the light that floods down between them. But it is probably most explicitly seen at the San Nicola Stadium in Bari (p178). Here the huge concrete upper tier of seating is not supported by the usual clutter of muscular structure, but hovers over deeply recessed columns, while the double curve of the flanges of the concrete beams that make up its underbelly seems to hang as lightly and softly as pleated fabric. This lightness is reinforced by the extraordinary sense of openness, or transparency, that the stadium achieves with its views in, through, and out, offered by the gap

14

1 San Nicola Stadium, Bari, 1987–90: the stadium exemplifies the constant quest for lightness in the way the heavy concrete upper tier seems to float over the recessed columns, the underneath of its beams seeming to hang like soft fabric.

2 The Menil Collection gallery, Houston, USA, 1981–86: section.

3, 4 Vesima Laboratory–workshop, 1990–91: section, **3**, and axonometric, **4**, show how it nestles into its site, inviting plants and ever-changing light inside, so that a sense of being at one with nature pervades the building.

1

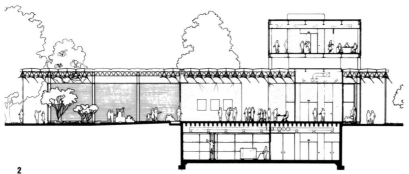

2

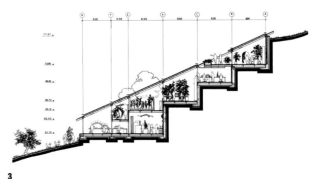

3

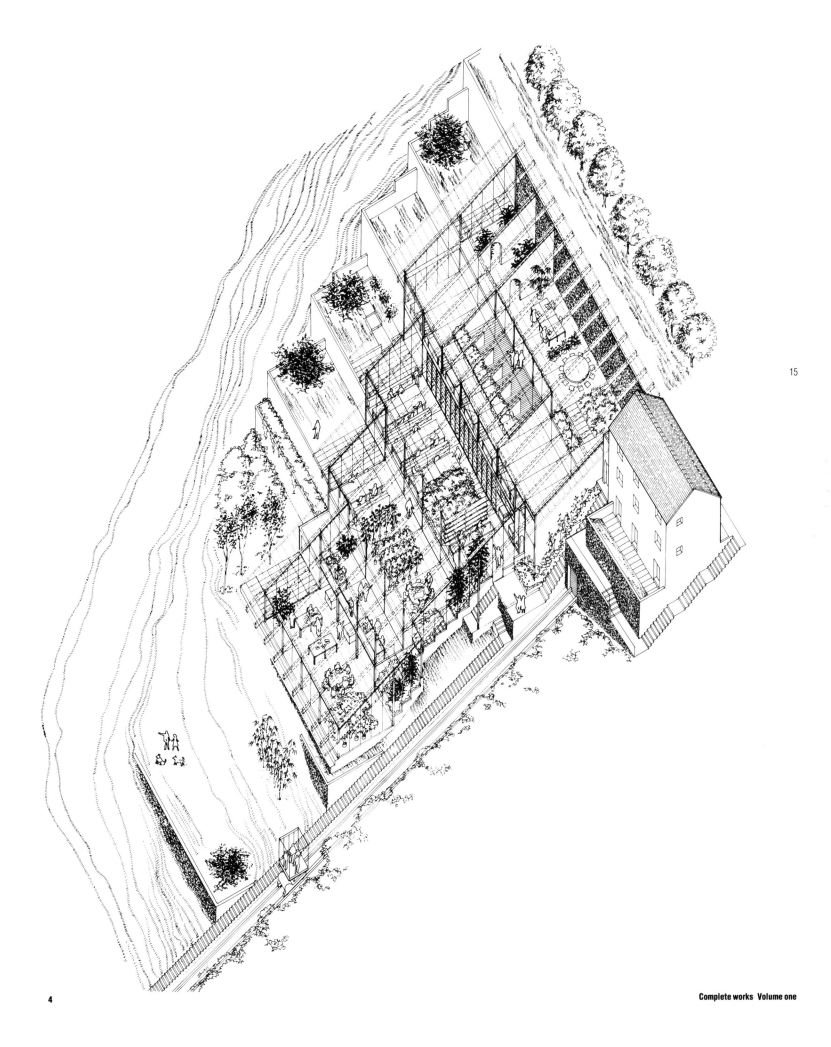

1

1 The Menil Collection gallery, Houston, USA, 1981–86: the museum is recognisable from its characteristic piece only, the composite of ferro-cement leaf and ductile-iron truss.

2–4 The experience of entry is typically emphasised by prolonging the approach through landscaping. At the Menil, **2**, the entrance is folded back into the building; at the Rue de Meaux Housing, Paris, 1987–91, **3**, entrances to the apartments are grouped around the central garden away from the street; at the Schlumberger Renovation, Paris, 1981–84, **4**, the approach is through a garden and by a bridge to each block.

between upper and lower tiers, and those between the banks of the upper tier.

The biomorphic shapes and openness to the surrounding landscape seen in the above example, reinforce another consistent trait of the architecture of the Renzo Piano Building Workshop: wherever possible it establishes an intimate relationship with nature, settling itself into natural or landscaped surroundings and inviting inside plants and ever-changing natural light as pervasive and potent presences. Again, Vesima illustrates these themes, as clearly as, say, the Menil Collection. But the buildings also strive for a more profound relationship with nature as they or, more usually, some of their components emulate the forms, and close fit of form to function, found in nature. The biomorphic light-diffusing 'leaves' and trusses of the Menil exemplify this – and also another trait of the Building Workshop's architecture. Leaf and truss together constitute the characteristic 'piece' of the Menil. The architecture of the Building Workshop consists, at least in part, of assemblies of tailor-made pieces, the identities of which are as intrinsic to that of the building as is that of a leaf to a tree, the buildings being similarly recognisable from their pieces alone.

The presence of the piece is usually clear in section or elevation but not in plan, and so too Piano's architecture, as exemplified again by Menil and Vesima, is usually far more distinctive in section than in plan.

These general traits, however, are the basis of the criticism that some of the intellectually dogmatic make of the Renzo Piano Building Workshop's architecture. The tendency to embed buildings in nature combined with Piano's constant quest for lightness (the antithesis of gravitas) lead to it being dismissed as intrinsically anti-urban – despite evidence to the contrary now offered by the two Paris buildings, the IRCAM Extension and the Rue de Meaux Housing (p214). The striking refinement of the pieces and their pervasive presence leads to the charge that the Building Workshop is the mere crafter of components. The predominance of the section over plan and facade is taken as further proof that this is not real architecture, for it lacks the resonances of conventional (and for these critics culturally and psychologically crucial) typologies and elements of architecture. There are sometimes no rooms or developed spatial sequences, nor walls, windows and heavily framed entrances.

In fact, in Piano's buildings the entrance is

3

2

4

5, 6 The Vesima Laboratory–workshop, 1990–91: the building has no conventional windows, only walls and a roof of glass, but the sense of being at one with the ever-changing moods of nature is as resonant as any framed view.

often given experiential emphasis, but this is done by prolonging it as a route flanked by planting that might even accompany one into the building. Yet, if attention is thereby drawn to the process of entrance, it is usually to stress continuities rather than play up discontinuities. The most extreme of such entrances are those by funicular railway to the Vesima Laboratory–workshop and the garden approach to the Schlumberger facilities in Paris (p90). But some equivalent is found at the Menil Collection where the entrance is folded into the building between shrubs, and at the Rue de Meaux Housing in Paris, where all entrances are off the central garden. The Building Workshop's architecture lacks nothing in the way of psychological and cultural resonances, but rather pursues different ones through different means than do buildings by other architects. Vesima may lack windows and those of the Menil that are not glazed screens might be awkward, but the sense both top-lit buildings offer of being at one with the moods of nature is as resonant as any framed view.

What is different about the architecture of the Renzo Piano Building Workshop arises not from any wilful quest for originality, but from a sense that we are living in and must be true to changing times. Hence, if some of the buildings seem unurban, it is probably because Piano senses that in some ways we are moving into post-urban times in which, thanks to electronics, the centre is everywhere. As at Vesima, we can now settle into nature and yet be instantly in touch with any part of the globe.

After Modernism's attempt to recreate the world from scratch, we have rediscovered in recent decades that roots in the past are vital to any unalienated sense of ourselves. But the sense of being part of our times remains equally important if one is to feel fully alive. Piano's strategy for being in touch with and part of his times is to trust his instinct and simply seek the design solution that seems most natural and least contrived, least constrained by architectural dogmas of any sort, and least cluttered by bogus 'creativity'. His inventiveness pursues no flights of fantasy, no fashionable or silly scenarios. Instead, his architecture is at the service of mankind and rooted in the everyday. The remarkable heterogeneity of the work results from his quest to be responsive not just to programme, but to both the specifics and tradition of the place and the potential of the latest technology. Such responsiveness and the readiness to use

17

5

6

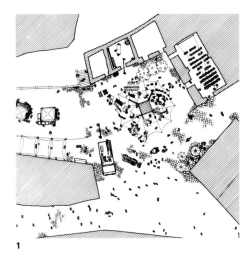

1

Different forms of participation, in its more
conventionally understood sense in architecture.
1, 2 UNESCO Neighbourhood Workshop in
Otranto, 1979: it provided a temporary multi-
purpose focus for the community, mobilising
them to regenerate their historic town.

any sort of material, again distinguishes Piano
from practitioners of doctrinaire High-Tech.

Certainly the Building Workshop experiments with, and exploits, leading-edge technology so that many of its buildings could not
have been conceived of, let alone realised, only
a short time previously. But Piano seeks to
combine, in the most uncontrived manner,
roots in tradition with the maximisation of
present potential – just as a violinist would
insist on using both his ancient Stradivarius
and the latest digital recording technology. To
build only with the materials and methods of
the past, or only with High-Tech ones, are
equally bizarre options. What matters is to
seek that ever-shifting and everywhere-differ-
ent point of balance where the union of the
local and traditional with the new and
imported seems obvious and unaffected.

Behind this attempt to do what is 'normal',
'natural' and uncontrived is a desire to be open
to and in touch with the world, to participate
in the way things are and so in the shaping of
the world as it changes and develops. This participation takes many forms. In architecture,
participation usually refers to the involvement
of users and community in determining design
goals and guiding design outcomes, or even the

empowering of people to perform these tasks
and the actual building or rebuilding work
themselves. These were processes that Piano &
Rice Associates raised to unprecedented levels
of sophistication with the Neighbourhood
Workshop developed for UNESCO and used at
Otranto (p68) and elsewhere. Another form of
participation is achieved by creating buildings
that users can adapt and reshape to their
specific needs. Piano & Rogers' Free-plan
Houses at Cusago (p51) and Piano & Rice's Il
Rigo Adaptable Housing at Corciano (1978)
exemplify this approach, as does the Pompidou
Centre, particularly in its original conception
with removable floors. But as a central
inspiration for Piano's architecture, the notion
of participation is here meant more generally,
though from the specific exercises mentioned
Piano learnt one of the keys to it: the art of
listening. Through attentive listening, his
architecture tries to grow out of, accommodate
itself to, or crystallise complex situations
rather than be a brutal and reductive impo-
sition of will or personal design idiom. To
pursue this ideal, the design process of the
Building Workshop is itself highly participatory, with clients, consultants, craftsmen and
subcontractors all contributing throughout the

2

process. The Menil, for instance, was shaped almost as much by the client and the consulting structural and services engineers as by Piano and his architects.

Participation, as it seems to lie at the heart of Piano's work, is not just with users and colleagues, but with the world at large, its places and communities, its history and traditions, and even with nature itself. To participate with the world, then, the Building Workshop's architecture does not impose upon a place, but rather, responds to and settles into it, adopting some local features and intensifying others by complement or contrast. Part of the quest for lightness and transparency is to avoid seeming to impose too much. To participate in history means not only responding to the past and carrying forward some of its traditions, but also living in the present by helping the future to be born. So, the Building Workshop does not just use the latest technology available, but also pushes forward the leading edge of that technology. And to participate with nature means not only to enjoy its presence, but to emulate it in one's own creations.

For architecture or technology to emulate nature neither necessitates nor excludes using natural materials and vernacular, or biomor-

phic, forms. But as science unravels nature's secrets, it is the leading edge of technology, which some may mistake for its most artificial and unnatural pole, that is most likely faithfully to approximate nature, especially in artefacts expressly created for some high-performance application. This artefact or component may have biomorphic form, not because it is styled that way, but because it happens to offer the economy, efficiency and exact fit for purpose found in organic creation. Hence the main structure of Kansai International Airport Terminal emulates nature not so much because it resembles a dinosaur skeleton, but because its forms simultaneously and economically span a large distance, are capable of resisting seismic stresses and follow the laminar flow of air, entrained without ducts. (The way in which Kansai exemplifies the ideal of combining the efficiency of a machine and the integrity of an organism, is illustrated in greater detail on the following pages.) And the roof canopy of the Menil, with its ossiform trusses and shapely leaves, also arose from the simultaneous solution of several issues: structural efficiency and method of manufacture; exclusion of direct sunlight and trapping a stabilising pocket of warm air. (*Continued on p26.*)

19

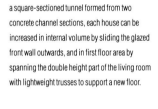

3 Free-plan Houses, Cusago, 1972–74: each home is partitioned according to the needs and taste of its owner.
4, 5 Il Rigo Housing, Corciano, 1978: occupying a square-sectioned tunnel formed from two concrete channel sections, each house can be increased in internal volume by sliding the glazed front wall outwards, and in first floor area by spanning the double height part of the living room with lightweight trusses to support a new floor.

4

5

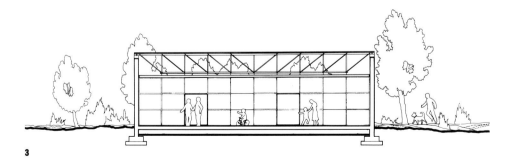

3

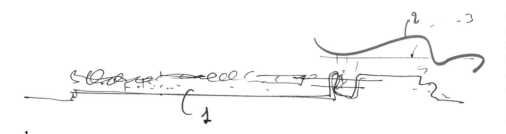

1

20 **Kansai International Airport Terminal** Osaka, Japan
Building Workshop, France, Italy, Japan 1988–

1 Piano's sectional sketch shows how the
asymmetrical curves of the terminal roof seem to
gather passengers arriving on the tree-planted
landside and visually propel them to the planes
on the airside.
2 Diagram showing how the curves of the
cross section are derived from the arcs of circles
of different radii.

Opposite page Main drawing is an exploded
perspective of some elements of the international
departures hall. Inset are computer images
studying the complex curves of the roof.

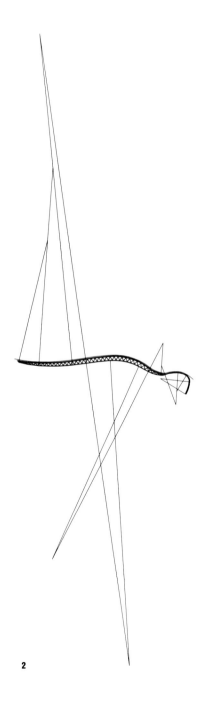

2

A competition-winning design now taking shape with startling rapidity on an artificial island offshore of Osaka, the Kansai International Airport Terminal clearly demonstrates a number of the ways alluded to in the introductory essay in which architecture can emulate and seek harmony with nature. The building is significant in other ways too. The last design for which Peter Rice was entirely responsible for the structure, it is a fitting climax to his collaboration with the Building Workshop, in particular with Noriaki Okabe and Renzo Piano, as well as with their long-time collaborator, Tom Barker, the services engineer from Ove Arup & Partners. At 1.7 kilometres in length, it is far and away the largest of their joint works, and probably the most thoroughly innovative too. It will also be a building that climaxes certain design ideals as thoroughly as did the Pompidou Centre in its time. It is certain too to be the building of its decade.

The Pompidou was the ultimate building-as-machine/building-as-kit-of-parts executed in a gung-ho, let-it-all-hang-out manner that is somewhat indeterminate in its seeming incompleteness. In contrast the perfectly symmetrical, smoothly curved and integrated terminal, with its obviously complete and finite form, is the ultimate machine-organism, culminating the Building Workshop's quest for a technology that emulates nature, a quest that extends back at least as far as Viollet-le-Duc. What makes Kansai a machine is how directly it is shaped by the circulatory flows of passengers and air. The curves aid these by unambiguously orienting passengers wherever they are and by entraining ventilation air without the need for enclosed ducts. But anatomical explicitness, the close fit of form to function, and these same curves and the finiteness of form they confer, make Kansai seem like a gigantic organism.

Metaphors the building conjures are both mechanical and organic too: hence it is both a glider and a dune-like form that with the surrounding trees 'naturalises' the tabula rasa of artificial land, lending it some of the identity of a natural island. With an archetypal island, the main town is around the harbour, the bay of which is a major topographical feature of the island. Here, the terminal's extended wings and curves embrace and take possession of the island as well as embed themselves in the trees so that together they suggest some favoured natural feature to which planes will come and go as naturally as do boats to an island harbour.

The basic organisation of the terminal came from closely following the brief (by the consultants Aéroports de Paris) and from a critical review of other recent terminals. For instance, non-directional structural modules such as used at Foster Associates' Stansted Airport, near London, were rejected as they confuse orientation by offering identical views in all four directions. The satellite system used at Stansted was also rejected, although shuttles are used to move passengers along the extended wings, which reach out from both sides of the main terminal building, and from which the planes are boarded. Also unlike Stansted, passenger routes for international departures and arrivals, and for domestic flights, are all to be found on different levels once passengers have passed through a tall tree-filled hall, called the 'canyon', in which they can orient themselves and change levels.

The interweaving of architecture and nature, as represented by the trees inside and outside the 'canyon', that is so typical of the Building Workshop was more developed in the competition design. In this, trees filled another long open 'canyon' between the two parts of what were double-sided wings. The structure at this stage, like the roofs, was a series of separate bowed elements. Neither architect nor engineer was happy with the solution. But to devise a

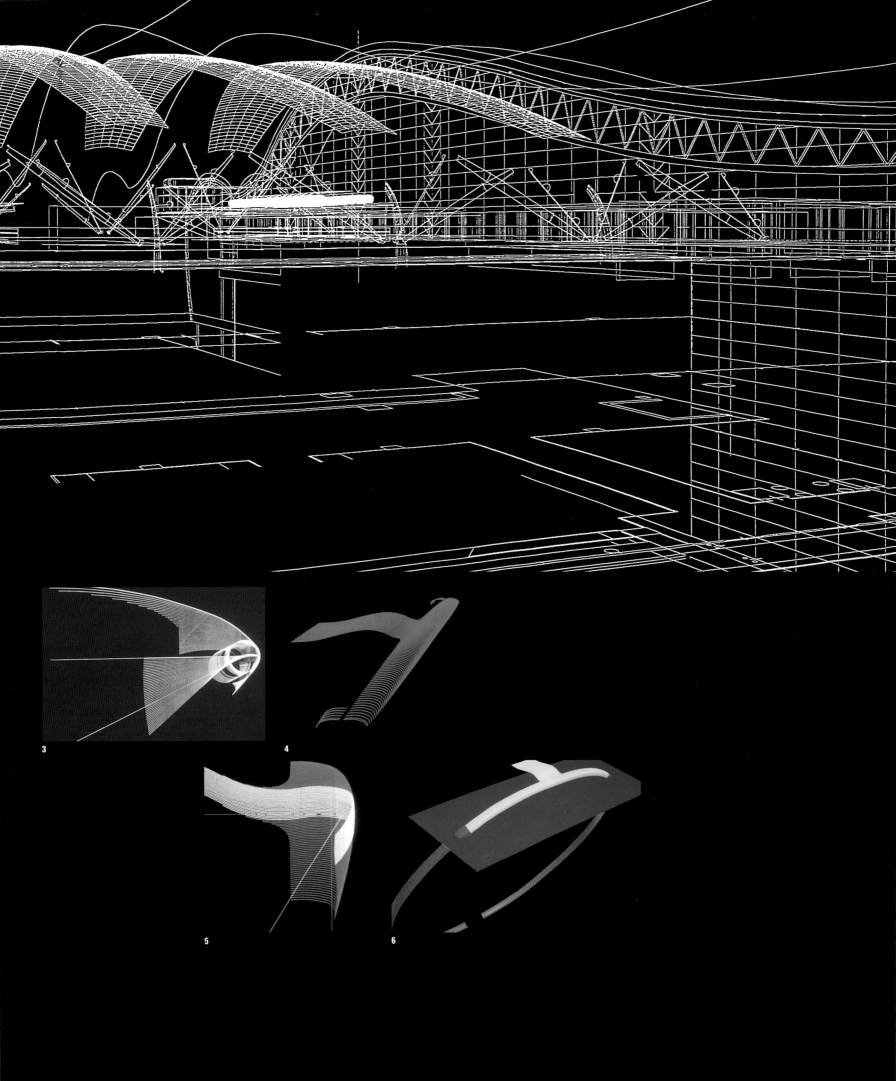

3

4

5

6

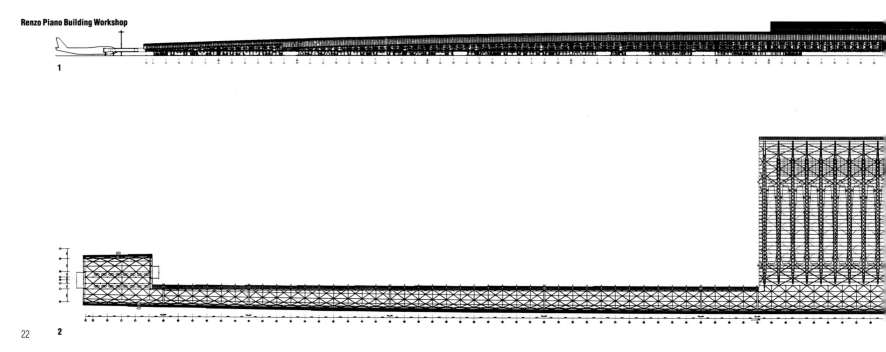

1

2

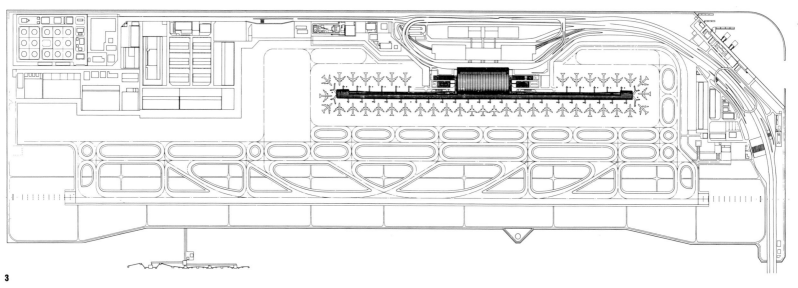

3

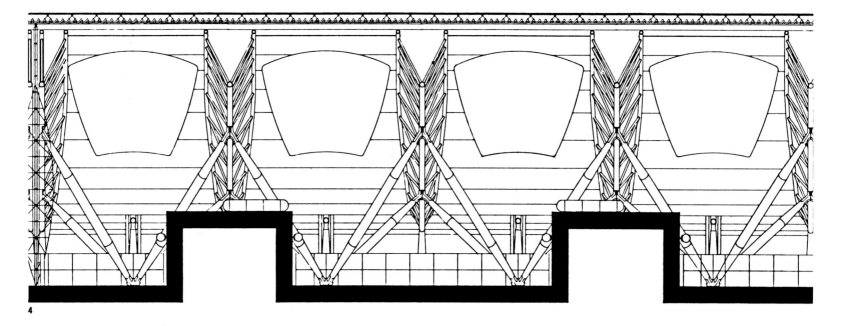

4

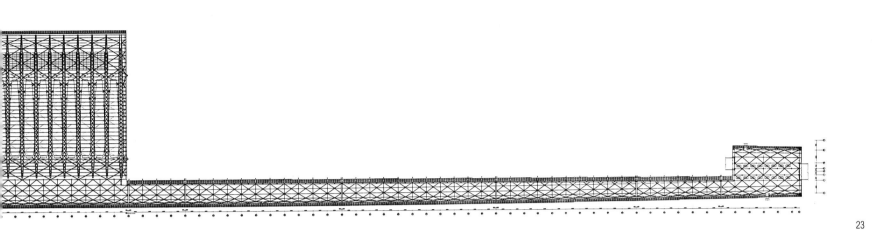

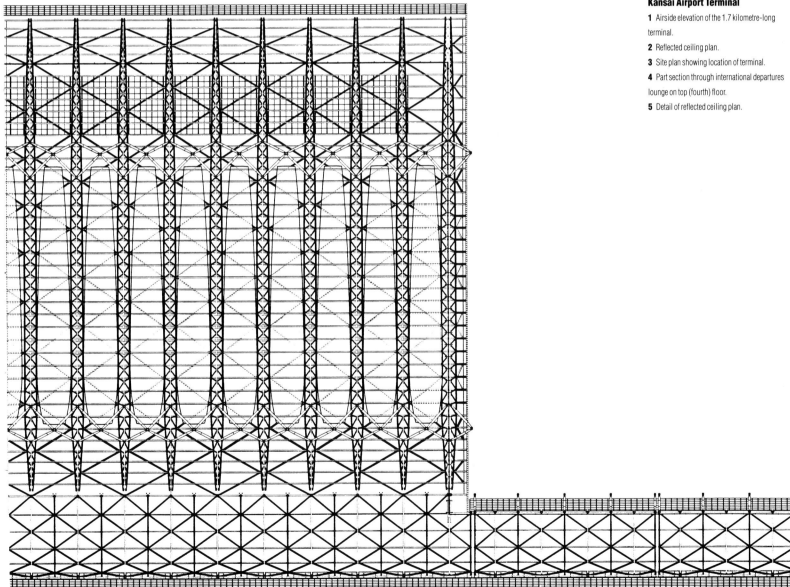

Kansai Airport Terminal

1 Airside elevation of the 1.7 kilometre-long terminal.
2 Reflected ceiling plan.
3 Site plan showing location of terminal.
4 Part section through international departures lounge on top (fourth) floor.
5 Detail of reflected ceiling plan.

5

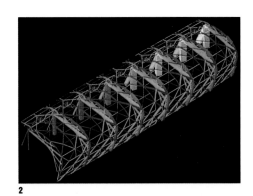

1

Kansai Airport Terminal

1 Diagram showing derivation of the geometry of the airside wing.

2 Computer analysis of forces in the structure of the airside wing.

3 Computer perspective of interior of the airside wing.

4–8 Sequence of perspective sketches showing how curves of structure and roof both lead passengers inexorably forward and unambiguously orient them.

4 View from fourth floor on landside, across canyon and into international departures.

5 International departures hall.

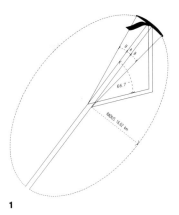

2

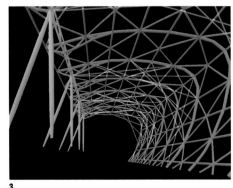

3

more integrated and synergistic solution involved so much computer calculation that this was put off until after the competition was won. Now the curves of the roof flow seamlessly one into the other. So too, the huge three-dimensional trusses flow into the bowed ribs of the wing, which in turn now function collectively as a shell structure, with considerable increase in efficiency in all parts of the structure. Hence if one dimension of nature has been diminished in the final scheme (the excluded

'canyon' along the wing) it is more than compensated for by the fact that the building has acquired a far greater organic unity – and a fabulous dinosaur skeleton-like structure.

Nature is emulated by the structural elements not just in the efficiencies and overtly biomorphic forms, but also in the visual explicitness with which they resolve stresses, and the sense of life given by the sprung shape of both the bowed wing-ribs and the asymmetrically-arched trusses. As a consequence, they elicit an empathetic relationship with passing passengers, as companionable presences that give character and intermediate scale between that of the person and the huge fluid spaces. The asymmetric arch was adopted to entrain air blown along the roof from landside to airside. Instead of closed ducts, open scoop-like forms guide the laminar flow of air and reflect light from uplighters, thus eliminating all other elements that would have cluttered the view of the structure.

The building's curves bring it near to nature in other ways

besides looks and conjured associations, structural efficiency and elicited empathy, and close fit to passenger- and air-flows. They conform to geometries not previously applied to architecture, yet are inspired by recent breakthroughs in chaos theory and topological mathematics that are giving new insights into the geometry of nature. Studies in these inspired the design team of architects and engineers to seek out new geometric disciplines to both shape the curves and allow maximum repetition of components. Here all 90 000 stainless steel cladding units will be identical, each designed to take up tiny accumulative tolerances. Identical too are all secondary structural elements and most primary elements. The rest of the latter are made from an identical jig and merely trimmed as required.

Once again the Building Workshop shows a considerable

4

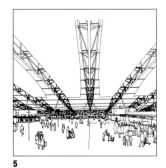

5

edge over other architects in understanding that while the computer may facilitate the making of whimsical forms and specials, it can also discipline complex forms so that they can be made with the intellectually and aesthetically satisfying sense of authentic economy found in nature. The extreme discipline that is such a satisfying aspect of the design of the airport terminal, was in part adopted because it was the only way to design and build such a vast building so quickly and cheaply.

The asymmetrical curves of the main terminal roof are fairly conventional, a series of circular arcs of differing radii. But the tapering curves of the wings, initially adopted to accommodate sight-lines from the control tower (by other, specialist architects) conform to a toroidal geometry. Conceptually the wings are cut from the top of a ring, of 16.6-kilometre radius and inclined at 67 degrees from horizontal. It is the subtle combination of these geometries that will give this immense building a sense of being a finite whole, as well as some of the light-sprung poise that the similar subtleties of converging columns and curved stylobate give to a Greek temple.

Client Kansai International Airport

Competition-winning design
Architect Renzo Piano Building Workshop, Paris
R Piano, N Okabe (associate in charge)
Engineer Ove Arup & Partners International Ltd (structure, P Rice), (services, T Barker)

Basic design and detail consortium for terminal building
Design leader and co-ordination Renzo Piano Building Workshop, Japan KK
Design: architecture, executive structural and services engineers
Renzo Piano Building Workshop, Japan KK
R Piano, N Okabe (associate in charge)
in collaboration with
Ove Arup & Partners International Ltd (P Rice), Nikken Sekkei Ltd (K Minai)
Concept, programme and shuttle design
Aéroports de Paris (P Andreu)
Negotiation with government departments and civil aviation authorities and airside planning
Japan Airport Consultants, Inc (M Matsumoto)

Glazing R J van Santen
Landscaping M Desvigne, K Nyunt
Acoustics engineer Peutz & Associates (Y Dekeyrel)
Quantity surveyors David Langdon & Everest, Futaba Quantity Surveying Co Ltd
Modelmakers Eikunion Model (J Fiore), Super Model (E Miola), Modelling Geimu (M Shimura), M Bassignani, D Cavagna

A full credit list for this project will appear in volume three

Kansai Airport Terminal

6 Computer rendering of junction of structural elements of airside wing.
7 Looking along airside wing and up to international departures from third floor after exiting from duty-free shops.
8 Departure lounge in airside wing.
9 Departure lounge at end of airside wing.
10 Cross section through centre of building.

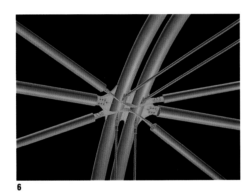

6

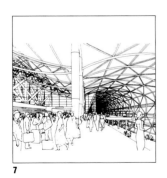

7

8

9

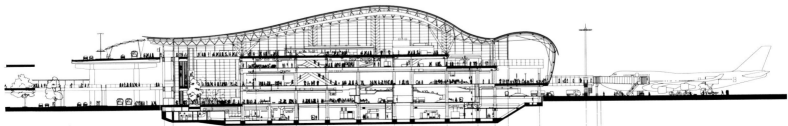

10

The Menil Collection offers further examples of other sorts of participation. It participates in place and community in its own way: it dons the clapboard cladding of the surrounding bungalows and distributes some of its functions among them to be a 'village museum' and not only offers the stoa-like surrounding colonnade as a generous gesture for public use, but allows views from it of such normally back-room functions as conservation and framing, so bringing these crucial functions to public awareness. The colonnade is also one of the most obvious devices through which the building participates in history, being both rooted in and transforming tradition by recalling the verandas of southern plantation houses and the Greek Revival traditions of American civic architecture. Furthermore, the detailing of steel frame and colonnade pays homage to Craig Ellwood and more recent American modern architecture. And if the design does give some suggestion of participating with nature, it is both in the biomorphic shaping and due-north (cosmic) alignment of the leaves and in the way it engages nature as an essential part of the architectural experience. Planting accompanies visitors as they approach the building and then provides a suitable jungle

backdrop to African art. More than that, galleries and art are brought alive by the way the light changes with that outside, so giving the visitor a sense of being alive to and in touch with this dimension of nature.

The Vesima workshop gives the feeling of being even more intensely in touch with a changing ambient nature, the weather, as well as with the planting that surrounds and continues inside the building. The workshop also conveys a strong impression that everybody on their different levels within the same space is participating in the same enterprise, all visible to and open to encounter with each other.

To participate fully in the unfolding of the future, and so in the present, the Building Workshop treats each commission as a research project. Beyond being alert to and keeping abreast of social and technical developments, research nearly always concentrates on two areas in particular: on a material, and on the piece. The truss and light-diffusing leaf of the Menil Collection, for instance, evolved from the exploration of ductile iron and ferrocement. Yet the material researched need not be new. Sometimes it is an old one for which new techniques or theoretical insights offer new potential. While the IBM Travelling Pavil-

1 The Menil Collection gallery, Houston, USA, 1981–86: the museum exemplifies how a building may participate in a place and its local traditions. It adopts the clapboard cladding of the surrounding bungalows and expressed steel frame of other neighbouring buildings. Its stoa-like colonnade is a generous gesture to the public realm that evokes both the verandas of southern plantation houses and the Greek Revival origins of American civic architecture.

1

ion explored polycarbonate and the very latest glues, the Padre Pio Pilgrimage Church now under development is pushing stone to new limits. The new techniques exploited here are those of structural analysis, whereby an arch can be calculated as an infinity of hinges rather than in terms of thrust lines; and precision stone cutting, which ensures that all parts of a stone block are evenly stressed. Both these techniques have only recently been made possible by the computer. From research such as this comes not just participation in the evolution of technology, but also an authentic creativity enjoyed by those who conduct it and, more importantly, the evidence of which is subliminally communicated to the viewer.

Though dependent on this research into materials, the shaping of the piece is even more central to both the Building Workshop's design method and to the qualities of the final work. The pieces are nearly always repetitive structural elements, and are always exposed to view from within the building. Usually it is the pieces more than anything, though not those alone, that give each building its particular identity. The pieces mediate between building and user in other crucial ways too, providing an intermediate scale to which people can

immediately relate and a sensually crafted presence that invites tactile contact, both especially pertinent qualities in buildings of large fluid spaces, as are many of the Building Workshop's.

The companionable presence of these pieces, almost as beings in themselves, and the visual and sensual satisfactions they offer, are intensified by a sense of aliveness acquired from their shaping and spacing. At its simplest, close spacing of repetitive elements can produce a barely perceptible optical flicker – as with the balcony louvres on the Rue de Meaux Housing. In shaping the piece, it is not just a degree of biomorphism that gives a sense of life, but the way it elicits empathetic identification through the expressively self-evident way the forms resolve stresses, often in sprung or suspended structures with shapely joints. The structure of the Kansai International Airport Terminal now under construction furnishes good examples, both in the huge trusses that span over the main terminal hall and in the bowed arches of the long wings along which the aircraft stand.

But there are other reasons for focusing so much attention on the piece. It is the piece that is most susceptible to sustained and objective

27

2, **3** Padre Pio Pilgrimage Church at San Giovanni Rotondo, Foggia, 1991–: computer projections of the arches and roof.
4 Rue de Meaux Housing, Paris, 1987–91: the facade is composed of abstract forms to give a sense of organic vibrancy through jumpy juxtapositions and close-spacings that induce a slight optical flicker.

2

3

4

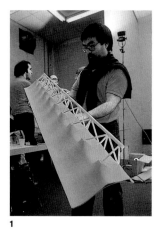

1

Emulation of nature: biomorphic form is not imposed so much as arises from attempting a similar close fit of form to both function and the potentials of materials.
1 Shunji Ishida studying a model of the Menil leaf and truss, the latter of which has not yet taken the bone-like cast shapes of the final castings.
2,3 The leaf of the Menil shows a striking similarity of form to those found in an x-ray picture of a digitalis flower.

refinement. Technical improvements to it are easily judged, and so are aesthetic ones. Many contribute to this refinement: architects, engineers and clients. And contributions can be made at all stages of development through sketching and drawing, hand-crafting of prototypes and preparing shop drawings. With all this input – intellectual, visual and tactile – the piece is the one element that might approximate both the precise tailoring to purpose and the satisfying sense of being exactly right that is found in the products of natural evolution. Often, too, the piece can, and does, continue to be refined long after the rest of the design has been settled. This allows each design to evolve as far as possible in a strategy analogous to neoteny in natural evolution, which can speed itself up by prolonging immaturity and with it the learning period of each generation, as happened with humans. Of course, in developing the piece the concern is not just with that component in isolation, but equally with what is created by the collective assembly of the elements. Obviously then, connections are important, and so too is the whole that results when the pieces are assembled with all the other elements. Those who see the piece as a mere component that can be taken up and

easily used in other designs profoundly misunderstand how intrinsic its role is in a specific building, its scale and place.

In its responsiveness to a place and its traditions, and in its refinement of the piece and the assembly of which it is part, the architecture of the Building Workshop may be characterised as an art of 'fitting in' and 'fitting together'. If the refinement of the piece has evolutionary analogies, then the way the architecture responds to place, respecting and fitting in with what exists while changing and enhancing it (like a new species entering and enriching an eco-niche) has obvious ecological analogies. (It is significant then that some of Piano's earlier buildings encourage continuing change, further adaptive evolution, once complete. The Pompidou is the most obvious example, but some of the early housing schemes exploit the same theme.) These are the most profound senses in which Piano's architecture can be said to be participatory, engaging in the unfolding techno-cultural evolution of the world and emulating the ecological reciprocities of nature that hold it all together.

The Building Workshop's engagement with technology then is quite different from that of High-Tech. It does not subscribe to the blind

2

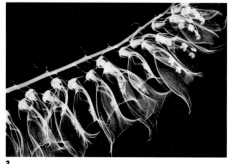

3

4

technological imperative of the latter, using advanced technology just because 'it is of our time' or 'it is there' and regardless of its appropriateness. And though the Building Workshop is committed to research and innovation, these are not fuelled by a competitive urge simply to do or use something first. All too often these lead, in architecture as in other fields, to a macho desensitising to the consequences of using this technology, and to its potentially deleterious impacts. Piano's approach is the antithesis because participation is not about technological assertion. Just the aspiration to participate heightens awareness and sensitivities, to vulnerabilities as well as potentials.

However, despite the differences between them, the Building Workshop and High-Tech share the same sources, specifically in the nineteenth century and the 1950s. Affinities with these periods are still pronounced in Piano's work. High-Tech is a latter-day version of Structural Rationalism as espoused by architects like Viollet-le-Duc. British High-Tech compounds this with nostalgia for the daring engineering seen in the public realm of the nineteenth century, in its stations and market halls. In a way it is the flip-side of British nostalgia for Empire and is symptomatic of that

country's continuing inability to define a relevant post-Imperial role. Even High-Tech's view of the future is nostalgic, still the relatively uncomplicated and optimistic one of the 1950s and 1960s, the last days of Empire. Yet already during the 1973–74 oil crisis, in the early stages of constructing the Pompidou Centre, some of those who were to become part of the Building Workshop recognised that it was a dinosaur that closed an era more than heralded a new one.

The strong affinities with the nineteenth century in Piano's approach are somewhat different in spirit to, or at least more complex than, those of High-Tech. Through his friend and mentor, Jean Prouvé, he has been touched by, and confirmed in, some of the craft and social ideals of William Morris. And just as Viollet-le-Duc sought to emulate the forms and structural efficiencies of nature with the skeletal cast-iron forms seen in his drawings, so Piano seeks to emulate nature in a similar way, as well as others. In works such as the Menil, he shows that he recognises that it is the use of the nineteenth-century technique of casting that gave the exposed engineering of that period its expressiveness and character. And indeed the Menil is very much a modern

29

4 A Pompidou Centre gerberette that resembles some gigantic finger bone.
5 Transmogrification of form from dolphin into cruise ship.
6 Crown Princess cruise ship 1987–90: the superstructure of which was designed by the Building Workshop.
7 Oxford Museum by Deane & Woodward, 1860: the sort of nineteenth-century building that is antecedent to Piano's architecture.

6

5

7

equivalent of Deane & Woodward's Oxford Museum, which combines the ideals of Ruskin and Morris with those of Viollet-le-Duc. Yet the similarity is not in nostalgia but due to shared ideals of showing art, celebrating craftsmanship and getting close to nature.

Both High-Tech and Piano have been influenced by Californian architecture of the mid-century period, an architecture that sought not to emulate but to embed itself in and co-exist with nature. Especially influential were Richard Neutra and Charles Eames, Ezra Ehrenkrantz and Craig Ellwood and the Case Study houses, by both them and others – particularly Eero Saarinen whose commitment to research and innovation in buildings such as the General Motors and the John Deere headquarters remains an inspiration. Buckminster Fuller, of course, was another major influence. Long before the Menil Collection gallery emulated Ellwood's steel frame detailing, Norman Foster and Richard Rogers (as two of Team 4) had modelled their Reliance Controls Factory on the same source. But British High-Tech got contaminated by Brutalism (largely under the influence of Foster and Rogers' teacher, James Stirling, who married the two so memorably at the Leicester University Engineering Block and

the Cambridge History Library), forgot the modesty and delicacy of Californian examples and became monumental and overpowering.

Piano remains far more true to the original ideals of California's mid-century Modernism. He is not interested in technology for its own sake, let alone flaunting it aggressively. Instead he seeks the lightness, openness and transparency that can be achieved by a tactful technology that stands aside for, rather than intrudes upon, human action and that also allows nature and technology to interweave and blend. Hence there is a lightness and liveliness in the architecture of the Building Workshop that is very different to the overwrought and/or overbearing ponderousness or lifeless perfection of so much High-Tech.

Significantly, both nineteenth-century Structural Rationalism and American architecture and design of the mid-century were touched by then-current ideas about evolution. If Darwin's ideas about the survival of the fittest were taken to legitimate capitalism and colonialism, then his theory of evolution also inspired the idea that an advanced and authentic technology would refine its forms to resemble those of nature. These ideas came together with others in a strand that conflated the organic

30   **1, 2** Cité International, Lyon, France, 1989: a galleria flanked by trade and business facilities stretched between the river and a park. This, like the 1992 Columbus International Exposition in Genoa, shown overleaf, is a large waterside, multi-use urban scheme.

2

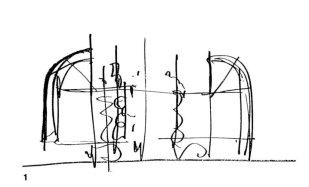

1

and the technical and has continued in various guises right through the modern period. In Europe it found its most caricatured expression in Art Nouveau and clearly continues in High-Tech with its explicit anatomy, exoskeletal structures and shapely joints. It found expression in the USA in the writings of Horatio Greenhough and in the architecture of Louis Sullivan and Frank Lloyd Wright. It continued with Wright's ex-employee, Neutra, and the Californians. Under the influence of Buckminster Fuller and others, including California-based cyberneticians, the idea emerged that design (or Comprehensive Anticipatory Design Science, as Fuller called it) was the means by which mankind could consciously intervene in and guide evolution.

At the time this was a magnificent and noble idea, that we could become co-creators in evolution, for the first time fully responsible for the consequences of our actions. But though still inspiring and useful, such notions now also smack of colossal hubris. They are particularly pernicious if married to an urge to control nature and the future rather than, to some degree at least, liberate the unpredictable. Since the development of the Gaia hypothesis and various other insights from

science and philosophy, we know the world is far too complex and our understandings inevitably always too partial for us to be able to predict the consequences of our meddlings. Besides, it is becoming apparent, the world is far wiser than we are and has its own teleological programme. What is necessary now is to abandon the arrogance that let us think we might control evolution. Instead we need to listen as best we can to the world, to let it continue its own evolution, rather than try to distort this to our own ends, and we must also urgently help the world to heal itself.

The deep appeal of the architecture of the Renzo Piano Building Workshop, and why so many instinctively feel it to be so significant, is that it is possible to believe that at one level it is shaped by some such intuitive realisation, even if still inchoate. If the question were asked, what sort of architecture would the world or evolution themselves bring forth spontaneously? then the only current architecture to which the result might have some resemblance is that of the Building Workshop. (This chimes with Piano's quest for an architecture that is natural and unforced, both as a piece of design and in its impact on its surroundings.) Not restricted to a personal idiom, it would be as

3, **4** Ravenna Sports Hall: **3**, model of half the roof, that resembles a scallop shell or palm leaf, and, **4**, sectional studies of the repetitive units from which the roof will be made show how Piano continues that bio-technical strand of Modern architecture that originates in the Neo-Gothic and strives to approximate the efficiencies and authenticity of natural form.

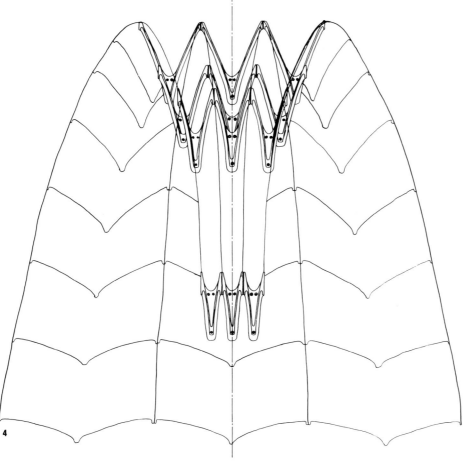

31

varied as its locations and programmes, and the technology available there and then. Conservative in the best sense of preserving still vital features of place and tradition, it would also embrace change: evolution is essentially about ever-accelerating change. And it would certainly exploit all available technologies and especially those of the leading edge (assuming these are benign of course), because why else would the world have evolved them and made them available now?

Questioning what sort of architecture the world itself might bring forth, in turn raises the notion that we might have reached a crucial turning point in our relationship with our evolving built environment, again something Piano seems to have intuited. Let's continue for a while to suppose that the world might bring forth architecture. Walking around historic towns, especially ones that have a feeling of organic rightness that has come from having grown relatively unplanned and unselfconsciously, it is easy to imagine that the world itself created them to herd people together so as to provoke encounters in constrained streets and squares, and thereby develop mankind socially. Similarly it has enclosed people in houses and rooms so that they might be secure

and undistracted enough to focus on and develop themselves as individuals. But eventually these benevolent gestures have resulted in such self-absorption by mankind that it has cost the earth dearly, bringing its very existence to the point of extreme precariousness.

Now our cities are fragmenting and the street and square disappearing as physical form and social mechanism. The same technologies that fuel this process and bring the world flooding into every room, also allow us to move out of the city. There we can settle into nature and be alert to its moods and cycles, and be in constant touch with the planet, its various processes and current pain. If the Vesima Laboratory–workshop does not enclose its occupants with solid walls and roof, where they might steal only framed views of the world, this does not result in psychological and cultural poverty, but rather might anticipate a still nascent psychocultural reality.

Just as double glazing, automatically adjusted shading and air conditioning allow us to open up our buildings and ourselves to nature, so also we might relate quite differently to such buildings. Perhaps we are outgrowing thick-walled and anthropomorphic abodes,

1, 2 Columbus International Exposition, Genoa, 1992: this restoration and reuse of the oldest part of the harbour began the regeneration of the historic city. New structures include the Bigo, **1**, a gigantic derrick evoking the naval past and supporting a panoramic lift and performance tent and the aquarium, on left of **2**.

3, 4 Bercy-Charenton Shopping Centre, near Paris, 1987–90: the grid warped into the sort of post-Euclidian geometry that only the computer can easily generate, and that the Building Workshop is increasingly exploring.

1

2

into the fabric of which our psyches can seep, while identifying with its forms and physiognomy. Instead, as Viollet-le-Duc long ago intuited, we might now prefer a more skeletal or vegetal architecture. No longer sheltering away from nature in the equivalent of a cave, we might now live in something closer to a grove or under a vine-covered pergola. Here, very aware of nature, we might rediscover our connections with, and responsibilities to, our living planet.

Such an architecture might be one of the forms that exactly suits the pluralistic culture now emerging around the Pacific rim – the civilisation of aerospace, electronics and international finance – and so also our first planetary culture. In civilisation's slow progress westwards around increasingly large bodies of water, each previous cultural ecology was distinguished by a quintessential architectural form or element. With the riverine cultures of Mesopotamia and Egypt, the harsh hierarchies of society under their priest- or god-kings were reflected in the forms of ziggurat and pyramid.

In contrast, Mediterranean cultures emphasised the rights of the individual across their far-flung empires and their colonnaded edifices dignified the being of each citizen/column,

which also stood for the standardised order that they represented wherever they were. The succeeding Atlantic culture is epitomised by the grid, in which nature is enmeshed by the grasp of reason and technology and abstracted in the quantifications of science. The grid organised the vestigial, largely decorative columns of Neo-Classicism, and then became the prime expression of the repetitive banalities of corporate Modernism. As such, the grid represents pure instrumentality, the diminishment of sensual experience, and alienation in its elimination of hierarchy and symbolic meaning.

Just as the pyramid persisted as the pediment of Classicism and the column, from J N L Durand to Le Corbusier, was reduced in symbolic status to marking the intersections of grid lines, so the grid will persist into the Pacific cultural ecology. But the reaction to the dead-hand of the absract and alienating grid of Atlantic culture is taking various forms, all seen or implied in the architecture of the Building Workshop. The lines of the grid will etherialise into intangible conduits of energy and information, or take tactile biomorphic form, while the taut hermetic skin that found its apotheosis with gridded mirror-glass crumbles and becomes more porous.

Nature itself, as buildings such as the Menil and Vesima so clearly anticipate, will no longer be suppressed by the grid, but will invade and flourish in it as the dominant sensual presence counterbalancing the intangibility of our electronic world in the high-tech/high-touch equation. Or the grid will fold into either the non-orthogonal geometries of space frames and 'tensegrity structures', or crystalline configurations with their cosmic associations; and the grid will also warp, bend and almost come alive in accord with the new topological mathematics that only the computer can easily generate – as exactly exemplified by the Bercy-Charenton Shopping Centre in France and the Kansai International Airport Terminal.

Now that we are moving on from the Atlantic culture in which architecture became abstract and arid, aloof and alienated from man and man's setting, it is to Piano and the Building Workshop that we must look to find its true antithesis. Theirs is an architecture that does not result in further fragmentation, as almost all current architecture does, but instead is thoroughly integrative in the way it seems an almost inevitable or natural part of its time and place, and participates in so many ways with people and nature.

33

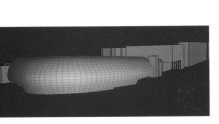

3

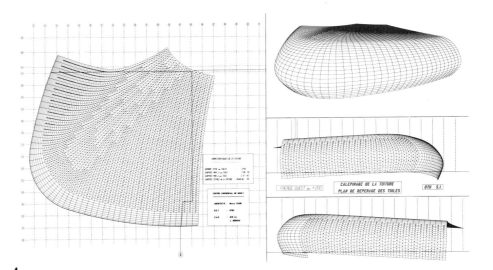

4

34

Spirit of the Workshop

All architects are aware that Man is an architectural animal. Not only are human culture and day-to-day life now unthinkable without architecture but so, some say, is modern thought itself, since the structures of our philosophical systems and psyches are arranged according to architectural metaphors. For most architects it is the final building and the living in it that is of greatest human significance. But for Piano it seems that it is the very physical act of making architecture that is the most natural of human activities. So the Renzo Piano Building Workshop is concerned with the making of architecture, its designs are about organising that making, and design development is about physically mocking-up and testing. Drawing only has value in so far as it serves these processes.

The way a design is developed by the Building Workshop and Piano's role in this process is entirely consistent with the architecture to which both aspire. Making buildings is not a solitary process, but one involving the skills of several people and various skills of each person. As far as possible the method is highly participatory, in contrast to what can be implied by the term multi-disciplinary. Too often the latter involves a design passing sequentially through a series of specialisations, to which each contribute in turn, as if on a production line. The Renzo Piano Building Workshop aims for a much more synergistically creative process in which consultants contribute right from the beginning and all the way through the design process as integral members of the team. In retrospect it is impossible to disentangle who contributed what to the design.

Just as all specialisations contribute at all stages of design, so the aim is that all facets of the people involved play their part. So that the

1

2

5

3

4

7

8

6

35

hand contributes as much as the head, Piano insists on many things being mocked up in model form or full-size in the workshop. This also allows precision of aesthetic judgement and so the resultant sensual tactility. For the Building Workshop, craft is as important as science, especially in giving soul to technology.

Piano is both more involved in a design and its development than other architects, and more detached. Although he makes copious sketches he no longer draws or even sketches much at his own board, but spends his time at those of others or discussing pinned-up drawings. After imparting his initial response to a design brief, and the ideas and images it and the site provoke, he tends to stand back and let others work up the design while he watches and guides. This detachment allows him to see more clearly and intervene more easily to redirect a design in which he has not become entangled in his own graphic knots, tics or seductions. For similar reasons he discourages 'sensitive' and seductive drawings, preferring bold and blatant ones, whose contents can be dispassionately assessed. In originally setting this style, and then making the first stabs at elaborating Piano's ideas, the role of Shunji Ishida was, and is, immensely important in

Genoa. Now, though, there are several others in Genoa and in Paris who work in this kind of intense interaction with Piano.

During the design process Piano mentally plays the roles of scout, actor and editor – as well as the more obvious ones of creator and refiner of form and space, and inventor and maker of their physical manifestation. The scout looks at the surroundings to find clues to generate the formal disciplines of the design. These often arise by extending elements he finds in the surroundings into the site and building. The Menil Collection is a good example of this, as the structural grid of its roof canopy is a microcosm of the suburban street grid. This canopy is supported on exposed steel columns derived from those of a nearby Philip Johnson building, which are infilled with the clapboarding of the surrounding bungalows. Paul Klee's painting *Blossoming* furnishes a good analogy of the way elements are drawn into and intensified in a design. Here the whole canvas is gridded, but towards the centre the grid breaks down in scale and the colours clash so that you can feel the flower bursting forth from the canvas as it draws sustenance from the rich and moist greens and browns around its edge. Some

36

1, **4**, **6–9** Architects at work in the Genoa office.
2 View down on the stepping levels of Vesima.
3 Members of the design team working on the 1992 Columbus International Exposition meet on site.
5 Studying a space frame made partly of bamboo as part of the research undertaken in the Vesima Laboratory–workshop.

1

2

5

3

4

6

7

8

9

10

10 Wall of the workshop in Vesima where models and full-size prototypes are crafted.

11 Interior view of the old Paris office.

12, 13 An increasing amount of the work is done on, and is only possible with, computers.

14 New premises of the Paris office: a glass-roofed court near the Pompidou Centre.

15 A craftsman in the workshop of the Genoa office.

16 Dante Cavagna, the craftsman who runs the workshop at Vesima.

17 Working on a computer in the Paris office.

18–20 Dante Cavagna at work: 18, on a model of the Palladio basilica in Vicenza; 19, beside a structural model of Fiat VSS Experimental Car; 20, crafting a joint at full size.

11

Building Workshop designs appear to be similarly rooted in, and intensifications of, their surroundings.

Piano the actor imagines himself as the kinds of people who will use the building. He conjures in the mind's eye the mood, speed and sense of expectation with which they will approach the building, the kinds of things they would like to do in the building, what characteristics and atmosphere will enhance these actions, what might suitably provoke or comfort them, and so on. Another one of Piano's greatest skills is as an editor of other people's elaborations of his ideas. Not only can he sense the most promising directions but he is also good at whittling away the unnecessary, and adjusting and refining what might already be very good proposals until they acquire an effortless and 'natural' feeling.

Though Piano's input is crucial in the design process, so is that of others. Many of the designs are utterly inconceivable without the engineer Peter Rice's contribution. Hence, too, the sophisticated toroidal geometries of the Bercy-Charenton shopping centre and the Kansai International Airport Terminal clearly come largely from Rice working with Noriaki Okabe and Jean-François Blassel, while the more stolidly robust Aluminium Research Institute and Rue de Meaux Housing are obviously the work of Bernard Plattner. This is consistent with the collaborative spirit of the Building Workshop. Yet these are clearly works by Renzo Piano, because of his considerable input into the designs, and because their authors are steeped in his approach, the influence of his very particular sensibility and the spirit of the Workshop he has created as a reflection of that approach and sensibility.

Design is not rushed. It usually proceeds by constant resketching, almost waiting for things to emerge rather than imposing them by act of intellectual or wilful clarification. Often the crystallisation of a design is postponed just as clarification and consensus seem to be reached. For Piano, an entirely instinctual rather than intellectual designer, such things need to steep in the subconscious. Only with this slow marination does he feel that crucial things are less likely to be overlooked. For him, a building is like an island placed in the river of life. Before intervening in that flow, all the river's streams and eddies must be charted to ensure that the building minimally obstructs, as well as fully enhances, the continuum of life and of the places where it is lived.

37

12

13

14

15

16

17

19

20

18

'Being an architect means you have to accept that you have to be a craftsman in a new sense of the word, a craftsman working with computers, tests, models and mathematics.' Renzo Piano

38

Early Influences

If the architecture of Renzo Piano Building Workshop is ultimately unlike that of any architect at work today, then it is particularly out of step with Italian architecture. Concerned with lightness not gravitas, technology not typology, and informed by wide-ranging instinctual sensibilities not narrow intellectual dogma, the predilections and forms of the Building Workshop are rather those of northern Europe and America. They owe nothing to the Classicist and Rationalist strains of Modern architecture, but instead belong to that strain which evolved from Structural Rationalism and Neo-Gothic into the bio-technic and Functionalist stream that sees equivalences between the organic and the mechanistic. The Building Workshop also subscribes to the social ideals that are part of this strand and shares its assumption that authenticity lies in the honest, and preferably innovatory, expression of structure and construction. As a result the work seems to arouse in Italy, as well as its due share of enthusiastic endorsement, misunderstandings and hostility that it provokes nowhere else.

Despite all this, the architecture of Renzo Piano and the Building Workshop is also profoundly rooted in Piano's family and Genoese background. His father and grandfather, uncles and brother were all builders and he grew up familiar with and fascinated by building sites, especially with the intricacies of how buildings are put together. A desperately shy boy, he kept to himself. His childhood domain was the roof of the family home in Pegli, a town just west and now part of greater Genoa. Here on the roof with its views over the sea he played among the bright billowings of windblown sheets, establishing early the themes of ever-changing natural light and airy lightness that still obsess him. And indeed his first executed structures were awnings of sheets

tensioned by the wind and anchored by himself and his infant sister, the person he felt most comfortable with as a collaborator.

In other company, Piano proved himself in his own private way, setting silent challenges against others who did not realise they were in, say, a running race. In awe of his father, whom he says he saw in almost mythic terms as 'this great guy who built great buildings', the young boy set himself the challenge of devising alternative means of achieving the same spans and enclosures, but with less and lighter materials. Again it was the ideal of lightness that he sought, and with it perhaps a shy and minimal impingement on people and place, another quality that obviously still guides his work.

The nearby city of Genoa, where Piano has lived as an adult and where the main base of the Building Workshop has always been, was an important formative influence, too. A strange and secretive city of contrasts and chaos, it is now (even after the 1992 Columbus International Exposition) surprisingly little known, even by Italians, who generally do not regard it as a particularly Italian city but rather as being north European in demeanour. Walled off from the rest of Italy by the mountains that hem the historic city tightly against its harbour, Genoa is, besides being the original city of international finance, a trading city of roving seamen like its most famous son, Christopher Columbus. As such it has always looked outwards to the larger world – a quality many see reflected in Piano's internationalism (though he has no lack of commissions throughout his native Italy).

But contrasting with this outward reach, Genoa is also famous for its introverted homes and family life. Several of its historic piazzas were private to the families whose palazzi enclosed them. The historic city is the most dense in Europe. Lack of land resulted in

1

Family and youth.

1 Renzo Piano as a child, Easter 1940.

2 Piano's grandmother with her two daughters outside her restaurant, where Piano grew up.

3 The architect's father, Carlo Piano, on site.

4 Piano's brother, Ermanno: like their father, a builder.

5 Carlo and Matteo Piano with their father, 1972.

6 With daughter Lia.

7 Piano in his first office–workshop, set up immediately after graduating as an architect.

8 Magda Arduino, Piano's first wife. A sociologist and video-maker, she collaborated on 'The Open Site' television programmes.

2

3

buildings being extended upwards, often more than once, with new construction on top of old that often had to be thickened to take the loads. Often too, what were once open porticoes have now been enclosed. The result is very narrow streets between towering buildings, the opposite cornices of which overlap in places. Piano's architecture, like the trompe l'oeil skies the rich Genoese had painted on their ceilings (perhaps a source of his predilection for roof-lit spaces), seems very much a reaction against the inert massiveness and stifling introversion, the claustrophobia of the old city.

For Piano, it was always Genoa's contrasting pole that appealed far more than the old city. The docks excited him with the promise of adventure from the open sea and the constant change of ships coming and going, loading and unloading. An avid sailor who has now built four yachts for himself (each time experimenting with a different material and/or building technique), Piano always experienced the old city as representing permanence and mass, and the docks as the exhilaration of transience and lightness. For him it is not just sails and sun sparkling on the water that represent lightness, but anything that floats, that bobs and moves upon the water, or anything easily lifted

by and hanging suspended from a crane. These qualities are celebrated in Il Grande Bigo, the gigantic derrick that supports a fabric roof and panoramic elevator that the Building Workshop built for the Columbus Exposition. But the influence of the docks might be seen even in the Pompidou Centre, which is like a foreign ship docked in Paris with thousands of passengers swarming up and down its suspended gangplank, and exhibitions coming and going like cargo. If the originally intended movable floors/hatches and 'electronic facade' of signs and festive lights had been realised, the parallels would have been even more pronounced.

The other major formative influence on him, Piano believes, were the times. As a youth he experienced the late 1950s in Italy as a period of immense confusion in which all traditional certainties were breaking down. Like other people at the time, he was attracted to the experimental and, in his case, also to the concrete, to what had been shaped and could be touched by hand. It was only what one had discovered through experiment and one's own hand that one could be certain of, and though this lead to naivety, it also gave one confidence in confusing times. And besides, it was only through experiment that one could discover

4

5

6

7

8

9

and help bring into being a less unsatisfactory world. Many of the other interests that now shape the designs of the Building Workshop, developed late. For instance, although Piano loved and sketched the historic towns of Italy, it did not occur to him until very much later that the study of old buildings might inform his own work in any way.

Even the social ideals that are now so clearly intrinsic to his work came later, from English sources. Through Richard Rogers he was influenced by the spirit of London's Architectural Association where, in student projects of the late 1960s, technological gadgetry provided flexible environments at the service of social experiment and liberation. And indirectly through Jean Prouvé he would be touched by the social ideas espoused by nineteenth-century English writers.

Piano studied architecture at the University of Florence and the Polytechnic of Milan, graduating from the latter in 1964. But these institutions shaped his personal approach to architecture far less than his childhood and family background and a number of formidable mentors, some of whom were Italian and others not, that he sought out during and after his studies. From all of these he learnt some-

thing, or as Piano puts it, 'stole some secret' that would guide his own development.

After his father, Franco Albini became his first mentor and employer. Albini was the architect of, among other things, a series of department stores, some of them very fine, for the Rinascente chain. Typically these sport a boldly displayed external steel structure, and are perhaps one of the forerunners of High-Tech. He was also responsible for some equally fine and influential historic restorations and conversions, a number of them in Genoa, as well as being a product designer of distinction. Piano had been impressed by the pleasure Albini took from materials and details and so sought work in his Milan studio when he transferred to the Polytechnic there. Still shy though, and fearing a rejection that others might hear about, he did not apply for a job but simply went along to the office early one morning – fortunately for him, a day upon which someone had just given his notice. His first task was to dismantle and then reassemble a television set to get a feeling for the problems and possibilities involved, before helping the master to design one.

Piano worked with Albini for two years during the period the latter was working on the

41

10

11

12

13

14

15

1

Genoa, a closed and claustrophobic city.

1 An introverted secret courtyard.

2–5 The narrow high-sided streets make it a city of slit-like glimpses: **2**, of the cathedral, San Lorenzo; **3**, of the raised loggia of a palazzo; **4**, of a cruciform of sky at a crossroads – in places cornices actually overlap; **5**, of a shady palazzo garden seen through a loggia in a Rennaisance street.

6 A rare patch of garden in the medieval city.

conversion into a museum of Genoa's Palazzo Rosso (in the famous via Garibaldi). For Piano, perhaps the most instructive experiences came during the lift he got home to Genoa each weekend: Albini would stop off in Pavia to meet a master-craftsman to check progress on the prototypes of wooden furniture that he was designing. They would spend up to two hours studying what were often the tiniest details and refinements. From this, and then the experience of working on the design of an adjustable shelving system, Piano learnt that Albini's design method, as is Piano's now, is largely one of eliminating the inessential, almost at times a process of dematerialisation.

It was during this same period that Piano first met Jean Prouvé when he dropped in several times where the latter taught at the Ecole des Arts et des Métiers in Paris. What impressed Piano there was how Prouvé set problems – such as making from a single sheet of paper a bridge that would be strong enough to support a pencil – that were to be solved by working directly with the hands, by manual manipulation as much as with the mind. Later when building the Pompidou Centre, for which Prouvé had been a crucial member of the competition jury, the two became close friends.

Prouvé's studio in the rue des Blancs Manteaux was only 100 metres from Piano's in the rue St Croix de la Brettonerie and the two often lunched together. But for all the obvious similarities in their work and for all Piano's (amply reciprocated) admiration for the older man, Prouvé was less of a formative influence than Albini. Instead he confirmed and reinforced, rather than changed, an already formulated and adopted approach.

Though Prouvé and Piano were both interested in new technology and materials, neither was interested in large-scale manufacture and standardised components. These lead to deadening uniformity in architecture and a loss of identity in individual buildings. Instead both believed in purpose-made components for each building, the identity of which should lie as much in the parts as the whole, and also in the importance of craftsmanship in both the shaping of components and in putting soul into technology. In stressing the tailored component and craftsmanship over industrial production, both of them might have seemed as conservative in the then current climate as they were progressive. For both of them, too, it was crucial that the designer-maker did not relinquish contact with the workshop, where the

2

3

4

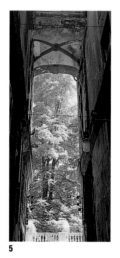

5

'Genoa, a shy and frugal town, cultured and silent, which is petrified memory, but also a mirror of the character of its inhabitants.' Renzo Piano

6

7

The harbour.

7 Genoa and its harbour started in the left (east) corner of the bay and together grew around it.

8 Historic view with harbour with sailing vessels.

9 The bustle of cranes and other machines, and the promise of adventure in distant lands always inspired Piano.

10 A wide street down to the docks cut through the historic core of the city in the nineteenth century.

11 The oldest part of the harbour was redeveloped by the Building Workshop to both host the 1992 Columbus International Exposition and initiate the regeneration of the old city.

12 Worker on the rigging of a performance tent built for the Exposition.

properties of materials are best explored and where aesthetic judgements are best made full-size, and not just by eye but by the feel of the hand too. A major but unimportant difference between them though is that Prouvé was a bender and a folder who worked up from two dimensions to three with sheet metal, while Piano tends to be a carver and a caster and starts from a cubic volume.

If Piano learnt the importance of craftsmanship and the workshop in part from his builder relatives, Prouvé had learnt similar lessons from his father. A founder of the École des Beaux-Arts in Nancy, which despite its name subscribed to the ideals of the Arts and Crafts movement and which became one of the most important centres of Art Nouveau, Victor Prouvé had been very influenced by the writings of John Ruskin and William Morris. Besides the interest in craftsmanship, these writings influenced the social and political ideals that were so much part of Prouvé's make-up. Although these were never explicitly discussed, Piano concedes that it is probable that conversation with Prouvé contributed to affinities between his ideas and those of these writers, particularly in relation to craftsmanship and social issues, and so furthered the

Anglo-Saxon rather than Italian cast to some of his ideas and sensibilities. Certainly Prouvé inspired his interest in and commitments to the social aspects of architecture. Piano was particularly impressed by projects like the housing for Abbé Pierre done in the early 1950s and noted that Prouvé's advocacy of houses built like cars was for the resulting social rather than technical advancement. And though the Pompidou Centre was conceived very much with people in mind, arguably Piano's first such building, his work after Pompidou and his deepening friendship with Prouvé becomes far richer in and more committed to its social ideas.

Another mentor, briefly, was the British-based engineer Z S Makowski who specialised in space frames and to whom Piano had sent documentation on some of his early experiments with lightweight structures. This resulted in an invitation to attend a conference on such structures at the Battersea College of Technology in 1966. Makowski was intrigued to find someone exploring instinctively territory where he was guided by calculation, while Piano was impressed by the engineer's intelligence and precision. Plans were formed to set up a company to specialise in lightweight

43

8

9

10

11

12

1

1 The architectural team that won the Pompidou Centre competition.

2 Elevation and, 3, corner of office–workshop Piano built for himself in Genoa in 1968–69. It had an internal space-frame structure and was lit through the roof.

4 Jean Prouvé, an inspiring friend and mentor.

5 Renzo Piano with Louis Kahn.

structures. But then Piano realised that this would be too limiting and that there was more to architecture than roofs and space frames. Yet the first office–workshop he built for himself outside Genoa (1968–69), with space frames supporting the walls as well as the translucent roof, owes a lot to Makowski.

A more lasting and pervasive influence that still lingers in the output of the Building Workshop came from Piano's discovery while in Britain of the comic-book visions of the Archigram group. Its various concepts of technology enveloping and extending the body, and of nature enveloping technology, probably influenced Piano's quest to bring technology and nature into happy harmony. Certainly Archigram's carnivalesque celebration of crowds, tents and electronics continues in the work of Piano and can be seen most clearly in the early drawings of such projects as the rehabilitation of the Lingotto Factory and the Columbus International Exposition.

In the academic year 1967–68 Piano was a teaching assistant in Milan to Marco Zanuso, a fine architect and product designer. From him and the course they taught together on the properties of materials, where students explored what each material could do and how

it could be worked before proceeding to design with it, Piano further honed his own feeling for and understanding of materials. During this period he also developed for Zanuso the roof, with its integrated natural lighting and ventilation systems, of the Olivetti Factory in Ivrea, Italy. This led on to working briefly – when already in Philadelphia teaching – in the studio of Louis Kahn. For Kahn, whose lasting influence is quite different to that of his other mentors, Piano helped develop the space frame roof of the Olivetti–Underwood Factory in Harrisburg, USA that owes something to the roof of the Ivrea factory.

Although the influence of Kahn's Richards Medical Research towers (1957–62) can be seen clearly in the projecting cores and spine walls of the QB Housing in Genoa (1968), Piano took little architecturally from Kahn. Piano's search for lightness and transparency, and for what feels like the 'natural solution' is very different from the essential archaism of Kahn's 'what does a building want to be?', and the four-square gravitas that always resulted. Instead Piano learnt from Kahn the importance of creating the right conditions and disciplines, of organising one's life, its rhythms and surroundings, so that creativity might flower.

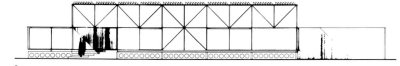

2

3

4

5

Piano Practices

When he founded the Renzo Piano Building Workshop in 1981, Piano had already had three previous practices. The two later ones had been partnerships with others, both of whom were based in London: with Richard Rogers, an architect born in Italy and raised in Britain; and with Peter Rice, an engineer born and raised in Ireland and working in London for Ove Arup & Partners. Though all the practices had been committed to technological experiment, each was quite different in character. Yet together they laid the foundations, each as a different kind of educational experience, for the sort of practice that the Building Workshop is now.

Particularly in his early years, Piano was fascinated with lightweight structures. These were for him far more intriguing and challenging than other forms of construction – and besides, lightness in a structure is an objective accomplishment that gave measure to the success of his experiments. With Studio Piano, his first practice, he devoted himself to designing lightweight enclosures, experimenting especially with plastics and tension structures. The engineer who made the calculations for these structures is Flavio Marano, who is still part of the Building Workshop, though now as the administrator. The builder was the architect's late brother, Ermanno Piano.

Right from these beginnings, Piano adopted his continuing commitment to design as a form of research. But here he concentrated only on technique and a few building components (though through these he also pursued his continuing aesthetic concerns with lightness and translucency). Generally the structures were assembled from a minimal number of different and repetitive purpose-made components that were each shaped in accord with the specific properties of the material. Reinforced polyester cladding panels, for instance, were in shapes that exploited the material's strength but also dealt with its low rigidity.

Pursuing economy of means as well as lightness, these early buildings were conceived of as ethereal and ephemeral. None exists any more. So it is fitting that this period concluded with an intentionally short-lived building, though Piano's most mature to date. This was the Italian Industry Pavilion at the 1970 Osaka Expo, a steel tension structure with reinforced polyester cladding and roofing panels. The building both anticipated British High-Tech's continuing obsession with exposed suspension structures and manifested the first of Piano's continuing parade of beautifully crafted joints.

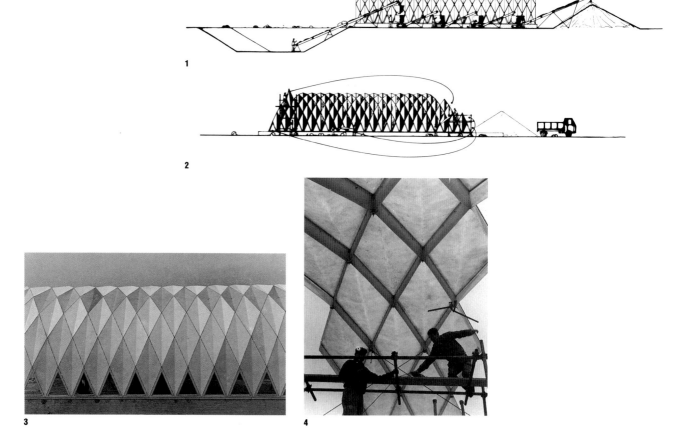

1

2

Studio Piano

3

4

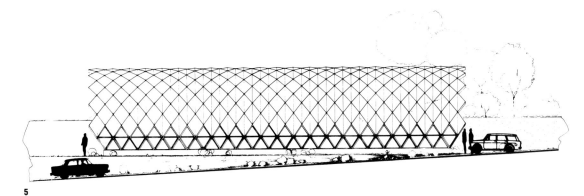

5

6

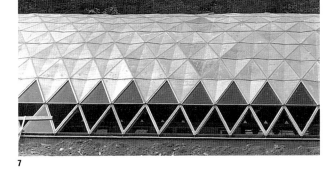

7

Studio Piano

Mobile Structure for Sulphur Extraction
Pomezia, Rome, Italy, 1966
Architect Studio Piano
Contractor E Piano Contractor

1 Long section.
2 Elevation: the vaulted structure is moved by taking panels off one end and reassembling them at the other.
3 Part of side elevation.
4 Construction view showing the vault being assembled from repetitive reinforced polyester panels.

Woodwork Shop Genoa, Italy, 1965
5 Side elevation.
6 Interior of vault that combined opaque and translucent panels to admit daylight.
7 Part of side elevation with clear glazing between structural props supporting panels above.

Reinforced Polyester Space Frame
Genoa, Italy, 1964–65
8 Trial assembly.
9, 10 Assembled on a roof, it achieves the lightness Piano the child sought with billowing sheets on his rooftop playground.

8

9

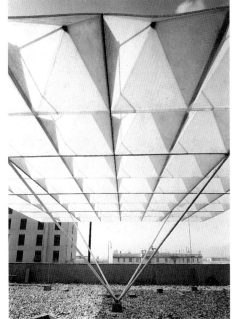

10

'At the beginning of my career, the piece-by-piece attitude gave me the opportunity to study, experiment and understand the logic of materials.'
Renzo Piano

1

3

2

3

48   **Studio Piano**

Shell Structural System for the Fourteenth

Milan Triennale Italy, 1967

1 Assembling a dome made of curved
rhomboidal panels clipped together.

2 Model of proposed roof structure.

3 Making the shell with sprayed glass fibre in the
factory.

4 Section.

4

Tensile Steel and Reinforced-Polyester

Structure Genoa, Italy, 1966

5 Section showing how pre-assembled sections
of the roof were erected.

6 Junctions of tensile elements that will support
the roof around the steel post.

7 Sealing a roof panel around the fixing at the top
of a compression strut.

8 Detail section shows roofing panels connected
by compression struts to ties to form an integral
structural unit.

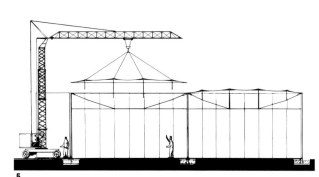

5

6

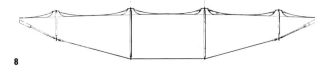

8

7

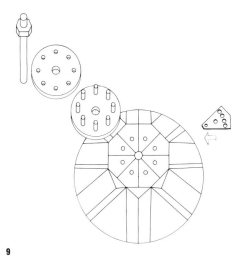

9

10

11

Studio Piano

Italian Industry Pavilion, Expo 1970

1969–70, Osaka, Japan

Client Italpublic, Rome

Architect Studio Piano

Design team R Piano, G Fascioli, T Ferrari,
F Marano

Contractor E Piano Contractor

9 Elements of the connector that joined the
centre of the reinforced polyester panel to
suspension ties.

10, 11 Construction views.

12 Corner of the completed pavilion.

13 Axonometric, which shows how the walls
and roof were made of the same cladding units
supported on a suspension structure.

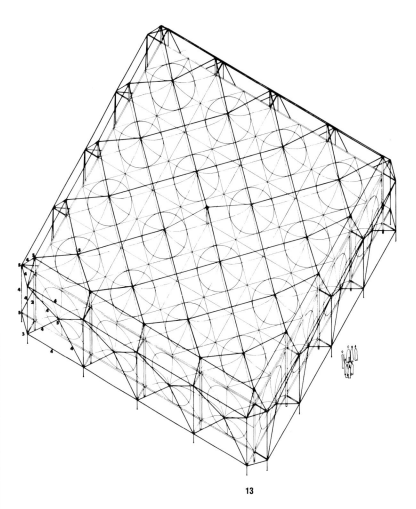

13

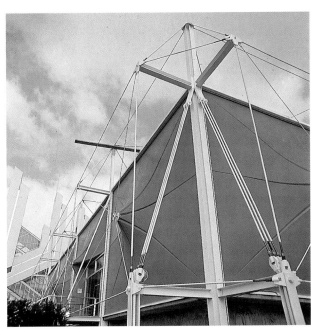

12

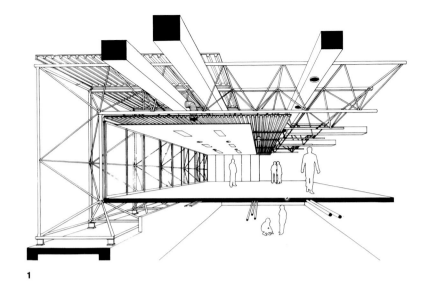

1

2

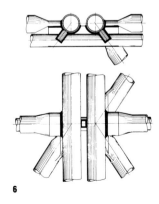

3

4

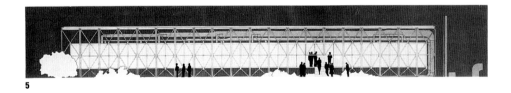

5

Piano & Rogers

6

If Studio Piano was a relatively modest and local affair, the next practice soon became something entirely different. Richard Rogers had barely begun to emerge as one of the two dominant figures in what was to become British High-Tech when Piano, discerning common interests, wrote to and then visited him in London. Though both did other work in this period, with greater or lesser degrees of collaboration, the partnership they formed was dominated by a single building that catapulted both of them, as still young men, to international prominence. The building is of course the Pompidou Centre (1971–78), which,

because it crystallised a large chunk of the *Zeitgeist*, caught the imagination of architects everywhere when selected as winner of an international competition by a jury that included Jean Prouvé. The other important collaboration was a spin-off from the Pompidou. The Institute for Research and Co-ordination of Acoustics and Music is buried under a square to one side of the Pompidou and was started after and completed before it (1973–77). Predominantly by Piano were the B&B Italia Offices at Novedrate near Como (1971–73) and the Free-plan Houses at Cusago, near Milan (1972–74).

7

8

B&B Italia, with its external structure and services, is a test bed for some of the ideas that were taken much further at the Pompidou. For the four houses at Cusago, deep lattice beams supporting a double roof with a ventilation void between them span between side walls over an open volume, interrupted only by enclosed service cores. These are placed to allow many options in further subdivision – or lack of it. If the roof probably derives from Ezra Ehrenkrantz, the influence of Nicholas Habraken and current thinking at London's Architectural Association is clearly present in the plan and its flexibility. In all of these sources, invention in technology and planning were intended to provide unprecedented choice for the inhabitant. Such notions, that Piano first encountered through his association with Rogers, were central to his architecture from this point onwards.

51

Piano & Rogers

B&B Italia Offices Novedrate, Italy, 1971–73
Client B&B Italia SpA
Architect Piano & Rogers
Design team R Piano, C Brullman,
S Cereda, G Fascioli, F Marano
Services engineer Amman Impianti

1 Perspectival section. All structure, plant and ducts are kept outside of clear open office space in this precedent to the Pompidou Centre.
2 Corner view, which shows how enclosed office floor is surrounded by an open structural frame that makes ample space for colour- coded ductwork.
3 Glazed bridge connecting the office block with existing buildings.
4 Detail of elevation, which shows an open loft for services between the two roofs.
5 Front elevation.
6 Typical junction of tubular-steel structure.

Free-plan Houses Cusago, Italy, 1972–74
Clients Lucci, Gianotti, Simi, Pepe
Architect Piano & Rogers
Design team R Piano, F Marano, C Brullman,
G Fascioli, G Luccardini
In collaboration with R & S Lucci

7 Garden elevation.
8 Interior as partitioned by the owner.
9 Site plan.
10 Section with deep double roof for cooling and clear spans.
11 Plan of house, unpartitioned except for the top-lit ablution cores.
12 View from garden.

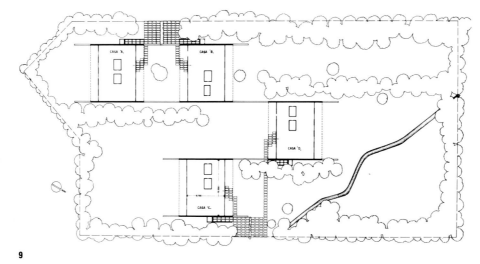

9

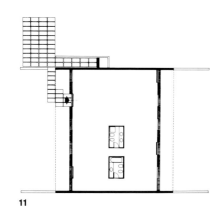

11

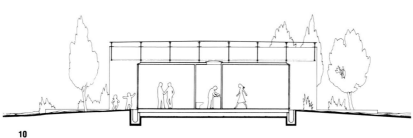

10

12

52   **Piano & Rogers**

Pompidou Centre Paris, France, 1971–78

1 Sectional sketch by Piano.

Views of a corner, showing aspects of the building-as-machine, building-as-kit-of-parts, building-as-indeterminate-process, as well as how visually explicit is the role played by each structural element.

2 Head of escalator tube seen from the external escape stair.

3 An 'empty' upper corner of the structure where it projects above the unfilled-in restaurant terrace.

Opposite page The building combines several kinds of kits-of-parts. Here the sensually sculpted primary structure contrasts with the too austerely unsensual elements, such as handrails and mesh, that visitors actually touch (an inversion of what is often found in nineteenth-century structures). The glazing system comes somewhere in between these extremes.

1

The most basic intention behind the design of the Pompidou Centre was to define a new relationship with culture. No longer elitist, culture was to come off its pedestal and enter the mainstream of life. Instead of being shut away in a temple- or mausoleum-like building, it was to be presented in a new sort of public forum, a bazaar of intense interaction between people and the arts. And this was to be only the major node in a nationwide network of such cultural exchanges. To achieve this vision, the design conflates and raises to an extreme a number of then current architectural ideas.

The Pompidou is the ultimate expression, even caricature, of the Modernist ideal of the building-as-machine and the more recent notion of building-as-kit-of-parts. It also exemplifies the idea of indeterminacy, the building-as-an-ongoing-process, never quite complete and final in form. But though intended as anti-monumental, the building has turned out to be a monument to the ideas of function and flexibility, neither of which in its imposing if exhilarating presence did it initially serve exceptionally well. But, unintimidated by culture or tradition, by historic setting or *La Gloire de France* that it is meant to exemplify, it

seemed so liberating, almost cathartically so, in its provocations and promises that immediately on completion and ever since it has proved immensely popular, and not just with architects. Yet, as recognised during the 1973–74 oil crisis by some of those working on it, the building was already a dinosaur. It climaxes and brings to an end such architectural ideals of the 1960s as megastructures and flexibility achieved through mechanical gadgetry, as much as it opens a period of new potential. For all their further refinements, none of its High-Tech progeny has been as exciting or convincing as the Pompidou.

Piano now tends to see the Pompidou as right for its time and the youth of its creators, but as perhaps too blatant in its presence and provocations. 'An act of loutish bravado', he justly calls it. Yet no matter how provocative and forward looking the Pompidou seemed at the time, in retrospect it can be seen as firmly rooted in Parisian history – and not just as the latest equivalent of what the Eiffel Tower once was. Aerial views of Paris show it has remarkable affinities with Notre Dame. Both loom larger than and isolated from neighbouring buildings, and, in a similar pursuit of

2

3

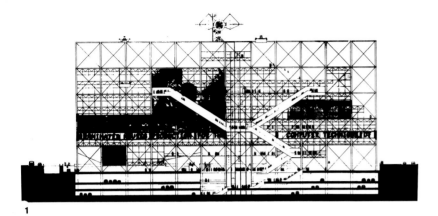

1

Piano & Rogers

Pompidou Centre

1 Elevation of competition design.

2 Members of the architectural team on site as it was being excavated.

3 Elevation and plan of cast steel gerberette that acts as a lever. It pivots on the column to which it transmits compression loads, the downward movement of the main beam it supports is counterbalanced by tying the outermost end to the ground.

4 Gerberettes awaiting finishing after being cast at a German steel works.

2

transparency, the length of both is rhythmically punctuated by external structure.

Most striking though are the similarities the Pompidou, especially the competition design (several crucial aspects of which were never realised), has with a particular stream of remarkable buildings and projects produced in Paris between the two World Wars. The originally intended removable floors recall those of the Maison du Peuple in Clichy (1939) by Jean Prouvé with Beaudouin & Lods, while the proposed electronic facade with its video screens and moving messages is strikingly like that proposed by Oscar Nitzchke for his Maison de la Publicité project (1934–36). And the intended translucency with the display of mechanical gadgetry has an obvious precedent in the Maison de Verre (1932). These projects, like others by Prouvé and Paul Nelson, as well as Le Corbusier's Maison Clarté in Geneva, marry Russian Constructivist influence with French Structural-Rationalism in a movement that seems to have been gathering momentum before being cut

short by the Second World War. Not too great a stretch of the imagination is needed then to see the Pompidou as almost latent and inevitable in Paris, and that without the intervention of the war something similar might have been built decades earlier. Again in retrospect, we might see this sensitivity to a place and its tradition – as much as the concern with advanced building construction – as the pointer to Piano's future direction as an architect. From now on he would prove that the latest technology need not be destructive of the particulars of place and tradition.

Building the Pompidou was formative for Piano in other ways too, especially in the experience of running such a dauntingly huge and complex undertaking. Here he learnt both determination and professionalism coping with and co-ordinating the various client bodies and consultants, contractors and subcontractors involved, as well as the various teams of architects, each concentrating on a different aspect of the building. Young architects, several of them exceptionally talented, gravitated to Paris from around the world to take part in what Piano has called the 'adventure in teamwork and international co-operation'.

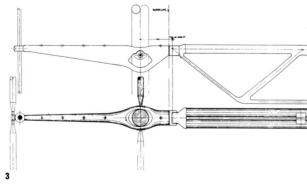

3

4

5

6

Pompidou Centre

5 Every night certain streets were closed so that the huge main beams that were made in Germany could be transported through Paris.

6 Construction view: the workman indicates the huge scale of the gerberettes.

7 Cross section through rue Renard, the Pompidou Centre and place Georges Pompidou.

Among those who came were the architects who have become the creative core of the Renzo Piano Building Workshop. Two of them are Japanese. Shunji Ishida left Japan because student unrest made it impossible for him to pursue his post-graduate studies and went to London where he worked for two years for the architectural practice Arup Associates. While there he became familiar with the work done by a nearby group of Ove Arup & Partners engineers, which was to include the structure for the Pompidou. Then, when in Italy to study Italian, he quite fortuitously met Piano who invited him to join the team in Paris.

Noriaki Okabe had worked for a big Japanese architectural firm before winning a scholarship to study in France, an opportunity he relished not only because it was the country adopted by Le Corbusier but because it gave him a chance to pursue further his enthusiasm for French philosophy. When his scholarship ran out he joined the Pompidou team. Bernard Plattner, who ran the Pompidou site, is a tough and down-to-earth Swiss who had previously worked in the office of Alfred Roth.

Ishida was to become Piano's right hand man in Genoa and amongst many other roles he is the self-appointed recorder of the Building Workshop's activities. (In any publication such as this many of the best photographs are by him.) Okabe, a very fertile designer, was chief architect in the Paris office. He now runs the Osaka office that is building the Kansai International Airport Terminal. Plattner, who ran the Paris office with Okabe, is now in charge there. The contribution of these three to the past and present output of the Building Workshop can hardly be overstated.

Equally or even more difficult to overstate is the role played by two other long-term collaborators who first worked alongside Piano on the Pompidou: Peter Rice, the structural engineer in charge with Ove Arup & Partners and Tom Barker, the services engineer, also with Arup's. Both have worked on nearly all the Building Workshop's major projects.

Much more than just a brilliant engineer, Rice's contribution to the Pompidou was crucial in every way. Having already faced the problems of building the Sydney Opera House, he provided the necessary strategic perspective without which the Pompidou could never have been realised. From then on, until he became ill in early 1992 and died towards the end of that year, he was to collaborate on almost all the major projects by Piano and the Building Workshop. Because his skills were so immense and wide ranging, and because his personal working relationship with Piano was so close, his contribution to these projects far exceeded what is normal for an engineer and extended to cover almost all aspects of the buildings.

55

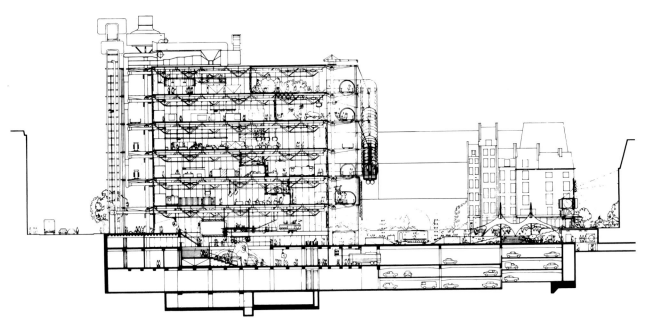

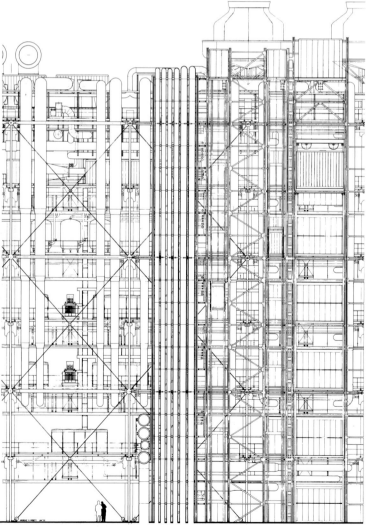

56 **Piano & Rogers**

Pompidou Centre

1 Part of the east, rue Renard, elevation that swarms with services of all sorts.

2 Main (west) elevation and place Georges Pompidou in front. The Pompidou Centre is an enormous machine-monument, celebrating technology in service of a populist view of culture, thrust into the historic centre of Paris. The public have responded by thronging outside as well as through the building.

1

2

3

58   **Piano & Rogers**

Pompidou Centre

1 Plan of typical floor. Structure, services and
circulation are kept to the long edges to leave the
floors unimpeded.

2 Roof and site plan showing the building and the
square in front of it.

3 Oblique view of east elevation on rue Renard
with its colour-coded ducts.

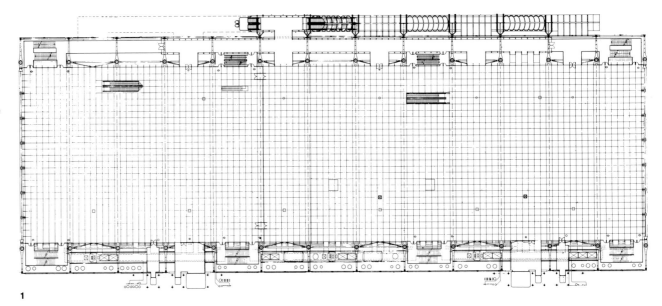

1

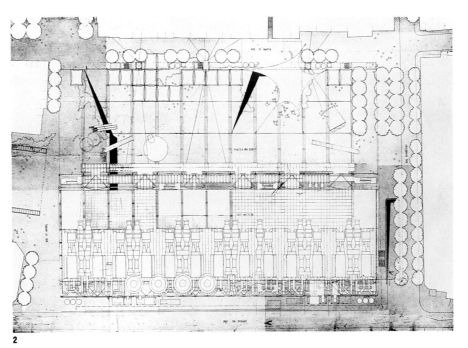

2

Piano & Rogers

Pompidou Centre

4 View from head of escalator through horizontal circulation tube and onto fifth-floor terrace of cafeteria.

5 Cross-bracing between beams on end elevation.

6 Night view of south elevation emphasises the transparency of the perimeter and the enormous clear spans achieved by the huge trusses.

1

60 **Piano & Rogers**

Pompidou Centre

1 View up to where the fourth-floor sculpture terrace opens up behind structure.
2, **3** Circles of spectators around performers are a constant feature of the sloping square in front of the building.

Clients Ministry of Cultural Affairs, Ministry of National Education
Architect Piano & Rogers
Design team R Piano, R Rogers;
competition, programme, interiors G F Franchini;
substructure and mechanical services W Zbinden, H Bysaeth, J Lohse, P Merz, P Dupont;
superstructure and mechanical services L Abbot, S Ishida, H Naruse, H Takahashi;
facade and galleries E Holt;
internal/external interfaces, audiovisual systems A Stanton, M Dowd, R Verbizh;
co-ordination and site supervision C Brullman, B Plattner;
IRCAM M Davies, N Okabe, K Rupard, J Sircus;
interior J Young, F Barat, H Diebold, J Fendard, J Huc, H Sohlegel
Secretaries F Gousinguenet, C Spielmann, C Valensi
Structural engineer Ove Arup & Partners (P Rice, L Grut, R Pierce)
Services engineer Ove Arup & Partners (T Barker)
Cost control M Espinoza
Contractors:
main contractor GTM (Jean Thaury, site engineer);
structure Krupp, Mont-a-Mousson, Pohlig;
secondary structures Voyer;
lifts and escalators Otis;
heating and ventilation Industrielle de Chauffage, Saunier Duval;
glazing CFEM

2

3

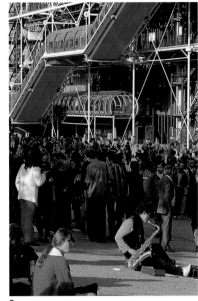

4

5

Piano & Rogers

Pompidou Centre

4, 5 The potent industrial presence of the Pompidou Centre attracts crowds rather than intimidates them.

6 As seen from a tower of Notre Dame, a building with which it shares some characteristics.

7 From the upper levels, as with the restaurant seen here, there are fine views of Paris, giving visitors a fresh appreciation of and sense of contact with the city.

6

7

4

62   **Piano & Rogers**

Pompidou Centre

Interior views.

1 A gallery installed on one of the upper levels.

2, **5** The library.

3, **4** The ground level 'Forum' inside the main entrance doors. Escalators in **4** lead up to the mezzanine level from which the outboard escalator tube is entered to climb the facade of the building in the reverse direction.

Opposite page The outboard escalators in their transparent tube command magnificent views of Paris and of the building itself.

1

2

3

5

4

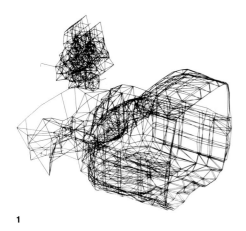

1

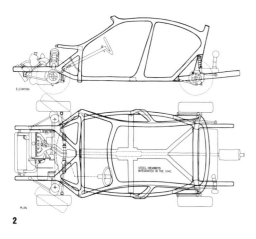

2

Piano & Rice Associates

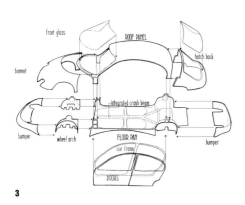

3

4

5

After the long and extremely arduous task of building the Pompidou Centre, Piano felt the need to sever the partnership with Rogers and return to Italy – though he did keep on a small Paris office. He wanted to take stock and recharge himself. He formed a partnership with Peter Rice, which, though short-lived (1978–80), was to be as seminal as that with Rogers. Together they embarked on an intensely experimental phase with very varied projects that led to an enormous broadening of the concerns and approach that has shaped all subsequent work. Not all these projects were architectural. Most show a deepened interest in the social and community aspects of architecture, as well as with all forms of process – and not just that of construction with which Piano had always been fascinated.

To work on these projects Piano took Shunji Ishida and Noriaki Okabe to Genoa with him. For one of the most important projects, an experimental car, they were joined in Turin by Bernard Plattner, and by Laurie Abbot and Alan Stanton who had also worked on the Pompidou. Developing the car, Piano and his collaborators learnt about industrial production and prototyping and also encountered new materials they were to later use in their buildings; making architectural history programmes for television, they focused not just on the final building, but also on the social co-operation, tools and assembly processes with which they were achieved; and in a housing project and a reconstruction exercise they became involved in community participation and other social issues. From all these projects, Piano says he learnt the art of listening, of patiently understanding people – a skill essential to serving them rather than striving for fame and self-glorification.

6

Piano & Rice worked on two experimental vehicles. One was the 'Flying Carpet', a sort of mechanical mule for use in North Africa, particularly Morocco. This was to consist of a locally-made chassis/loading platform of ferro-cement to which were mounted standard imported Fiat components: engine and transmission, steering and suspension. Onto this cheap and rudimentary vehicle could be attached a number of modular secondary components to create a range of different models.

The ferro-cement, which Piano was familiar with from boat-building, was to be only 1cm thick increasing to 4 or 5cm where connections were to made. Though this project went no further than concept stage, Piano was to return to ferro-cement for the leaves of the Menil Collection. The other vehicle was the VSS Experimental Car developed over a period of two years (1978–80) with Fiat engineers. Many of the breakthroughs made on this are now incorporated in the Fiat Tipo, which started production in 1988.

Fiat's brief was to reconsider the car from first principles. The assumption was that as outsiders to the industry, and free from myths about styling and marketing, Piano & Rice might come up with something fresh. This they did. Basically, they rejected standard monocoque construction, which though good in crash performance can be low in buckling rigidity and which because difficult to calculate often acts in unpredictable ways after seemingly minor styling changes. Instead they proposed a separate tubular steel structural frame with plastic body panels. Such a structural frame, even once adapted to robot assembly, is not only superior in performance, but can be more

confidently calculated in terms of strength, corrosion (from which it is well protected) and fatigue. Because cladding panels are separate, the same structural frame can serve several current models as well as future styling changes. Also the car body is 20 per cent lighter and more sound absorbent than other models.

But if Piano & Rice re-introduced the separate frame and panel of building construction into car design, they also learnt a lot from the motor industry, which is generally far more advanced than the building industry. It was here that they first encountered such materials as ductile iron, used for parts of the chassis, and plastics such as polycarbonate, as well as new glue technologies that could secure the plastic panels directly to the steel frame. Ductile iron was later used for the trusses of the Menil Collection, and the polycarbonate and glues on the IBM Travelling Pavilion.

65

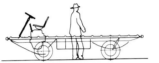

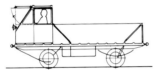

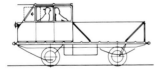

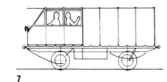

7

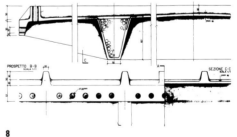

8

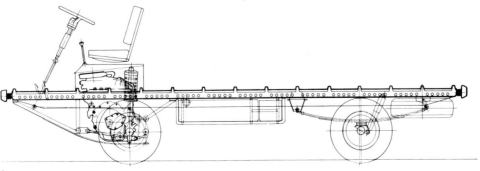

9

1

Piano & Rice Associates

'The Open Site'

Television programmes, 1979

Client Radio Televisione Italiana, Channel 2

Director G Macchi

Producer V Lusvardi

Production Piano & Rice Associates

Production team R Piano, P Rice, S Ishida,
N Okabe (associates), R Biondo, M Bonino,
G Fascioli, R Gaggero, G Picardi, S Yamada

Text and screenplay M Arduino Piano

1 Shunji Ishida's wife, Sugako, with a model that
shows the lattice structure of a Mongol yurt.
2–4 Structures being erected for use in the
television programmes to explain their structural
principles and potentials.
5 Renzo Piano demonstrating how plywood
panels can be tensioned into curves to provide a
lightweight but stable emergency shelter.

2

3

'The Open Site' was a series of
10 television programmes Piano
made, with the assistance of
Ishida and Okabe, in 1979 for
the national Italian network.
The director, with whom Piano
has kept in close contact, was
Giulio Macchi and the script
and screenplay were by Piano's
then-wife, Magda Arduino,
a sociologist and video-maker.
The intention was to show
architecture as a product of
technological invention – in
tools, building methods and
materials – as well as of
social organisation.

Using models and mock-ups they
analysed the Gothic cathedral
(which involved the
collaboration of the whole of the
city that it towered above as it
pushed forward the bounds of the
possible), the mobile Mongolian
yurt (prefabricated in three kinds
of components by men, carried
by animals and easily erected by
women), and the American
balloon frame house (a frugal and
efficient enclosure made only of
local wood and imported nails).

The year before, Piano & Rice
had been commissioned to design
an industrialised housing system
and then use it for the Il Rigo
housing scheme in Corciano near
Perugia (p18). The system
consisted of large concrete
channels, one inverted and
superimposed above the other
to create the floor, roof and side
walls of each unit. Lightweight
steel trusses supported an
intermediate floor, and light steel
glazing frames closed off either
end of the house. The idea was
that within the volume cheaply
enclosed by the concrete channels,
the occupants could select for

themselves how much space they
wished to be enclosed at any
moment and could re-position
the glazed facade accordingly.
Similarly they could add or leave
out parts of the intermediate
floor. Though a prototype unit
was successfully built and tested,
the rest of the scheme was built
conventionally. Yet if actually
building such a prototype was an
uncommon achievement, the idea
of such a flexible unit had been a
recurrent one during the previous
decade or so. It was seen as one
way of offering to occupants
choice and limited participation
in shaping their immediate
environment. Much more radical
and far-ranging were the forms
of participation offered as part of
a strategy devised to regenerate
run-down historic towns and
tested at Otranto.

4

5

6

7

Piano & Rice Associates

'The Open Site'

6 Renzo Piano and Noriaki Okabe demonstrating methods of structural testing.

7 Stills from one of the television programmes explaining the tools and community organisation that built the Gothic cathedrals.

8 Chart by Renzo Piano planning what was to be shown in each of the 10 programmes.

9 Models used to explain the construction of a cathedral.

8

9

68   **Piano & Rice Associates**

UNESCO Neighbourhood Workshop
Otranto, 1979
Client UNESCO (S Busutill, W Tochtermann)
Architect Piano & Rice Associates
Design team R Piano, P Rice, S Ishida,
N Okabe (associates in charge), E Donato,
G Fascioli, R Gaggero, R Melai, G Picardi,
R Verbizh
In collaboration with M Arduino Piano,
F Marano, M Fazio, G Macchi, F Marconi
Engineers Ove Arup & Partners,
IDEA institute, G P Cuppini, G Gasbarri, Editech
Main contractor
G F Dioguardi

1, 2 Typical views of the picturesque but run-
down historic town.
Opposite page Poster on one of the worn walls
of the town announcing the forthcoming arrival of
the Neighbourhood Workshop in the local Piazza
del Popolo.

Perhaps partly inspired by insights gained in making the television programmes, the Otranto experiment with the UNESCO Neighbourhood Workshop (1979) is one of the most seminal of all Piano's projects, both in expanding and redefining his own approach to architecture, and in the evolution of strategies for rehabilitating historic urban fabric. It is particularly significant for the way it proposed using the most up-to-date technology to empower a traditional community and its craftsmen to repair their ancient town.

The first in a series of projects Piano has undertaken for UNESCO, this research was commissioned to find a strategy that would save not just isolated historic monuments but whole historic centres with their vital communal ties and traditions. Urban redevelopment, a panacea of the previous decade, had been immensely destructive of what was now recognised as precious historic fabric, as well as of the social fabric. And if conservation and restoration did not result only in preserved monuments surrounded by increasingly mouldering mundane fabric, then they tended to disrupt the community too because they led to gentrification and rising

property values. The brief for Otranto, the ancient southern Italian town closest to Greece, was to devise an alternative approach and then to test its feasibility in the field.

In line with what was happening elsewhere at the time, the adopted approach was participatory, highlighting process as much as end product and involving the community in all stages and facets of that process. Instead of disrupting and displacing the community and marginalising its knowledge and skills, the Otranto project sought to let the locals determine the future shape of their town and homes and to execute this transformation themselves. What is more, the community would, in the process, develop a renewed cohesion, confidence and sense of purpose.

Participation has too often been only an intellectual exercise in the early stages of a project, in which an ill-prepared community is asked to make binding decisions – a process both intimidating and abrogating of professional responsibilities. What was sought instead at Otranto was an ongoing involvement best achieved by physical participation. The key people to involve were the local artisans and craftsmen who

1

2

1

Piano & Rice Associates

UNESCO Neighbourhood Workshop
The stones of Otranto.
The town is built entirely in local limestone that has now weathered, revealing the patterns of its formation which differ depending on which quarries it came from, so adding to the historical memory of the town the vast temporal dimensions of geology. All these patterns had to be studied and different methods devised of preventing further deterioration of the fabric.
1 Pressure testing a sample of old stone.
2 Roofscape of the old town shows that even many of the roofs are stone paved.
3–10 Some of the patterns in the weathered stone, all of them trace telling tales of the primeval organic life of the region.

constituted a pool of skills and wealth of knowledge that are often ignored today. Their participation was to be elicited by the introduction of specially designed or selected tools that they could easily master, or which, if used by an expert, would complement rather than negate their contribution.

It was with this emphasis on tools that the devised approach differed from and improved upon most other participation exercises of the time, and where it chimed, unconsciously apparently, with the contemporary ideas of the

social critic, Ivan Illich. For Illich the difference between a product and a tool is crucial. A product belongs to the 'heteronomous' mode of industry that reduces people to passive consumers. In contrast a tool can facilitate the autonomous mode whereby individuals actively shape their environment and future. The prime tool proposed and tested in Otranto was the mobile Neighbourhood Workshop. This was itself a multi-functional tool as well as container of many other tools, some of them extraordinarily simple, and

others from the absolute leading edge of technology.

The Neighbourhood Workshop was a 2.4-metre cube brought in by truck and set up in a piazza. There its four sides were unfolded below a sheltering tent roof, revealing their contents and defining a series of spaces for a wide range of activities open to and inviting the curiosity and participation of local citizens. Each side was dedicated to a different facet of the reconstruction process.

The first contained some of the most sophisticated equipment available for quickly and easily surveying the exact condition of the physical fabric of the town. But besides such advanced forms of survey as photogrammetry and thermography, others were cunningly improvised, such as the rudimentary aerial photography achieved with an ordinary motor-driven camera, which was held aloft by balloon and walked around the town.

The second side was where proposals were formulated and their feasibility tested, and where community and craftsmen were inculcated in new ways of doing things. Here the primary resource was not equipment but expert

2

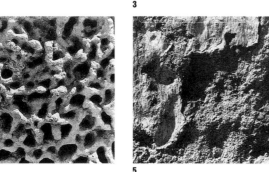

3

7

4

5

6

8

Piano & Rice Associates

UNESCO Neighbourhood Workshop

11–13 Street floors, like the walls of the town, are in stone, all in a rich variety of patterns and textures. **11**, shows one of the houses in which novel techniques were applied to repair the structure without displacing the tenants.

14–16 Further examples of the contrasting patterns revealed in the weathered stone.

71

13

11

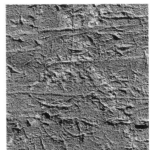

14

9

12

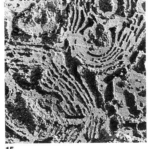

15

16

10

1

2

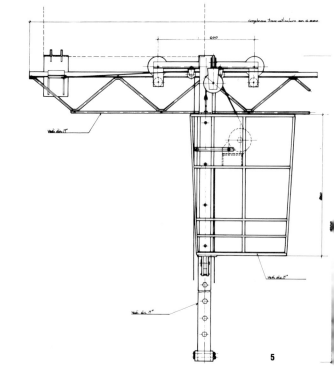

5

72   **Piano & Rice Associates**

UNESCO Neighbourhood Workshop

The strategy adopted emphasised tools that would
to be used by local craftsmen and the community.
1–4 The prime tool, the Neighbourhood
Workshop, itself housing many other tools, being
delivered, opened up and sheltered by a tent roof.
5 Elevation of cradle that could move along, up
and down from a parapet-attached truss, so
obviating scaffolding in narrow streets.
6, 8 Balloon-tyred electric tractor and trailer
designed for narrow streets and stairs.
7 Making lightweight trusses in the street.

3

4

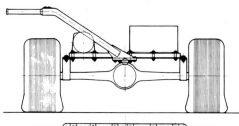

6

7

8

9

advisers. The third side was for documentation and discussion, and the fourth was devoted to actual construction. Included in this fourth side were many ingenious tools that could be easily manipulated and mastered by local artisans and that could be used in constrained contexts.

The transport of building materials was by battery-powered tractor driven by someone walking beside it, its low-pressure tyres allowing it even to scramble up staircases. Simple electric hoists lifted materials and movable parapet-attached cradles eliminated the need for scaffolding in very narrow streets.

The tools that best exemplified this alternative approach to conservation and reconstruction were those with which a couple of artisans could purpose-make components on site, which they then could equally easily erect. An example was the metal bending tool with which light steel trusses were made to exact fit, to support collapsing ceilings and vaults without even the need to disturb the furniture below. Here normal industrial process was reversed and the plant not the product, which was itself a one-off rather than standard, was brought to site. Hence 'progress' adapted itself to the historic fabric, rather than the reverse as is usual, and the community was empowered in, rather than pre-empted of, its capacity to manipulate and preserve its built environment.

Although much time had gone into conceiving this strategy and the form and contents of the Neighbourhood Workshop, in this initial instance it was only set up in Otranto for a week. This was just long enough to demonstrate the potential of the strategy and of the regenerative energies it could unleash, but not to effect much of a transformation of the town. However it did lead on to the successful application of a very similar strategy to restructure and repair part of the island of Burano in the Venetian lagoon (1980–84).

The Otranto experiment also led to several other such projects by the Renzo Piano Building Workshop, as the practice became known when Rice ceded his partnership. Some of these successive projects were again undertaken with UNESCO, and others independently for local authorities, some of which had corporate sponsorship. A modified form of the Neighbourhood Workshop was set up the year following Otranto in nearby Japigia near Bari (1980), where it was sponsored by a prominent local contractor, Gianfranco Dioguardi, who helped with the administration of the Otranto experiment.

73

Piano & Rice Associates

UNESCO Neighbourhood Workshop

9 Parapet-attached cradle in action.

10, **11** Installing a tailored-to-fit lightweight truss to support a sagging upper floor without moving even the furniture.

12, **13** Aerial photography was cheaply achieved with a motor-driven camera lifted aloft by a helium balloon, which was walked around the streets.

14 Making the trusses seen in **10** and **11** with simple tools in the street.

15 Testing types of impregnated damp proofing.

16 Testing stones from different areas.

10

11

12

14

13

15

16

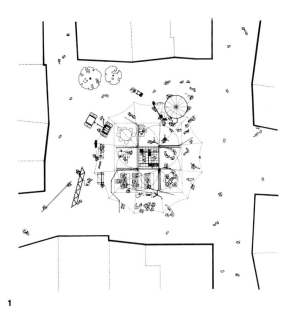

1

One of the most ambitious and interesting of such urban regeneration schemes was that for the rehabilitation of the ancient Molo quarter alongside Genoa's docks. Here the upward extensions characteristic of the old parts of that city have resulted in buildings that are seven or eight storeys high with very narrow streets between them, and very poor ventilation and natural light.

Besides solving the latter with such ingenious means as mirrors to reflect down sunlight, it was proposed to stratify the functional uses. On the bottom levels commercial uses were proposed, in the middle housing, and on the upper levels an active public realm of schools, bars and other such uses. These would all be connected by a series of high-level bridges like those commonly found giving access to the upper levels of apartment blocks on the steeper slopes of Genoa. Although this scheme was never executed, it was the seed that eventually flowered as the 1992 Columbus International Exposition and therefore led to the rehabilitation of several fine old warehouses and the reintegration of the old town and historic docks.

Other schemes studied for UNESCO were for Senegal (1978), where a mobile unit was to have operated, Khaniá, Crete (1985), the town of Rhodes, Greece (p76) and for Valletta on Malta (p74). Similar studies for other clients were prepared for the Sassi quarter of Matera in southern Italy (1987) and for visitors' facilities for Pompeii (1988).

74   **Piano & Rice Associates**

UNESCO Neighbourhood Workshop
Community participation.
The Neighbourhood Workshop, the way it folded open to create inviting spaces, and its contents were all devised to encourage the community to become engaged and participate in the process in a wide variety of ways.

1 Plan showing the Neighbourhood Workshop opened out to create spaces for different activities.
2 Audience at a nightime meeting.
3 Old men in a bar: a pool of knowledge and one of the resources of the town.
4 Seeing the town afresh: people viewing an exhibition of photographs of Otranto.
5 Each undertaking drew its own group of spectators and helpers.
6 Renzo Piano addressing a community meeting.
7 Children watch videos while adults discuss around the table.

2

4

3

5

6   **7**

8

9

Piano & Rice Associates

UNESCO Neighbourhood Workshop

8 In the evening relevant documentary films are shown.

9 Young and old gather to watch a replay of a video documenting the ongoing process.

10–13 Each of the four sides of the Neighbourhood Workshop opened into a zone serving a different purpose: **10**, diagnostic and analysis sector with photogrammetry and thermography equipment, as well as equipment for more simple surveys such as aerial photography; **11**, construction sector with its specially devised tools; **12**, planning and design sector; **13**, documentation and feedback sector.

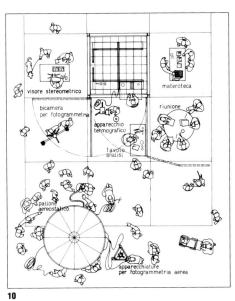

10

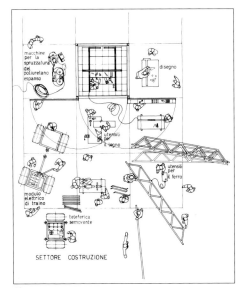

11

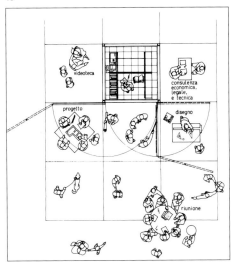

12

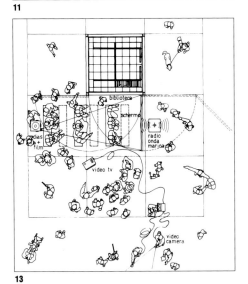

13

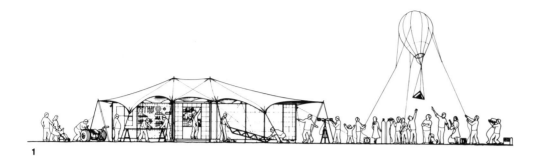

1

Piano & Rice Associates

UNESCO Neighbourhood Workshop

Community participation.

As well as individual, informal and small group-participation meetings, such as seen in **1** and **2**, there were regular evening meetings for the whole community.

1 Elevation showing a range of both simple and sophisticated tools being used by members of the community.

2 People studying an exhibition while a community meeting is in progress.

3, **4** Neighbourhood Workshop serves as an illuminated stage and focus for community meetings.

2

3

4

78

Renzo Piano Building Workshop

In 1981 Piano's partnership with Peter Rice was dissolved because it was attracting insufficient work, particularly of the sort that benefited from the integration of architectural and engineering input, such as the experimental car. The Genoa office then took the name Renzo Piano Building Workshop. (The French office only changed its name from Atelier de Paris sometime later.)

The name is virtually a statement of intent. Being in English it makes explicit Piano's very un-parochial perspective and international ambitions – though Workshop might also conjure associations with Florentine *botteghe* of the Renaissance, thus evoking the humanistic values and emphasis on practice as much as theory that Piano espouses. And adding Building, rather than architecture to Workshop, emphasises further a pragmatic and experimental approach, concerned with actually making and not just drawing. The name might also imply that everybody mucks in in a way that is participatory and not too hierarchical.

The Building Workshop has become an increasingly international enterprise with work in far-flung parts of the globe. Besides having bases in Paris and Osaka as well as Genoa, where there is now another outpost in nearby Vesima, it has projects not only in several parts of Europe, but also in the USA and Japan.

On taking this new name, Piano's architecture enters its mature phase. All the experiments and lessons of the previous practices and the stable core of his multinational team of collaborators and consultants are consolidated in producing works that are more complex and complete than what went before. Yet the works are no more uniform or less experimental. The commitment to start each design afresh remains. Materials, whether new or old, are explored for new potentials and components are refined until they achieve novel organic integrity. But now context in all its spatial and temporal, physical and cultural dimensions also heavily conditions design, as can be seen in most of the buildings in the rest of this volume. These factors ensure the striking freshness of each design and their collective heterogeneity.

A new and consistent characteristic of these works is the way technology and nature are always brought together in intimate interrelationship. Thus at the Schlumberger site, Paris, (p90), nature as landscaping and internal planting comes together with technology as new glazing and services to convert an old factory into pleasant modern premises. The IBM Travelling Pavilion (p110) used natural materials and biomorphic forms to create a technology that would be at home in park settings. The Menil Collection at Houston, USA (p140) uses new technology to admit and modulate natural light in its ground floor, which is pervaded by pockets of planting. At the Aluminium Research Institute, Novara (p166), planting penetrates the front face of the slot-together concrete and aluminium building to relate it to the park across the street. At the San Nicola Stadium in Bari (p178) the presence of the surrounding landscape can be sensed in all parts of the introverted concrete structure. And in Paris at the IRCAM Extension (p202) and Rue de Meaux Housing (p214), the warmth and weathering of the 'natural' terracotta elements tempers the cold steel frames or glass-reinforced concrete panels they face.

As well as preparing a design for a retrospective show of some 500 pieces by Alexander Calder, the Building Workshop was asked to look at how the Palazzo a Vela might be used for future cultural events. Built for the Turin International Expo of 1961, the hall subsequently had proved difficult to use. Its huge size and height (a span of 120 metres rising to 30 metres) overwhelms most exhibits and even the largest artworks, while the glazed walls flood it with sunlight, adding glare and further heat to that admitted through the uninsulated roof.

The response to these problems was to mask the 7 000 square metres of windows with aluminium panels: a natural silver surface faced outwards to reflect heat, and a dark blue surface faced inwards. Together with fans that moved the air, and water sprinkled on the roof, these simple devices lowered temperatures inside by some six degrees centigrade. The blue helped provide a feeling of cool tranquillity, while the darkness masked the immensity of the hall in which spotlights kept the eye low and focused on the artworks. The result was an atmosphere that was relaxed, but encouraged concentration.

To gather up visitors, lead them into and through the show, and out to where further works were displayed, a long straight promenade was created. This led people past an outdoor bar, under huge suspended steel letters spelling Calder's name, through the hall with the exhibition to one side and service rooms and auditoria to the other, and out again past another bar to an outdoor pond.

Inside the hall, long partitions, lit by rows of spotlights held on arms that reached out from the heads of the partitions, radiated from an eccentrically placed focus towards which visitors were funnelled by those partitions closest to the promenade. In this brightly lit focus were three large stabiles over which swung a few mobiles. On the partitions, hung paintings and similar flat(ish) works, and where the partitions opened out away from the focus were placed more sculptures. These sat on raised white islands that like the water outside prevented the works from being tampered with.

80 **Installations**

Over the years, the Renzo Piano Building Workshop has been involved in a number of installations, mainly for exhibitions. The first two works executed after the office took its present name were both temporary installations. The first was for a large retrospective of the works of Alexander Calder held in the Palazzo a Vela in Turin. The other was a setting for Luigi Nono's opera *Prometeo*, which housed singers, musicians and audience within the embrace of the same wooden structure. This is a work that remains a favourite with several members of the Building Workshop.

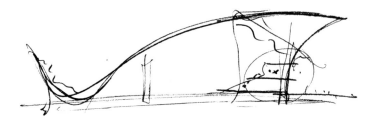

Calder Retrospective Turin, Italy **Building Workshop, Italy** 1982

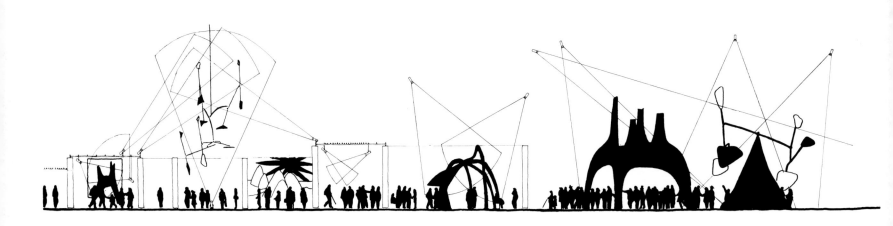

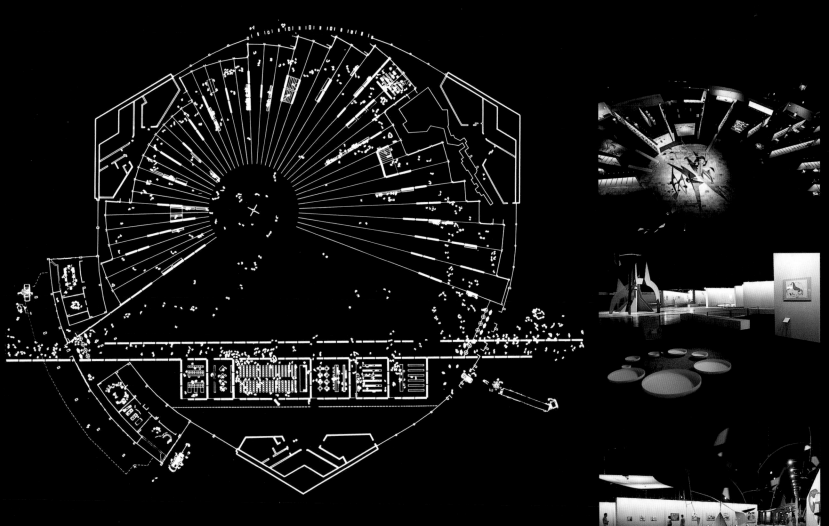

1

82   **Calder Retrospective**

1 Interior view showing partitions radiating from the central focus.

2 Site plan with promenade created to run right through Palazzo a Vela from the site entrance and parking on the north to the lake in the south.

3 View along the promenade that leads past outdoor sculptures and the bar, and under suspended lettering, into existing Palazzo a Vela.

4 Night view of entrance with sculpture and suspended lettering.

5 Close-up view of a suspended steel letter.

6 Lake with sculptures seemingly floating above its surface.

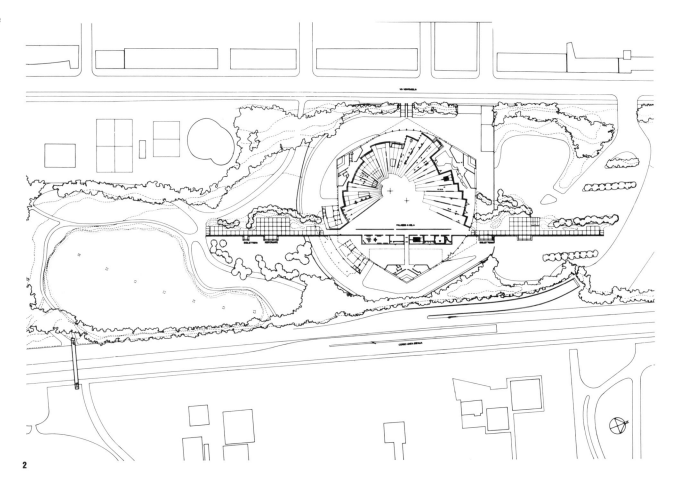

2

3

4

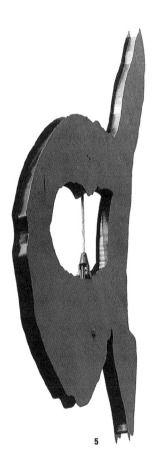

5

6

84

An enormous musical instrument that was simultaneously stage and set, auditorium and reverberant sound box, was tailor-made for an opera by Luigi Nono, which was first performed during the 1984 Venice Biennale in the church of San Lorenzo. In the centre of this wooden 'opera ark', of material chosen for its acoustic warmth, the audience of 400 listened to how the sounds from performers who moved among the audience, as well as on the three galleries around it, reverberated and mingled. The chairs were specially designed to allow some reclining and swivelling so that the audience could better follow the action.

The installation was made of prefabricated laminated timber structural elements and fireproof plywood panels. These were chosen not only for acoustic and fire resistance purposes, but also because they were easy to make in curves or to bend, to transport by barge through the canals of Venice and to erect. The laminated timber elements served as beams for the raised floor as well as curving up to become the columns of the outer walls of the installation. Connecting the columns were tubular steel rails that supported the plywood cladding panels and the galleries.

Once erected, the whole that somehow embraced the heavily ornamented arch in the centre of the double-aisled church resembled the still-unfinished hull of a ship. This impression was enhanced by the way the performance/listening area floated in the space, raised on metal props to create a foyer underneath that would otherwise not have been possible in the cramped volume. Raising the installation also brought it closer to both the entablature that rings the old interior and to the vaults of the roof that provided further sound reflecting elements. Some final tuning of the acoustics was possible by adjusting the position of the plywood panels, and by the placing and combination of the curved and straight panels.

The transportability and ease of erection of the installation were proved again when it was transported to Milan the following year and set up in a factory in Ansaldo.

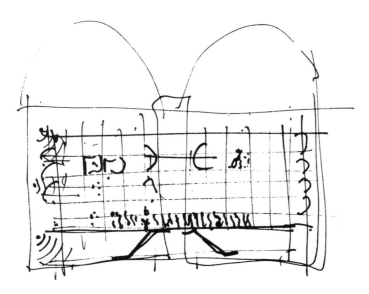

Setting for *Prometeo* Opera Venice and Milan, Italy **Building Workshop, Italy** 1983 and 1984

Client Ente Autonomo, Teatro alla Scala, Milan
Architect Renzo Piano Building Workshop, Italy
Design team R Piano, S Ishida (associate in charge), A Traldi, C Abagliano, D L Hart, M Visconti
Structural engineers M Milan, S Favero
Music L Nono
Libretto M Cacciari
Director C Abbado
with R Cecconi
Contractor G F Dioguardi SpA

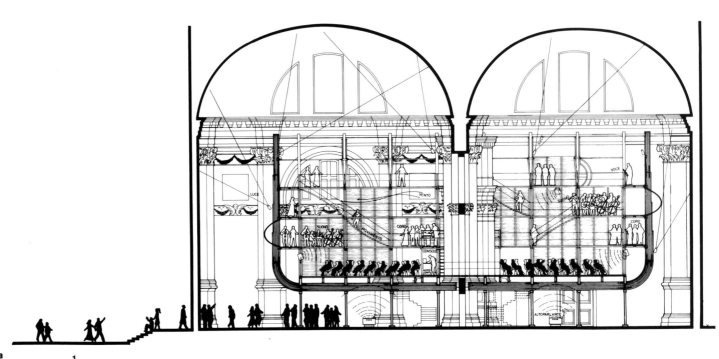

1

86 **Setting for *Prometeo* Opera**

Installation in San Lorenzo, Venice.

1 Section.

2 Plan.

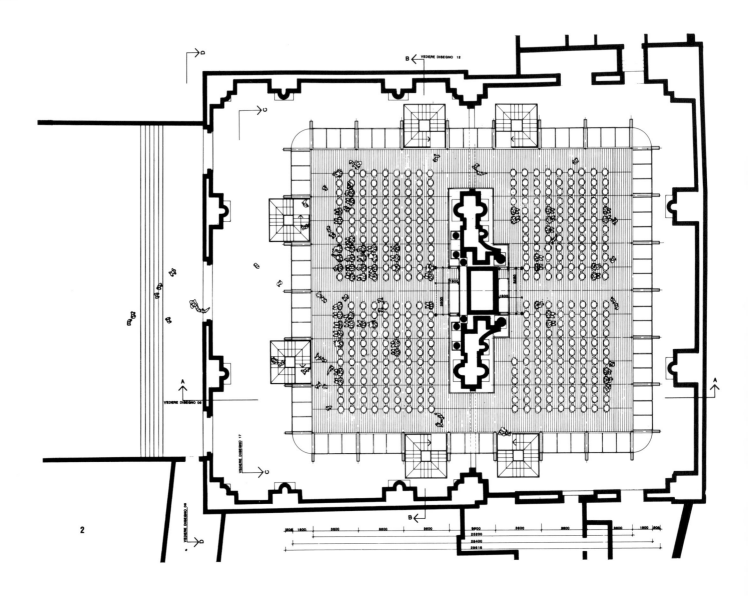

2

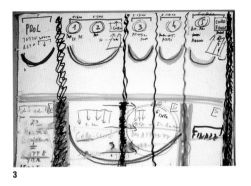

3

4

5

'The music in 'Il Prometeo' is not projected into perspective, over the heads of the audience as in a traditional opera house, but instead inundates the audience, which becomes fully immersed in the performance.' Renzo Piano

Setting for *Prometeo* Opera

3 Notes for score by Luigi Nono.

4 Performers' galleries with the old walls of the church behind

5–7 Performers in rehearsal. Note how some plywood panels were curved to vary the acoustic reverberations.

8 Performance in progress. The installation served as both stage and auditorium as performers encircled and moved amongst the audience.

9 Sketch studies for stairs between performers' galleries.

6

7

8

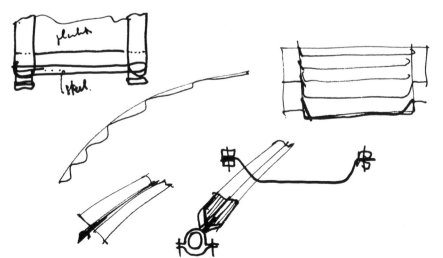

9

Setting for *Prometeo* Opera

Opposite page: corner of installation in San Lorenzo, which shows clearly the contrast in scale and detailing between the huge laminated timber members and the spindly steelwork. All parts were sized for easy transport by boat and truck.

1–3 Installation being assembled in Milan.

4, 5 Construction drawings: **4**, details of junctions of tubular steelwork; **5**, part section.

6 Close-up view of junction of steel tubes.

7 Sketches of tubing junctions.

1

3

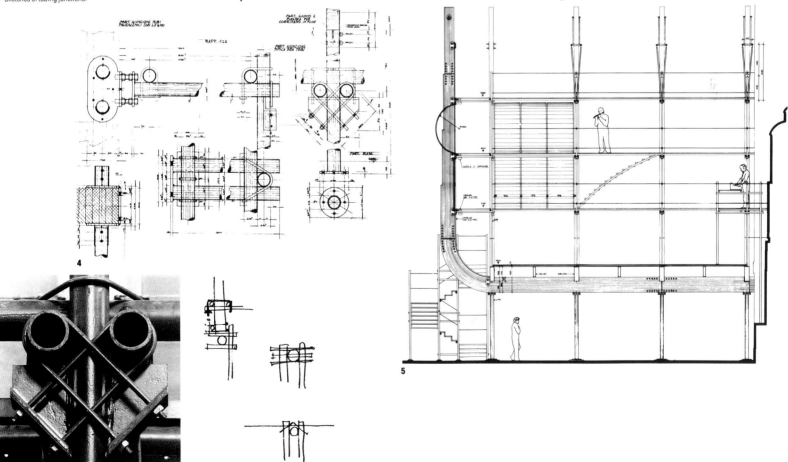

4

5

6

7

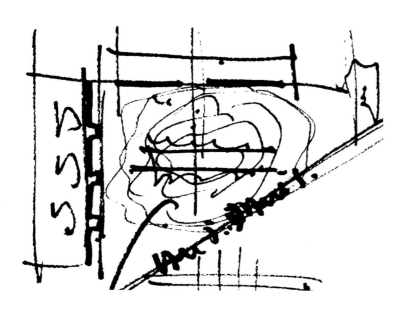

Schlumberger Renovation Paris, France **Building Workshop, France** 1981–84

To convert a densely developed old industrial complex into pleasant and efficient modern research and office facilities for Schlumberger, new technology and nature have been brought together symbiotically with each other and with the old fabric. As well as the Teflon tent that shades a 'street' between communal facilities built above a submerged new parking garage, the new technology takes the form of new lifts and air conditioning, windows and partitions. Nature takes the form of a landscaped garden that accompanies workers into the circulation cores and even into the office and research spaces, serving as a tactile counterpoint to this technology and that with which the employees work.

Coming together here for the first time, in this its first large-scale work, are key themes that still dominate the work of the Building Workshop, but that Piano had explored only separately in earlier projects. As with the UNESCO reconstruction experiment at Otranto (p68), modern technology is used to revitalise the legacy from the past. And as with the IBM Travelling Pavilion (p110), designed, built and travelling while Schlumberger was in progress, technology co-exists

harmoniously with, and even emulates, the forms of nature – here most obviously in the shapes of the tensile structure and its components. So the initially daunting prospect of converting grimy and unprepossessing old buildings on a strictly limited budget and for a very demanding client (though a good working relationship was enjoyed with the chairman Jean Riboud and the co-ordinator Alain Vincent, who subsequently joined the Building Workshop), became a seminal project consolidating past experiments and laying foundations for the future. For instance, the rehabilitation of the Lingotto factory now in progress not only introduces new technology and landscaping but as here uses a pre-designed kit of parts to retain some overall consistency throughout the various interventions.

Schlumberger's industrial plant in Montrouge, a southern suburb of Paris, grew piecemeal from 1925 until the eight hectare site, that is bisected diagonally by the avenue Jean-Jaurès, was completely filled in the 1950s. At one time there were not just factories and some office and research facilities, but also workers' housing. However, in recent decades the company has developed away from heavy engineering production to become a multinational specialising in electronic equipment for use in detecting and extracting oil. As a result, different and much cleaner manufacturing premises were required and a larger proportion of the workforce (there are now 2000 on site) is involved in administration and research.

Land costs prohibited building elsewhere in Paris and so the decision was taken to renovate the five-storey blocks around the edges of the site while demolishing the single-storey factories in the centre. Only after proposals had been sought from more than 20 other architects was the Building Workshop selected and commissioned.

While the old blocks to be kept needed new windows, the Building Workshop otherwise

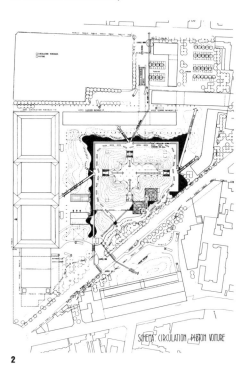

1

Schlumberger Renovation

1 Aerial view of the site as it was, densely
developed with single-storey factory sheds
framed by five-storied blocks.
2 Site plan of original design has a diagrammatic
clarity loosened in the executed design.
3 Inside one of the now-demolished factories.
4, 5 Equipment that was made by heavy industrial
processes in the factories, the memory of which
Piano did not want to obliterate entirely.

2

proposed to remain true to, and
highlight, the plain and frugal
character of the exteriors that
had become part of the historic
identity of this industrial area.
Inside though, more extensive
intervention was required to
bring the blocks up to
contemporary standards. But
wherever possible the proposal
was to do this using a
standardised strategy and kit of
parts. And in the space to be
vacated by the demolished
factories would be a garden that
would not only enhance the
Schlumberger premises, but also
be a visual oasis in this greenery-
starved area. To keep this as
large as possible, the required
new communal facilities would
either be concealed below the

earth or sheltered in tensile
structures that would be a semi-
festive focus of the garden.

The park-like garden now
provides a flattering foreground
to the rehabilitated but rather
mundane old blocks, and an
attractive slowly changing
outlook both for them and for
those passing along the avenue
Jean-Jaurès. Also, by providing
an extended and pleasant
entrance route, it distances those
arriving from the dreary
surroundings. Approach from
the street is by paths that,
unbeknown to visitors, are
along the edges of the roof of a
submerged parking garage for
1 000 cars. Stairs rise up through
the corners of the garage to these
paths. From them, bridges cross
the ponds that flank three sides of
the sunken garage to lead to the
circulation cores of each block.

Between these paths, on the
middle of the parking garage roof
and under a planted mound of
earth bermed against and swept

over them, are such central
facilities as a restaurant and bar,
bank and travel agency,
gymnasium and auditorium.
These are ranged on either side
of a pedestrian 'street' that
bisects the mound, and are
collectively referred to as the
Forum. A Teflon awning floats
over the crest of the mound to
shelter the street. The tenting is
supported on a tensile structure
with minimal compression
elements, one row pin-jointed to
the facade of the street, the other
row supported over the street by
tension cables only. Viewed from
above it resembles the shell of
some giant crustacean. Hence the
only entirely new and visible
construction in the whole scheme
is expressed, either through its
shape or by putting a berm over
it, as part of nature, even though
it shelters that quintessential
urban element, the street.

Beyond the Forum, one of the
bridges ramps up across a pool to
pass through the now-exposed
concrete frame of the most
prominent old building and
penetrate the circulation core at
first floor level. Here the original
windows and brick infill have
been removed and the new
glazing recessed to form a screen
behind, and independent of, the
old concrete frame. Above, the
red tile roof has been removed to
expose the delicate old trusses
and purlins – and leave exposed
the motor room of the new lifts

3

4   5

6

Schlumberger Renovation

6 Aerial view of the site as it now is with the single-storey factories demolished and replaced by a park-like garden and central facilities along a tent-sheltered 'street'.

7, 8 Electronic equipment now assembled in the 'clean' factories on site.

9 The tent-roofed street of the Forum of central facilities.

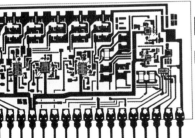

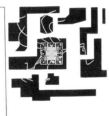

7

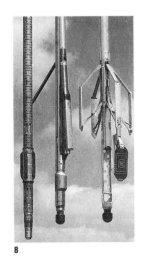

8

9

that are also visible behind the old concrete frame. This is an extreme example of the tactic used elsewhere in the scheme, whereby the old building seems to have been eroded, its infillings and coverings removed to leave the old structural frame evident.

Breaking down the scale of and animating the drab and monotonous old blocks, these erosions, far from being gratuitous and decorative, actually exemplify the spirit of the conversion. They highlight the differences between old and new, and yet, by also conspicuously interweaving them, simultaneously integrate them too. The implied agent of this erosion is an active nature that has come in with the new garden; in the prominent block beyond the Forum, it has also eroded the bottom two floors where the glazing is again set back behind the concrete frame, almost as if this has been clawed clean by the plants that penetrate

beyond it. So these erosions not only interweave old and new into a fresh unity, but do the same for architecture and nature, at least for the latter as landscaping.

At the circulation cores, nature in the form of planting invades the buildings to swarm up the stairs, take over landings and enter the offices and laboratories. (In the most extreme instance, again the core into which the bridge enters at first floor level, and in a trick taken from Neutra, a pond extends under the glazing and into the bottom of a stair-well, down towards which creepers cascade). Nature thus furnishes not just visual outlook in the garden, but also a companionably tangible presence inside to offset the numbing abstractness of so much contemporary work, a counterbalance sometimes referred to as high-tech/high-touch. And outside, the planting was chosen by landscape architect Alexandre Chemetov, to provide a pronounced sequence of colour changes through the seasons, so marking these cycles for those in the stabilised state of air-conditioned interiors full of evergreen plants.

Sheathed in continuous glazing, the central circulation core is like a tall conservatory. The stairs and balustrades are from the kit of parts used throughout the scheme and are in the same yellow steel as the

bridges and balustrades outside. This further blurs the distinction between inside and out. In their spindly delicacy, which matches that of the exposed old roof trusses, these stairs and balustrades – like the new green window frames – seem to intimate that they too are part of the intrusion by nature.

Besides stairs, balustrades, bridges and window frames, the kit of parts includes lifts, street furniture and facing panels. All are designed with a restraint compatible with the old buildings and both they and elements of the old buildings are colour coded – grey for existing concrete, red for old structural steel, green for window frames, yellow for circulation elements and blue for air conditioning. Again the strategy is to make distinctions between the parts that thereby become more equal and so are drawn together into a new whole. As is typical of the Building Workshop, the elements of this kit are designed so that they too seem to be made up from a kit of parts, back into which they could easily be disassembled. This results in a rather distractingly didactic quality to the detailing, and constrains some of these elements from coming together as an elegant unity.

Beyond the circulation cores a common strategy is used to convert the old factory blocks into modern offices and laboratories. Because of their 16-metre depth, the floors have been subdivided into naturally lit cellular spaces on both sides of a wide circulation zone, in which there is a central row of rooms for photocopiers, storage and so on. And because of the high cills of the original windows, a 30cm raised floor has been installed throughout for telephone and

93

1

2

94 **Schlumberger Renovation**

Some of the street furniture and smaller structures are overly elaborated into individually expressed parts in a distractingly didactic manner.

1 Reception kiosk.

2 Bus shelter.

3 Corner of escape stair.

4 Cutaway isometric of typical refurbished floor. A raised floor accommodates cabling and reduces the window cill level. Because the windows rise to soffit of shallow beam, new suspended ceilings stop short of them, with glazed partition panels rising into this slot. A row of central service rooms fills the area in the wide block between outer office/laboratories.

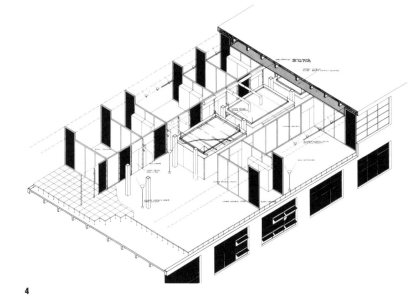

4

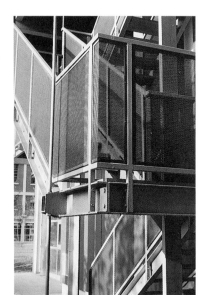

3

electricity cables and heating pipes. But the windows reach up to the bottom of a perimeter beam that barely descends below the slab. So the suspended ceiling installed to hide the messy soffit of the slab and the purpose-designed, aluminium-framed partitions stop short of the windows, with the resultant gap filled by glass. This transparent perimeter and the double central corridor give to even this highly constrained conversion the fluidity of space and light, and so a certain sense of ease, that Piano always seeks.

Although the basic elements and their positioning persisted, the design changed considerably from first proposals to final execution. As its graphic presentation emphasises, the initial design is something of a period piece that looks back to British architecture of the 1960s, including that of Cedric Price. It has a diagrammatic clarity rather lacking in the final design.

Although the parking is submerged as in the executed scheme, its presence is more strongly revealed by a clearer expression of the roof as a rectilinear island, with a free-form edge to the water on the opposite bank, and where it extends beyond the sunken garage. From taxi drop-offs on the edge of each side of this island, enclosed bridges (on the then *de rigueur* diagonal) lead to the circulation core of each converted block. From the same spots open bridges cross to a meandering waterside path. Adjacent to each drop-off is an entrance to the parking below and to the awning-sheltered central Forum. This was much more of a hub for the whole scheme than the built equivalent.

As executed, the street of communal facilities is central, but no longer pivotal. However, along with this loss of clarity the scheme has lost a certain sense of contrivance and datedness, an example perhaps of Piano's search for the solution that feels natural and not forced or over designed. Yet for all its attractiveness, the landscaping seems too 'natural' and mock rural. Mostly shrubs, grass and water with few trees, it is a landscape to walk upon rather than be enveloped by; it can be looked at with great pleasure but not really used.

More formal and traditional French urban landscaping, such as Chemetov apparently first proposed, might have worked better. Then visitors might have been immediately welcomed into a gravel-floored room, colonnaded with the trunks of horse chestnut trees and roofed with their foliage. Shady in summer, sunny in winter, such a room would also be usable, for sitting, trysts and boules. On the other hand, the aloofness from the street, the sense of corporate identity and exclusiveness, that the present landscaping confers is perhaps just right for such high-security premises for rarefied research.

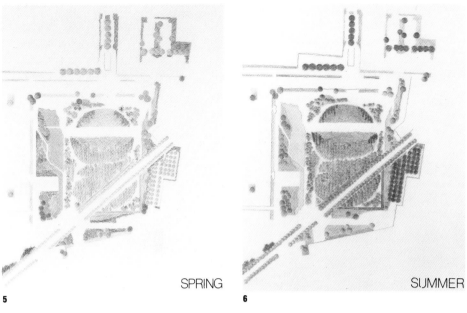

SPRING

5

SUMMER

6

Schlumberger Renovation

Landscaping: plants were chosen and placed for their colour changes through the seasons. This provides an ever-changing outlook for those in the stable conditions of the interiors.

5–8 Planting plans, which show colours through the seasons.

9 Chart plotting colour changes through the year of different plant species.

10–13 Details of the landscaping, seen in different seasons.

10

11

12

13

9

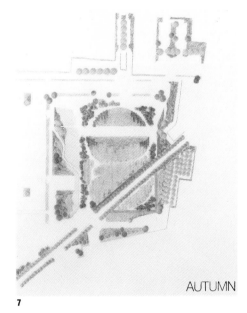

AUTUMN

7

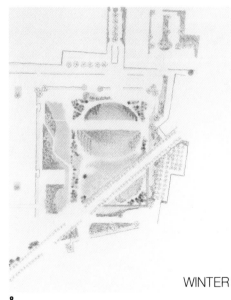

WINTER

8

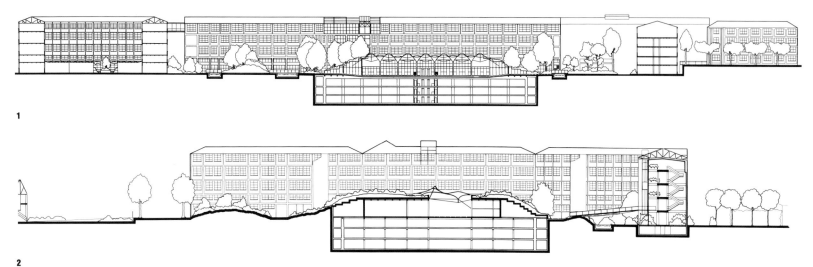

1

2

Schlumberger Renovation

Previous pages View north into the site from near the main entrance. The pedestrian entrance is to the right, along the edge of the pond and over the various footbridges. The tent roof that shelters the central 'street' of the Forum crowns the mound to the right.

1 Section through the refurbished blocks, garden, subterranean parking garage and 'street' of the Forum.

2 Section across avenue Jean-Jaurès and through parking garage, Forum and conservatory-like circulation core.

3 Site plan and ground floor plan. The site is bisected at an angle by avenue Jean-Jaurès.

Opposite page Close-up view, which shows how the old building has been eroded at the conservatory-like circulation core, leaving the old concrete and steel frames exposed, behind which is set the new glazing and glazed external lifts.

Following pages View from near entrance to parking garage, through trees and past mound and tent roof of top of central block with conservatory-like circulation core.

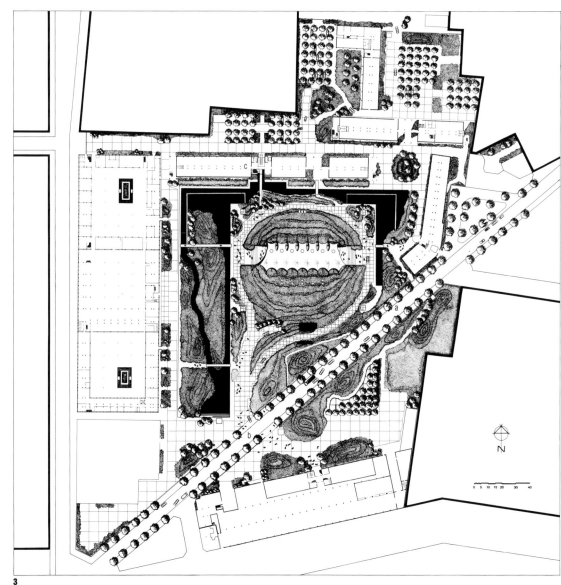

3

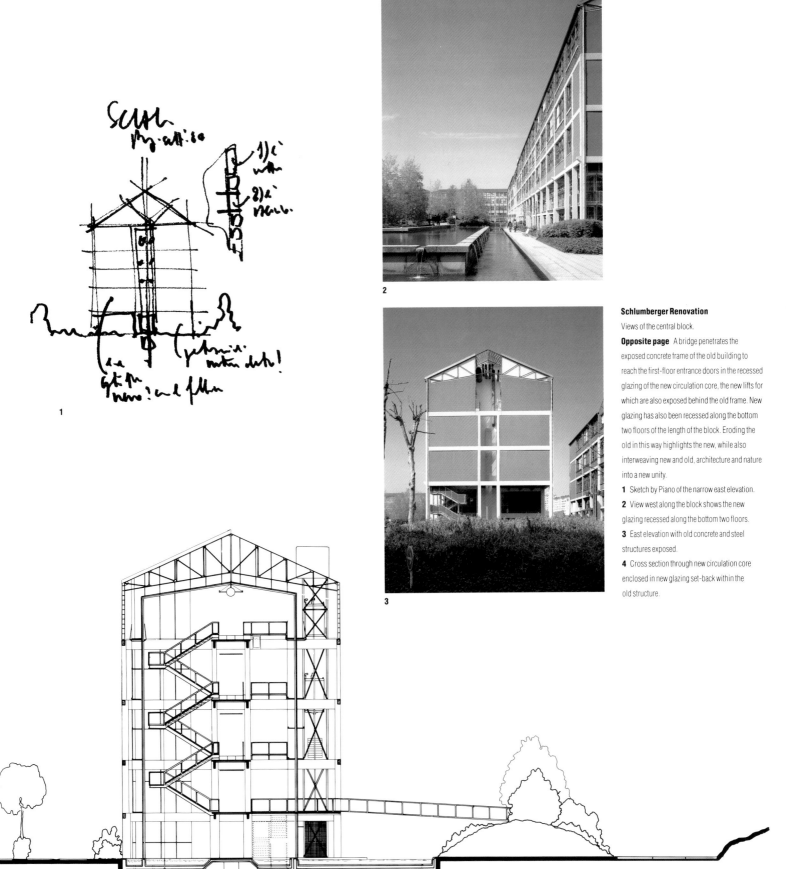

Schlumberger Renovation

Views of the central block.

Opposite page A bridge penetrates the exposed concrete frame of the old building to reach the first-floor entrance doors in the recessed glazing of the new circulation core, the new lifts for which are also exposed behind the old frame. New glazing has also been recessed along the bottom two floors of the length of the block. Eroding the old in this way highlights the new, while also interweaving new and old, architecture and nature into a new unity.

1 Sketch by Piano of the narrow east elevation.

2 View west along the block shows the new glazing recessed along the bottom two floors.

3 East elevation with old concrete and steel structures exposed.

4 Cross section through new circulation core enclosed in new glazing set-back within the old structure.

104

1

2

3

4

5

6

Schlumberger Renovation

Interiors.

1–4, 7–8 Views of the conservatory-like circulation core in the central block.

1 The top floor overlooking the well that rises behind new glazing to the glass roof.

2 Pond at bottom of the well, which seems to extend the water outside inwards.

3 View from near the new lifts across the well – where the plants seem an inward extension of the landscaping outside – to the new stair.

4 View from the landing on the new stair to the wind lobby, through which the entrance bridge passes before bridging the well.

5 Top floor reception area.

6 Office/laboratory space in the north-lit ex-factory block, south of avenue Jean-Jaurès.

7 New steel and glass stair, colour-coded yellow to denote that is a circulation element.

8 Sky-lit top of the circulation core, with the exposed old roof structure, air-conditioning ducts and stairs all colour coded.

9 Construction drawing: cross section of new circulation core.

7

8

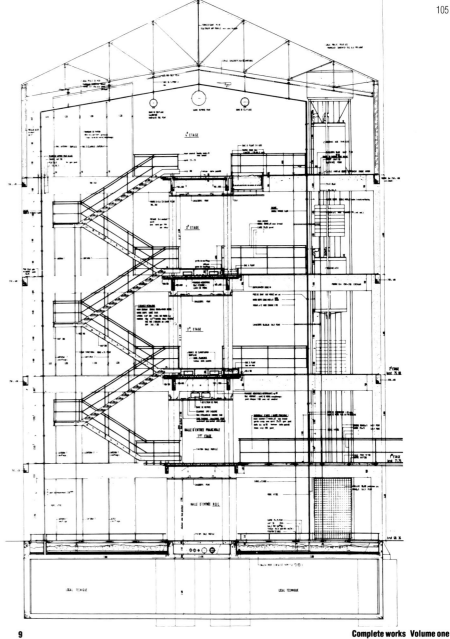

9

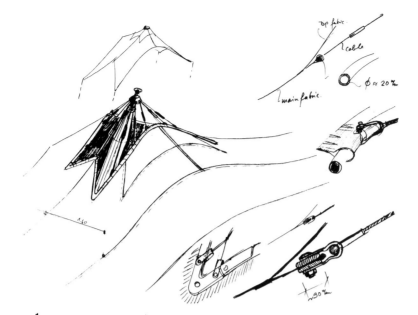

1

Schlumberger Renovation

Construction views and details of the tensile
structure and fabric roof of the Forum.

1 Sketches of details for securing the tent fabric.

2 Section and plan sketches of the tent by Piano.

3–6 Views of early stages of erection.

7 Plan of Forum. On the north side of the street
is a post office, magazine shop, cafeteria, travel
agent and bank as well as the lifts down to the
parking garage. On the broader south side is
a multi-purpose gallery, an auditorium and
a gymnasium.

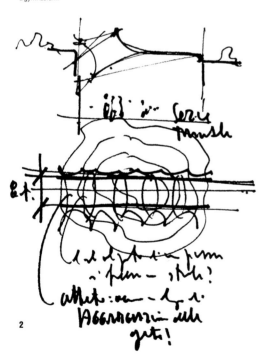

2

3

4

5

6

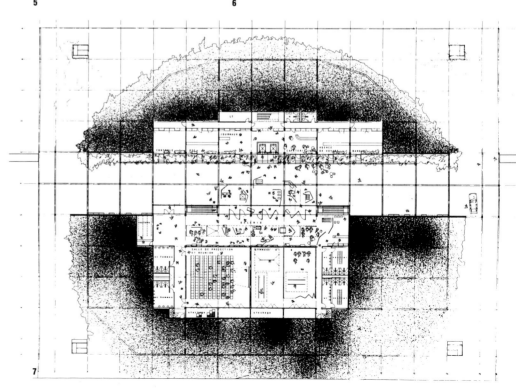

7

8

9

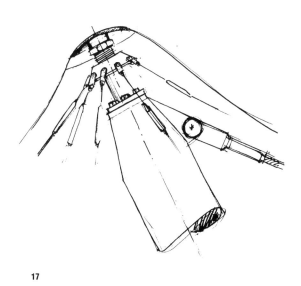

17

Schlumberger Renovation

8 Aerial view of the erected roof and planted mound.

9, 12–15 Close-up views of the connections between tension guys and tent fabric.

10, 11 Construction views, which show the fabric roof just in position.

16, 17 Sketches of details, which show how the fabric is attached to the compression supports.

10

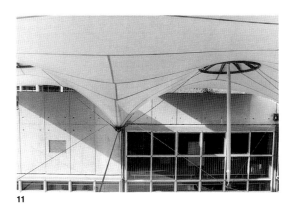

11

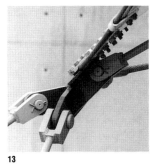

13   14

12

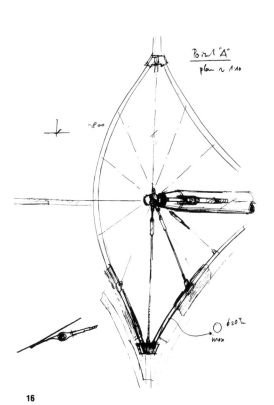

Point "A"
plan ~ 1:10

~800

Ø20
max

16

15

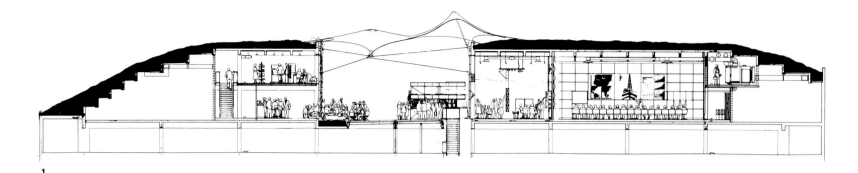

1

108   **Schlumberger Renovation**

The Forum.

1 Cross section through the central facilities under the mound and across the street.

2 'Palmier' compression element.

3 Original design of the palmier, which was simplified in manufacture.

4 Part plan of the tensile structure and fabric roof.

5 Detail of the aluminium frame of the glazing along the street. The cruciform element that projects outwards secures a wire for climbing plants to cling to.

Opposite page The street with its fabric roof supported by the elegant tensile structure with palmier compression elements. The perspex-filled metal frames on the right are later additions by the client.

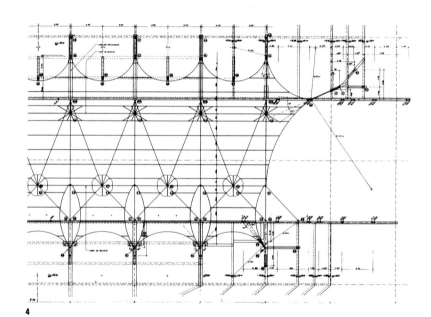

4

2

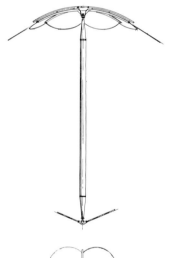

3

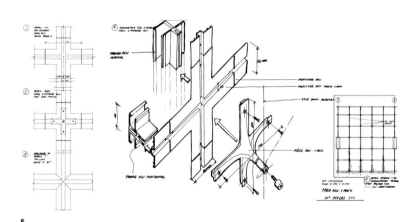

5

Client Compteurs Montrouge (Schlumberger Ltd)

Architect Renzo Piano Atelier de Paris

Design team R Piano, N Okabe, B Plattner (associates in charge), S Ishida (associate), T Hartman, J Lohse, D Rat, G Saintjean, J F Schmit, P Vincent

In collaboration with M Alluyn, A Gillet, F Laville, G Petit, C Susstrunk

Cost control GEC Paris (R Duperrier, F Petit)

Engineer for tensile structure P Rice

Landscape architect A Chemetoff, M Massot, C Pierdet

Interiors M Dowd, J Huc

Contractors GTM, Albaric Rontaix, BATEG

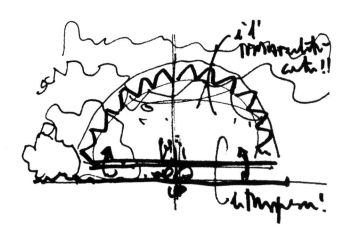

IBM Travelling Pavilion   European tour 1984–86 **Building Workshop, Italy** 1982–84

Like a modern-day equivalent of the circus, the demountable IBM pavilion travelled from city to city in a fleet of specially-built and emblazoned trailers. But there most similarities end. Instead of showing off the physical feats of man and beast, the exhibition that the pavilion housed, though similarly intended for young people (of all ages), showed off the more intellectual and abstract capacities of machines – IBM's computers. Also, the pavilion was not set up on bare open ground, but among the trees of lush city-centre parks.

Moreover, though fabric awnings defined some more intimate pockets within it, the pavilion was no shabby closed tent pitched on the dirt. Instead it was a pristine barrel vault of transparent polycarbonate pyramids with shapely wooden struts and metal joints, the whole poised above the grass on its raised structural floor.

The IBM Travelling Pavilion's real precedents were the greenhouse as developed in the nineteenth century and the contemporaneous and demountable exhibition pavilion, the Crystal Palace. As with these, its transparency and purity of form were animated by the repetition of identical precision components. In this case though, many of the components were of sculpted biomorphic form, and some of these carved in wood. This suggested a particularly intimate relationship between the pavilion and the foliage it nestled in, which also provided a backdrop and some sun-shading to the exhibition. Arranging for the computers to be seen against a natural backdrop accorded with a basic intention of the exhibition, which was to present computers to young people as an entirely natural part of daily life.

The travelling pavilion also continued themes from Piano's earliest explorations into lightness, transparency and construction with repetitive units. The demountable and movable, vaulted structure that sheltered sulphur extraction in Pomezia (1966) could for

instance be seen as one of its ancestors. Yet the pavilion also differs markedly from these earlier structures by Piano, both in the rich variety of materials used in a single work and in the celebration of craftsmanship. Instead of the flimsy insubstantiality of the earlier structures, the wooden struts and their cast aluminium joints have a sensually tactile presence that invites the hand of the visitor. (In concept it is almost as if the huge, cast gerberettes of the Pompidou Centre have come down to the scale and height of the hand.)

Hence the wood and aluminium 'pieces' not only give warmth and character to the structure but have also become intermediaries between not just building and setting, but between building and visitor/user too. Their crafted sculptural shapes temper the abstractness of the overall form and also invite a more intimate relationship than any earlier Piano work.

Yet, with the wood and the biomorphic shapes evoking organic resonances and helping to suggest that the structure was at home in its verdant settings, this was the first Building Workshop design to express so explicitly the ideal of a technology that emulated and embedded itself in nature. As such it was a seminal work for Piano and his collaborators. If at Otranto they explored how technology could be introduced in an undestructive manner into historic towns, here they explored how technology could be at one with nature.

The most immediate precedent for the pavilion in Piano's work is the Fiat VSS Experimental Car. It was here that he and his colleagues became familiar with new plastics, such as polycarbonate, and with the new glues that could bond them directly to other materials such as metal, a technique used here to bond the apexes and bases of the polycarbonate pyramids to metal. Glue was also used in the finger joints between wood and cast aluminium. It was the desire to explore both a combination of

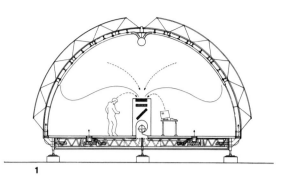

1

IBM Travelling Pavilion

1 Cross section showing mechanically assisted air flows. Air was pumped in through circular outlets in the floor and grilles along its outer edges as well as from nozzles set in small ducts branching off a central overhead duct. It was extracted via freestanding elements along the centre of the pavilion.

2 Computer simulation of anticipated light levels inside the pavilion when set up on a particular site (with deep shade from tree on near right) and with opaque shading elements in place along middle of vault.

3 Cast aluminium element that joined two wooden struts and the flexibly mounted spacing bolt that slotted into it to take up the differential expansion of the different materials – a simple solution to a conceptually tricky problem.

4 Longitudinal section of initial design with slot-together joints.

several materials, and these in particular, that initially generated the design, not a concern with joints as has often been assumed by some people.

The pavilion essentially was a transparent vault, 48 metres long by 12 metres wide and 6 metres high, made up of 68 half arches (forming 34 three-pin arches) each consisting of six polycarbonate pyramids held together by laminated timber struts with cast aluminium joints. The half arches were in fact three-dimensional trusses, with the polycarbonate serving as both the cladding membrane and the structural web between inner and outer chords.

Although Piano's use of polycarbonate as both cladding and structure was ingenious and conceptually elegant, it presented Peter Rice with a tricky engineering problem because the rates of expansion of it, the wood and the metals are so different. Yet the eventual solution devised to take up these differential rates was simple: a spacing bolt between the base of the pyramid and the inner chord of the truss where it was flexibly mounted into the cast-aluminium element that connected consecutive wooden struts.

The original design was to be of complete arches with slot-together joints in which the aluminium ends of each strut fitted into cut-outs in an aluminium disc. Although this solution was conceptually as elegant as the individual joints, which would otherwise have been too distractingly dominant, this would have resulted in modules that were not easily

dismantled and transported. The complete arch was too large to move, individual pyramids too labour intensive. For these and other structural reasons the half arch was chosen, resulting in a large unit that could be quickly disassembled and yet easily manipulated by a couple of workmen. These half arches also stacked against each other for easy transport in the 18 specially built trailers, two of which always remained by the functioning pavilion. One contained the mainframe computer; the other, air conditioning and other electrical plant.

Once erected in any new location, a process that typically took three weeks, a computer simulation was run of outside light and thermal conditions, taking account of the orientation of the pavilion, position of shading trees and so on. This determined the exact placing of opaque pyramidal elements, which were fixed inside the transparent ones, and of mesh screens. Together these controlled glare and heat loads. At one stage, double-skinned

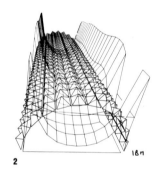

2

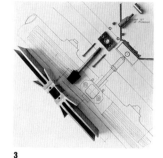

3

4

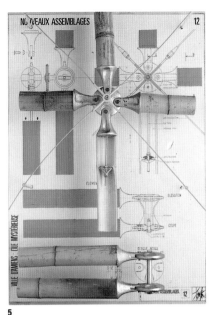

5

IBM Travelling Pavilion

5 Jules Verne Leisure Park, Amiens. A panel from the 1986 competition entry shows a later proposal to use struts of a natural material, this time bamboo, with cast aluminium joints as part of a cheap, appealingly rough and rustic building system.

6 Piano's sketch of how the stalk and veining of a leaf inspired the aluminium connector that was finger-jointed to the wooden strut.

7 Components arriving on the Paris site in one of the specially built trailers with Renzo Piano and Noriaki Okabe in the foreground.

8 Pavilion assembled in Milan with one of the two trucks containing mainframe computer and plant that remained beside it while open to the public.

9 Pavilion in place in York attracting throngs of visitors, as it did everywhere.

Following page The pavilion nestled in greenery in a park in Milan. The shapely wooden struts were obviously organic in form and resonance, but the crystalline vault also conjured associations with the exoskeletons of small organisms.

'IBM is very organic, because of course everything becomes organic when you look for extreme optimisation, lightness and perfection.'
Renzo Piano

6

pyramids had been considered with opaque or photosensitive gas used to exclude heat, an idea that others have also proposed but nobody has yet managed to make work. During cold spells, condensation on the pyramids was prevented by blowing warm air onto them from nozzles identical to those used on aircraft and set into small ducts that branched from either side of a large duct that ran the length of the pavilion, suspended from the central pins of the arches. Other air-conditioning ducts and cabling were accommodated within the structural depth of the floor that was raised and levelled on jacks.

Over three years the pavilion visited 20 cities in 14 European countries. If the Pompidou Centre is the Piano building most visited by European architects, the IBM Travelling Pavilion must be the next most familiar. At the time it caused quite a stir. Architects who associated Piano with the Pompidou and High-Tech were surprised at the liberal use of wood. As well as for structural struts, it was used for the floor, end partitions and the bases of exhibits. The beautifully crafted components and connections also made a strong impression. That the prototypes for these had been lovingly crafted at full size and by hand was as obvious to everybody as the resulting tactile and friendly, essentially humane quality.

But if associating Piano with High-Tech had been a mistake, the IBM joints also led to a common misapprehension about his work. Many architects and critics saw (and some still do)

Piano as a consummate crafter of components and connections. To them his buildings were mere assemblies of these rather than real architecture. But then the buildings in which these components come together in a larger unifying idea or device, and with many contextual resonances too, were still in the future.

The great popular and critical success of the pavilion led IBM to commission the design of the smaller, unrealised IBM Ladybird Pavilion (1986). This again exploited natural materials and metaphors. Again with laminated wood struts and cast aluminium joints, this went further in not only being mobile, but in actually unfolding in an action inspired by that of bat and bird wings. The mix of cast aluminium and a natural material, this time bamboo, was also proposed in a competition entry for the Jules Verne Leisure Park in Amiens, France (1986).

113

7

8

9

1

2

3

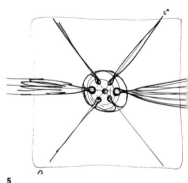

4

116   **IBM Travelling Pavilion**

Crafting the components of the initial slot-together design (abandoned because it broke down into parts that were either too large or too small for easy transport and quick assembly) and test-assembling a complete arch.

1 Components were first modelled full-size in wood.

2 How the components came together: a glued finger joint cements wooden strut to cast aluminium element that slips into one of the slots in the node-joint.

3 Test assembly of components into arch on a beach near Genoa.

4 Triumph on completing test assembly of a single arch.

5, 6 Piano's sketches of joints.

7 Cast aluminium element being checked in workshop and...

8 ...being slipped into position in the node-joint.

9, 10 Final finishings to moulds for the cast aluminium components of executed design.

5

6

7

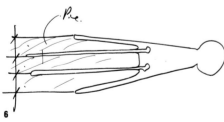

8

9

10

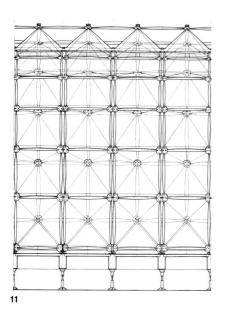

11

IBM Travelling Pavilion

The structure of the slot-together scheme, like that which was built, consisted of 'pieces' made of very different materials that came together in a hierarchy of larger pieces.

11 Part elevation shows how pronounced, almost decorative, the node-joints would have been.

12 Assembled arch, the major piece, in process of erection shows off the shapely sub-components and joints, the minor pieces of which it was made up.

13 Study of proposal for pyramids as two layers of polycarbonate forming pockets filled with photosensitive gas to control admission of heat and light.

12

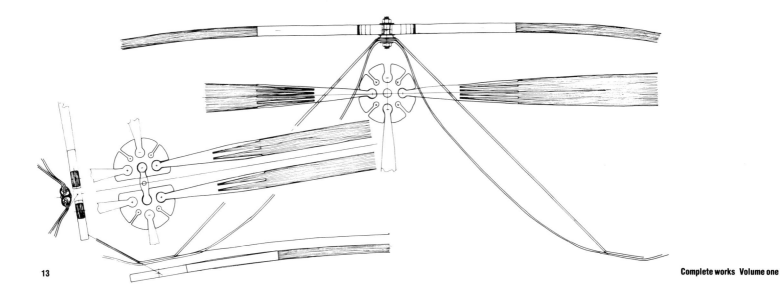

13

1

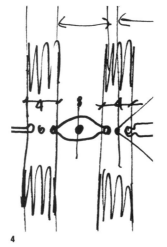

2

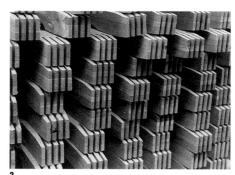

4

3

118   **IBM Travelling Pavilion**

Repetitive, yet crafted, components and the complex junctions they formed.

1 Polycarbonate pyramids.

2 Ends of laminated wooden struts await gluing to cast aluminium elements.

3 Finished struts. On the left are the ends of the inner chord struts that met in a pin-joint at head of vault, on the right are the opposite ends of the outer chord struts that terminated at the apeces of the bottom row of pyramids.

4 Sketch by Piano.

5 Ends of inner chord struts.

6 Wooden struts and aluminium connections glued together.

7 Isometric showing pin-jointed junction of inner chords of adjacent arch-trusses at head of vault.

8 Isometric of junctions between struts of inner chords of adjacent arch-trusses with ring to secure ventilation duct and flexibly mounted spacing bolts securing polycarbonate pyramids.

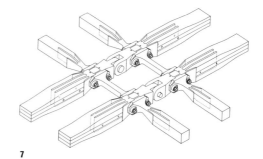

5

7

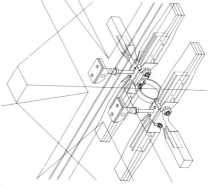

6

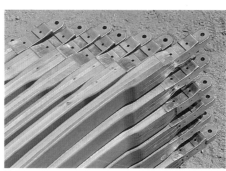

8

9

10

IBM Travelling Pavilion

Factory-assembly of crafted components into
arch-trusses.

9 The polycarbonate pyramids were formed in
units of three.

10 Connecting aluminium and stainless steel
fixings to polycarbonate pyramids. The arch-truss
to the right is ready for transport, the
polycarbonate pyramids already secured to the
inner chord by spacing bolts.

11 Laminated wood and cast-aluminium
elements being glued in jig to ensure alignment.

12, 13 Assembled and exploded isometric views
of junction of inner chords and polycarbonate
pyramids with edge of floor-chassis of pavilion.

11

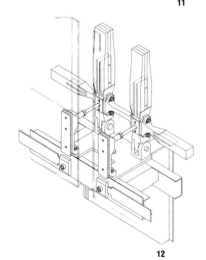
12

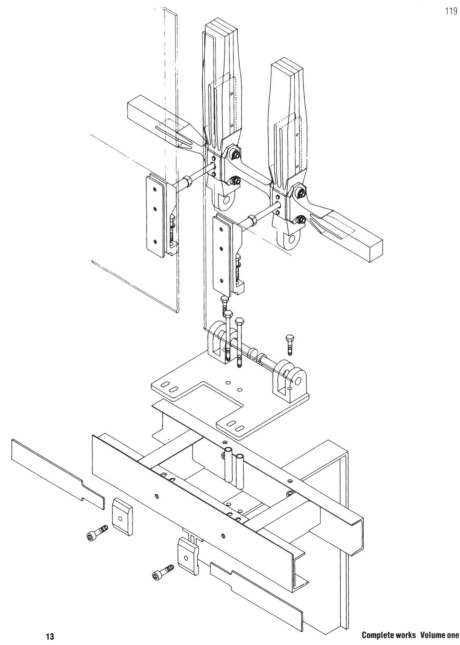

13

1 **2**

120 **IBM Travelling Pavilion**

Cast-aluminium connections.

1 Pin-jointed junctions of inner chords of
adjacent arch-trusses to edge of structural
chassis.

2 Junctions between struts of inner chords of
truss and webbing strut, with spacing bolt
securing polycarbonate pyramids.

3 Cross section.

Opposite page Telephoto view of junctions.

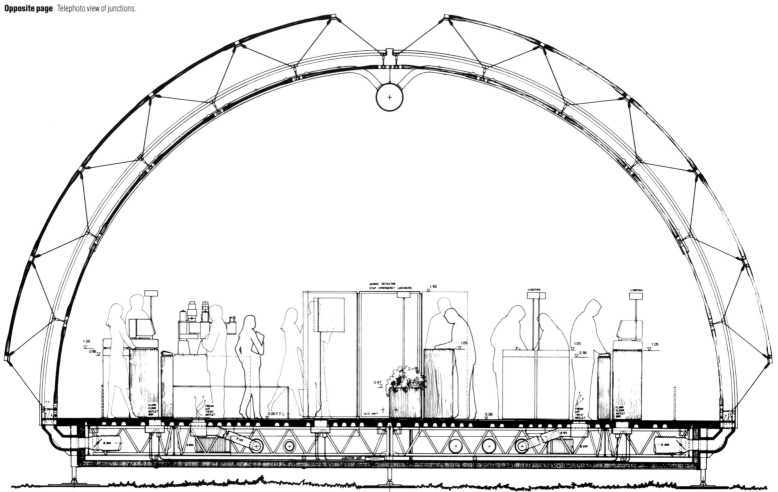

3

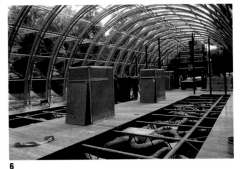

122 **IBM Travelling Pavilion**

Site assembly.

The arch-trusses were designed for easy
manipulation and assembly, and a special
hydraulic tool was designed to ease these
processes and facilitate precision assembly.

1 Arch-trusses being bolted together around the
pin-joint at the head of the vault.

2 The specially developed hydraulic tool
supporting an arch-truss.

3 In foreground arch-trusses wait to be pinned
and bolted into position to form the vault seen in
the background.

4 An arch-truss being manoeuvered into position
with the hydraulic tool.

5 Vault in place at either end of the pavilion with
part in between yet to be assembled.

6 Vault is complete and flooring is being laid over
the structural chassis packed with services. The
freestanding units in the centre house the air
extract units.

IBM Travelling Pavilion

7 Polycarbonate pyramids being cleaned, once assembly was complete.

8 An arch-truss being unloaded for assembly, or loaded after dis-assembly.

9 Construction drawing shows detail of external elevation, section and internal elevation, and cross section.

7

8

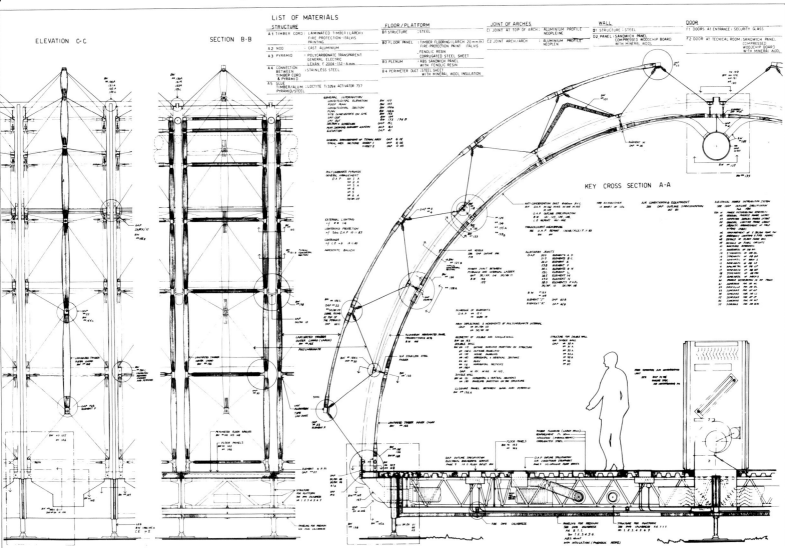

9

124 **IBM Travelling Pavilion**

1 Part elevation.

2 Diagrammatic plan with exhibition layout.

Opposite page The heterogeneity of the elements that made up the pavilion can be clearly seen in this close-up view. The abstract form and transparency of the polycarbonate pyramids contrasts with the tactile warmth and sculpted form of the wooden struts, and both of these contrast with the smaller scale complexity of the metal elements. The gutters between the pyramids were transparent pvc held in aluminium channels glued to the polycarbonate.

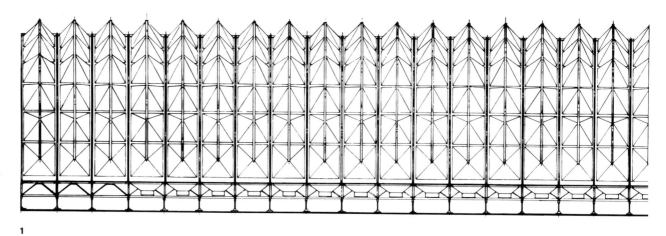

1

2

2

1

126   **IBM Travelling Pavilion**

The pavilion travelled throughout Europe and was
sited on prestigious and verdant city-centre sites.

1 One of the specially built and emblazoned
trucks arriving in Paris.

2 In the Parc du Champ de Mars in Paris.

3 Outside the Natural History Museum
in London.

4 Aligned on axis with central tower of Schloss
Charlottenburg in Berlin.

5 Looking over the pavilion at central Lyon.

6 Against the medieval and leafy backdrop of
Stuttgart's Schlossplatz.

3

4

6

5

7 If the other views on these pages show how at ease the pavilion seemed in its various settings, then this close-up view of it in York suggests how at ease the public felt with its unintimidating and welcoming presence.

8 On a barge in Bonn, the only place where it had no shade from adjacent trees.

9 In front of the Castel Sant'Angelo in Rome.

10 Site plan of placing in Milan amongst temporary site works.

11 Juxtaposition with Gothic ruins in York emphasises how the pavilion belongs to the bio-mechanical strand of modern architecture that originated in Neo-Gothic.

12 In Amsterdam's Vondel Park.

7

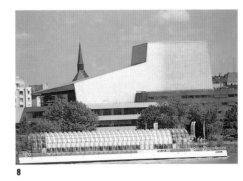

8

127

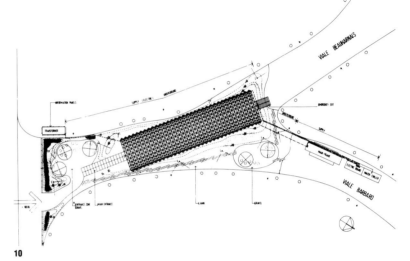

10

9

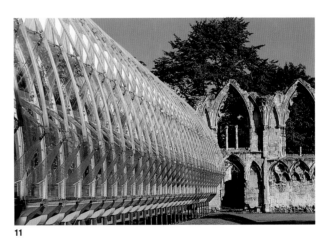

11

12

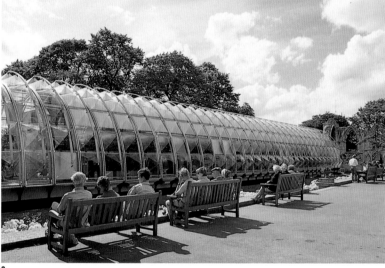

1

128 **IBM Travelling Pavilion**

The pavilion in use, introducing the capabilities of computers to the public, particularly young people.

1 Set in the wooden end wall that was recessed to create a welcoming porch, the entrance doors were wide inviting sheets of frameless glass.

2 Mime artists invite uninhibited encounter with the computer.

3 While many thronged through the pavilion, others contemplated it from outside before and after their visits.

4 Concerts also brought in visitors. This view emphasises the transparency of the pyramids.

5 Opaque elements placed in many of the pyramids shut out sun and glare while suspended fabric created more intimate pockets and screened glare off some screens.

2

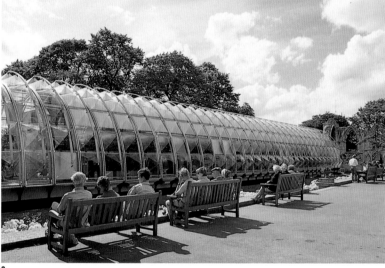

3

4

5

IBM Travelling Pavilion

6 Visitors queue for admission.

7, **8** Contents of the pavilion were tantalisingly
visible from outside .

6

7

8

130 **IBM Travelling Pavilion**

Interior seen from a high viewpoint shows how nature and natural materials were used as an immediate and vibrant counterfoil to the abstractions of computing. Inside were plants and an abundance of unpainted wood. And outside and very visible through the transparent polycarbonate were the trees that were such an essential part of the architectural experience.

Client IBM Europe

Architect Renzo Piano Building Workshop, Genoa

Design team R Piano, S Ishida (associate in charge), A Traldi, O Di Blasi, F Doria, G Fascioli

Co-ordination on site Renzo Piano Atelier de Paris (N Okabe, P Vincent, J B Lacoudre)

Structural and services engineer Ove Arup & Partners (P Rice, T Barker).

Contractor Calabrese Engineering Spa, Bari

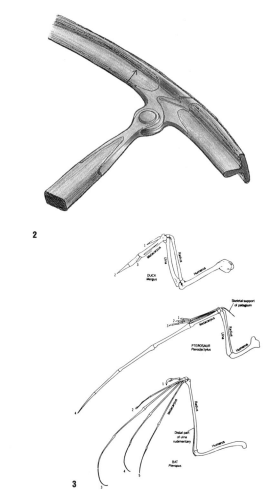

2

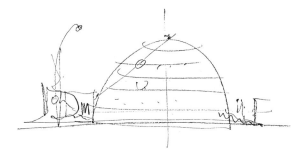

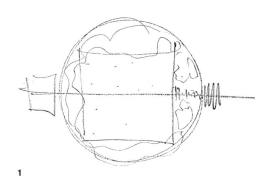

3

132   The great popular and critical success of the Building Workshop's first pavilion for IBM led the company to commission the design of the smaller, unrealised IBM Ladybird Travelling Pavilion. This also exploited natural materials and metaphors. Again with laminated wood struts and cast-aluminium joints, this went further in not only being mobile, but in actually unfolding in an action inspired by that of bat and bird wings.

1

IBM Ladybird Travelling Pavilion Unexecuted project Building Workshop, Italy 1986

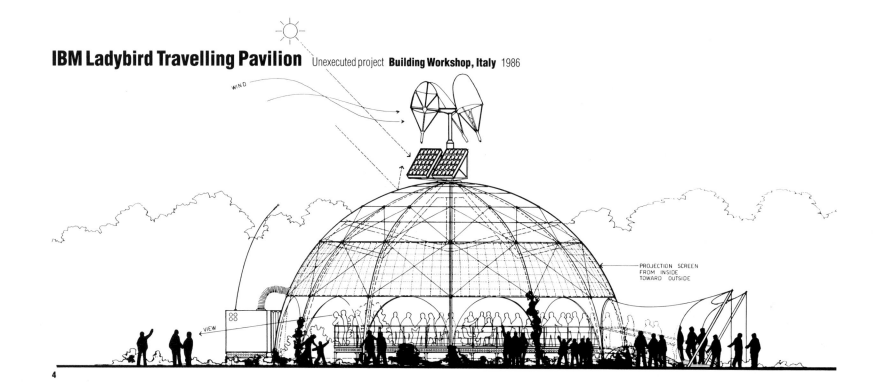

4

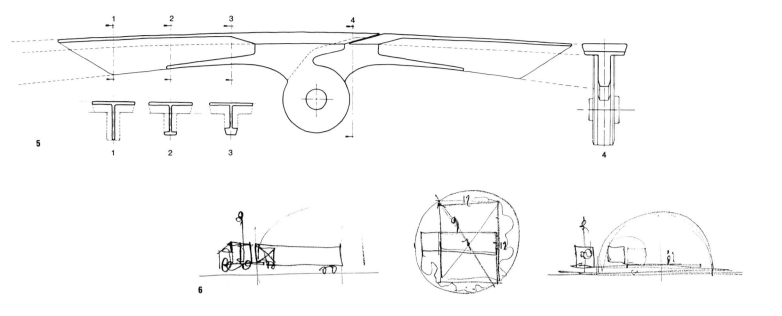

5

6

IBM Ladybird Travelling Pavilion

1 Section and plan sketches by Renzo Piano.

2 Cast aluminium folding joint in wooden arch, with T-section to serve as a fixing rail for the fabric cladding.

3 Skeletons of wings that inspired the structure of the folding arches.

4 Elevation of the pavilion in use.

5 Elevation and section details of a folding cast aluminium joint in an arch.

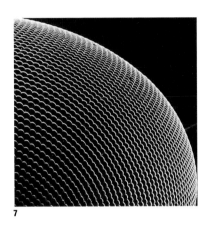

7

133

9

10

6 Sketched sequence by Piano of pavilion being set up. A lorry unhitches the trailer that unfolds to create the exhibition floor and to reveal a cabin that contains air-conditioning plant. Straddling the floor are unfolded the arches of a hemispherical cage of structure. Over this is draped the cladding – a triple-layer skirt of translucent waterproofing and insulating materials.

7 Magnified surface of fly's eye, one of nature's creations that inspired the design of the cladding.

8 Plan.

9,10 Model views show the structure of the pavilion unfolding.

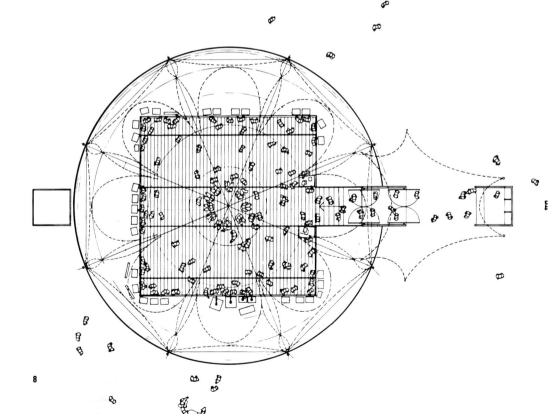

8

Below the sagging curve of its roof, the long open expanse of the Lowara office building houses the sales and administrative departments of a company that makes electric pumps on a semi-rural site outside Vicenza. The un-partitioned interior was a stipulation of the client who wanted employees always to be aware of their relationships with and responsibilities to a company that imposed no fixed working hours. The 15-metre-deep by 150-metre-long block is built across one end of an older and much larger factory from which it is separated by a corridor. This also gives access to such necessary cellular spaces as conference rooms that are partitioned off within the volume of the old factory with the same glass panels as line either side of the corridor and enclose the office space. Together, corridor and cellular rooms provide some acoustic isolation for the offices from the factory.

Although quite different from the blocky, blank-sided factory buildings around and behind it, and though it was adopted also for microclimatic advantages, the tent-like roof and transparent walls of the new block are a direct response to contextual pressures. In particular they recognise the presence of and

Lowara Offices   Montecchio Maggiore, near Vicenza, Italy **Building Workshop, Italy** 1984–85

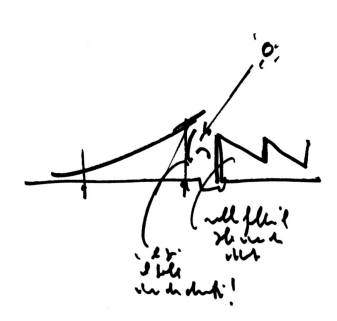

try to cement some relationship with the agricultural fields, distant villages and Palladian villa that the block overlooks.

With modern architecture's abolition of such rhetorical elements as pedimented porticoes, one of the few ways left with which to address the distance, such as the vestigial Arcadia found here, is by doffing an upward sweep to a canopy or roof edge. The office block now establishes a connection between the factory it screens and the countryside that the complex once ignored, in a manner analogous to the way the aerodynamic spoiler on the cab roof of a truck makes an implicit connection between the trailer behind it and the road ahead.

At Lowara, of course, the only movement involved is visual and metaphorical. Yet the distinct impression is given that some natural energy emanating from the countryside has caused the roof to curve up and crash like a wave against the old factory; while in the interior below, the downward sag of the ceiling pushes attention outwards through the fully glazed front wall to focus it on the countryside. The roof's resemblance of a marquee also emphasises whatever is natural in the setting and outlook. Complementing such a reading is the *Bürolandschaft* layout of furniture and plants, and the rockeries that extend under both ends of the roof where the glazing has been set back.

The curving roof also mediates with nature, or at least its ambient phenomena, in other ways to provide passive environmental controls for comfort and energy efficiency. Where the roof reaches highest, a clerestory not only lights one long side of the space, but also admits southern sun from above the shadow of the existing factory. Besides bringing welcome warmth in winter, these same elements of curved roof and high clerestory also aid summer ventilation from northern breezes by helping exhaust the space with a combination of convection and the Venturi effect. In summer,

too, if a certain temperature is exceeded, a row of sprinklers along the outside of this upper edge switch on automatically to wet the roof so that evaporation cools both it and the office space below. In winter, heating is by warm air from a single duct placed high up towards the clerestory. The air from this cools as it disperses and descends to extract grilles in the floor, the pattern of air movement obviating the stratified layers of air at different temperatures that sometimes plague large spaces. The exhaust air ducts are beneath a raised floor where telephone and electricity cables are also accommodated.

Lightness and natural light, the recurrent themes in the architecture of the Building Workshop, are once again celebrated. The curve of the roof hangs, seemingly as soft and light as fabric between the leaning props that support it. Inside, the roof seems to float in the light that washes along it, from both the bright strip of the clerestory and the fully glazed north wall, to reflect off the crests of the corrugated steel ceiling. Both curve and corrugations emphasise the enlivening play of shifting natural light and they efficiently reflect and diffuse artificial light from uplighters.

The corridor is also naturally lit to magical effect. Windows below the clerestory are the hidden source of this light, which is reflected – by a corrugated steel scoop that billows into the office space – onto the curved ceiling of the corridor, which is again of the same material. This natural light is so abundant as to help illuminate the open office and cellular spaces on either side of the corridor. The curved ceiling of this extends out beyond the building to create a welcoming canopy that leads to and emphasises the entrance. From here, the whole length of the bright-lit scoop, ceiling and corridor are clearly visible.

The main structural props, which lean on more slender elements standing just inside the glazing, slant into and articulate pockets of space along the long

1

2

136 **Lowara Offices**

1 View to the north is of a vestigial arcadia with which the design in several ways cements a connection.

2 Pin-jointed footing of V-prop outside one end of office block.

3 Plan: **a** open offices, **b** existing factory, **c** cellular spaces, **d** lavatories, **e** entrance canopy, **f** parking, **g** potential expansion

4–7 Diagrams of ways ambient conditions are tempered: **4**, natural ventilation is aided by Venturi effect; **5**, evaporation of water sprayed on the roof cools both it and the space below; **6**, the cellular spaces partitioned off in the existing factory and the corridor provide an acoustic buffer for the open offices; **7**, the flow pattern of the mechanical ventilation prevents layers of static air forming.

sides of the office space. Along the northern side these props are 3 metres apart. Those supporting the opposite side, where the ceiling rises to 7.2 metres (from a low point of 2.4 metres) form Vs, each pair sharing a base at 6-metre centres. Between the heads of each pair of long and short props hang inverted arches welded from bent lengths of steel angle arranged back to back. Between these arches spans the corrugated ceiling, a deep profiled steel sheet more usually used as permanent shuttering in bridge building. To resist up-draughts, here the steel sheet carries a dead load of concrete, above which is the insulation and the waterproof membrane.

Most Building Workshop designs start simultaneously with and give equal emphasis to considerations of both the general (context, overall layouts and so on) and the particular (materials, details and so on). Although as always the joints, such as the footings of the props,

are finely detailed, the Lowara office block gives the impression that here for once the general has predominated. Especially because the curved roof reads as single unit, it is difficult to say what is the repetitive piece that encapsulates the identity of the building, although it is probably a single bay of roof and structure. The result is that the building seems a little glib. Yet not only does the play of light give a highly nuanced richness to the seemingly simple structure and section, the form of the latter deals simultaneously with several issues. To summarise: it creates a fitting response to context; provides a number of benefits in terms of internal environmental conditions and vividly demonstrates Piano's persistent concern with light and lightness – and with suspended structures as the means to achieving the latter. The factory has now changed ownership and the long fluid space has been cut up with floor to ceiling partitions.

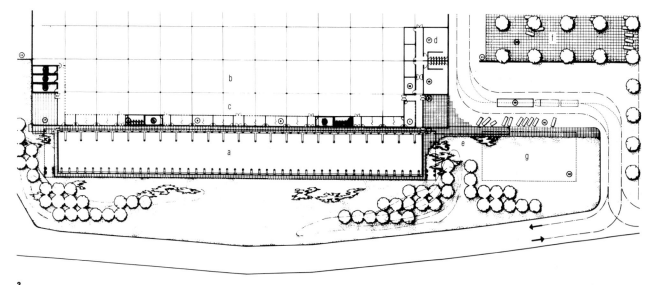

3

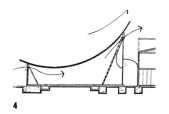

4

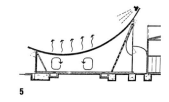

5

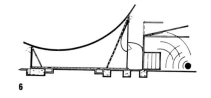

6

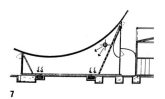

7

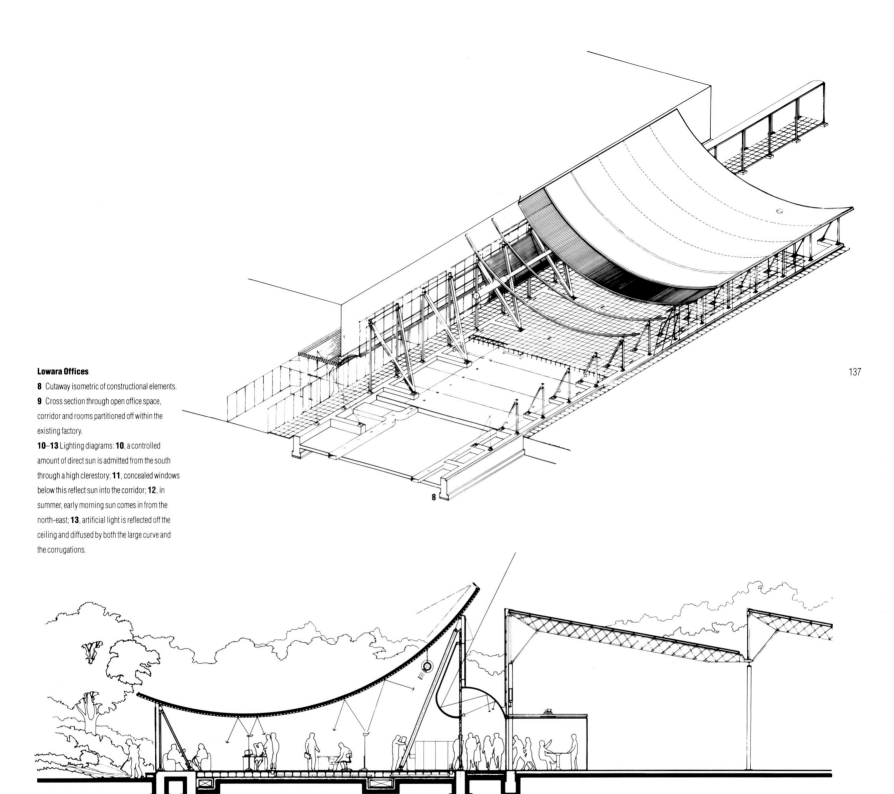

Lowara Offices

8 Cutaway isometric of constructional elements.

9 Cross section through open office space, corridor and rooms partitioned off within the existing factory.

10–13 Lighting diagrams: **10**, a controlled amount of direct sun is admitted from the south through a high clerestory; **11**, concealed windows below this reflect sun into the corridor; **12**, in summer, early morning sun comes in from the north-east; **13**, artificial light is reflected off the ceiling and diffused by both the large curve and the corrugations.

8

9

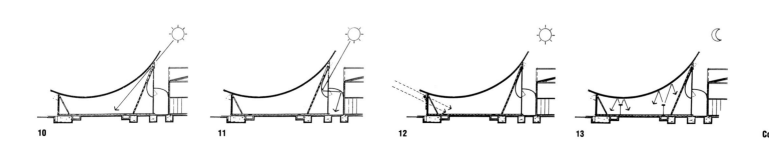

10   11   12   13   **Complete works Volume one**

1

138 **Lowara Offices**

A play of curves and transparency, of light
and lightness.

1 The long block of open-plan offices is naturally
lit along both sides. The sag of the ceiling helps to
draw attention to the view outside.

2 The corridor is lit by natural light from hidden
windows, which is reflected by the curved element
on upper right onto the ceiling. This bright light
helps illuminate the adjacent spaces, through the
glass walls that line both sides of the corridor.

3, **4** Night and day views of the narrow entrance
end of the offices.

2

3

4　　　　　**5**

Client Renzo Ghiotto, Lowara

Architect Renzo Piano Building Workshop, Genoa

Design team R Piano, S Ishida (associate), O Di Blasi (architect in charge), G Fascioli, D L Hart, M Mattei, M Varratta

Structural engineer M Milan, S Favero

Landscaping Studio SIRE

Contractor Trevisan Tachera

Lowara Offices

5, **6** Views out from entrance end, from the open offices, **5**, and from the corridor, **6**. The latter shows how the curved ceiling of the corridor extends outwards past a wind lobby to become a welcoming canopy.

6

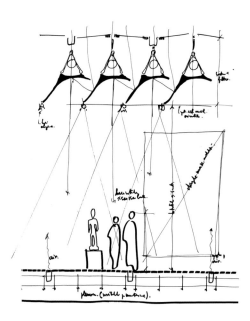

The Menil Collection   Houston, USA **Piano & Fitzgerald, Italy and USA** 1981–86

Discounting the Schlumberger facilities, which are only a conversion (no matter how large and well done), and the IBM Travelling Pavilion, which was mobile and impermanent, the Menil Collection might be seen as the Building Workshop's first really mature work: calm and coolly stated, yet richly resonant.

As his first major all-new building since the Pompidou Centre, and as one again for the study and display of artworks, the Menil shows clearly just how far Piano's approach had developed in the decade between initiating the designs of the Pompidou Centre and of this museum and study centre in Houston. Of course, many of the differences between the buildings reflect those of place and programme rather than maturity. Nevertheless the Menil does show Piano's shift to seeking the 'natural' design solution, one that feels relatively unforced and in harmony with local conditions, rather than one that might be intrusively assertive or unduly provocative and mechanistic. So, if on its city-centre site, the Pompidou rudely flaunts its technology in the face of, and so as to face up to, the glorious historic monuments of Paris, the Menil Collection in contrast wraps itself in the same clapboarding as the surrounding bungalows so as to settle almost shyly into its suburban setting.

The Pompidou is a huge intense machine built to house and provoke the unpredictable, and through which vast throngs pass daily. The Menil, though, is a study centre for an established private collection, with public but quietly contemplative galleries for a rotating selection of these works. Yet even it has leading edge technology on prominent display in the form of the light-diffusing 'leaves' that, together with the truss they are an integral part of, constitute the characteristic 'piece' of the design. These are arranged so that natural light permeates everywhere in the ground floor galleries, an impossibility in the stacked and immensely deep floors of the Pompidou. And if

that building's mighty trusses verge on the overbearing, the leaves of the Menil neither overwhelm nor distract from the art below them as they float, indeed seem to swim upwards, in the magical light that floods down between them. And if now it is possible to claim some (arguable) resonances with history and context at the Pompidou, these are more intentionally and obviously present at the Menil. Indeed, to foreign eyes at least, one of the most remarkable things about the Menil is how quintessentially American it seems. More than that, what it evokes of American precedent are some of the most admirable examples of its architectural legacy.

Dominique de Menil and her late husband John started collecting in Paris in the 1930s, encouraged by the Dominican monk Marie-Alain Couturier who was later instrumental in Le Corbusier being commissioned for Ronchamp and La Tourette. They then became major supporters and patrons of the arts in Houston as well as amassing a most exceptional private collection. Now some 10 000 pieces, it focuses mainly on modern art, with many Max Ernst and René Magritte paintings, and on African art, but also includes pieces from other periods and places, such as Cycladean and Oceanic art.

The de Menils had long intended to make their collection available for serious study and public viewing. In the early 1970s they commissioned Louis Kahn to build for these purposes. But after John de Menil died in 1973 and Kahn the following year, the project was shelved, though Dominique de Menil never lost her enthusiasm for it. She continued to think about her requirements and to visit museums so as to clarify them, but failed to find the architect she deemed right for the job. In late 1980 Pontus Hulten, then curator of the modern collection at the Pompidou Centre, introduced her to Renzo Piano. Thus started an extraordinary relationship: Piano always

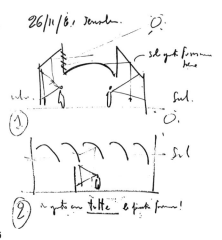

142   **The Menil Collection**

1 The client, Dominique de Menil.

2, 4 Two of the porch-fronted, grey-clapboarded bungalows that surround the museum.

3 View between two bungalows of part of the long south elevation of the museum, which shows how it is clad in the same grey clapboarding and is surrounded by a colonnade that suggests some reciprocity with the bungalow porches.

5 Renzo Piano's sketches of his original inspiration for the natural lighting, that of a gallery on an Israeli kibbutz, and his response for lighting wide and flexibly subdividable space.

6 Dominique de Menil's initial sketch of the 'treasure house' as a drum with a circulation core and segmental storerooms that can be opened up at one end to natural light.

7 Piano's response to the client's concept sketch: an elongated linear arrangement with art works leaving the elevated treasure house for short-term public display.

8 Sectional diagram showing mechanical circulation of conditioned air.

9 Corridor of the treasure house, a simple and severe space that nevertheless has a suitably ceremonial quality.

Following page East elevation. Clearly displayed are some of the key elements of the design: the elevated treasure house; the canopy of glass roof and light-diffusing leaves that extends outwards as a colonnade.

acknowledges what an exceptionally important role she played in the conception and refinement of the design, a role that far transcended that which is usual with a client.

One of Dominique de Menil's foremost requirements was that all art on display must be seen in natural light, and that this light be handled in such a way that visitors are alert to its constant changes with time, season and weather. Such changes bring alive both the galleries and the art – as she knows well from living with these works in her house. As part of her strategy for achieving this, the artworks were to be stored in ideal conditions of darkness, constant temperature and humidity, in a 'treasure house' – where they are nevertheless immediately available for study. Those works selected for short-term display in the public galleries can then be quite brightly lit without harm.

These requirements were crystallised while travelling with Piano and his team and her assistant Paul Winkler, who formulated the detailed brief and oversaw the project for her. (He is now director of the collection.) The solution to the lighting was inspired by that of a small gallery on the kibbutz of Ein Harrod in Israel, on much the same latitude as Houston and where the light is reflected from monitors. But the desired atmosphere was found much nearer home, in the Media Center or 'Arts Barn' on the campus of Rice University, which was also sponsored by the client. Within its warehouse-like exterior it has a rather domestic interior, but one charged with the various activities of restoration and research. The client insisted that conservation and exhibition planning in the new museum should not be shut away in the equivalent of the usual attic or basement, but placed where the public would be aware of these important activities.

Another crucial concept arose, at least in part, from the setting. The client wanted a building that though spacious inside should not seem overbearingly large outside, and that though dignified and contemplative should not be pompous or intimidating. To achieve this, she and Piano conceived of it as a 'village museum' with some of its functions dispersed into the bungalows that the Menil Foundation already owned around the campus on which the building is sited. In fact one of these balloon-framed bungalows was moved across a road to make way for the museum. The clapboarding then not only settles the building into its surroundings but also implies this connection. And the colonnade around it seems both a reciprocal response to the bungalow porches and stresses the welcoming, public nature of the building and surrounding campus.

The client's original concept, which she sketched for Piano, included a drum-like treasure house with segmental storerooms that scholars entered from a central core and that could be lit by opening up shutters on the outside wall. Piano's response, which remains the basis of the design, retains the essential ideas but straightens the ring of storerooms into a row along a corridor, all held aloft above ground-level galleries that bask in light admitted through a deep roof with light-diffusing baffles.

The museum as built consists of three contrasting levels, each the same length and organised along a circulation spine, but each different in width and very different in character. The ground floor is much the largest, almost all of it lit through the glass roof and light-diffusing leaves. Here are the public

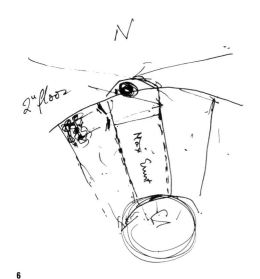

6

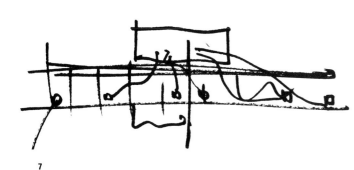

7

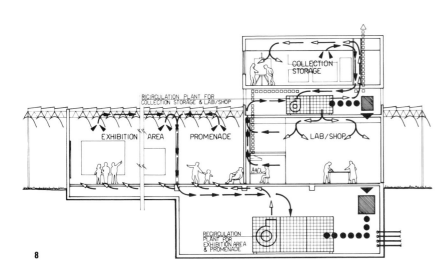

8

galleries, both for the short-term display of small selections from the collection, and for visiting exhibitions. Pockets of space off the circulation spine, or promenade as it is called, can be used for the display of the smaller objects the collection abounds in, or for reading material related to an exhibition. Also on this level are a library and rooms for exhibition planning and preparation, conservation and framing. Several of these are organised so that the public may glimpse them from the colonnade and so have a sense of these other museum functions.

Both the way the treasure house is held aloft above this ground floor, and the way its rooms are strung out along a plain yet almost ceremonial corridor, are suitably symbolic gestures of homage to its fabulous contents. Here the 10 000 artworks are kept in ideal conditions, yet are immediately available for study when shutters

are slid aside to reveal windows. These admit a side light very different from the diffused top-light below (but their square shape does sit a little uncomfortably on the outside elevation). Below ground are various plant and service rooms and workshops. The boiler room and a stand-by electricity generator for the security systems, which are noisy, smelly and potential fire and explosion hazards, are not included here but are in an isolated building connected by a trench.

Just as the whole building is a sandwich of three contrasting levels, so too is the main gallery level: the ceiling-canopy, the walls and the floor are each quite different in idiom and character. Above are the light-diffusing leaves, their sensual curves swimming in the bright light that they suffuse. Together leaves and light provide the building with its very memorable identity and atmosphere. The upper part of each ferro-cement leaf also serves structurally as the lower chord of the ductile iron truss that supports the roof of ultraviolet light-excluding glass and the return air duct threaded through it. The rest of the leaf curls down to hide most of this, to block direct sunlight and to scatter the light reflected off the upper part of the neighbouring leaf.

The materials and manufacture of the leaf and truss, both of which are immaculately crafted castings, are updated versions of older technologies. And the resultant canopy they

form appears to be both mechanical and organic, a high-technology analogy of a forest canopy or vine-clad pergola.

Below this bio-technical level is a conventionally abstract–modern zone of plain white wall planes, some of which can be rearranged to vary spatial subdivisions and display sequences. And then quite different again is the floor – black painted pine boards of local domestic tradition. Especially as this shows signs of wear, it adds a friendly familiar touch to offset the austerely abstract and functional levels above. Insisted upon by the client, the boards are an inspired choice, giving an intimacy to the serene and spacious galleries and promenade. Under the floor are the inlet ducts for the air conditioning, the black grilles for which fit almost imperceptibly into the floorboards.

The presence of yet another contrasting element pervades most of the ground floor. Beneath the canopy but otherwise outside, pockets of planting penetrate the surrounding colonnade to be protected from summer sun and

143

9

The Menil Collection

1 Leaders of the design team: Peter Rice, Renzo Piano and Tom Barker.

2 Diagrammatic cross section showing passive climatic controls.

3, 4 Early studies of the 'leaf'. The initial idea, **3**, was of a curved ferro-cement element that would reflect and diffuse both natural and concealed artificial lighting, and would also provide diagonal bracing for a tubular-steel truss. At an intermediary stage, **4**, the leaf served, as in the final version, as the bottom element of a three-dimensional truss, but with further development became more substantial and complex in shape.

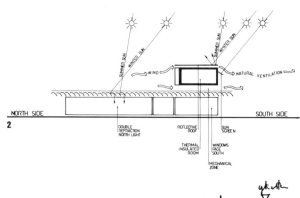

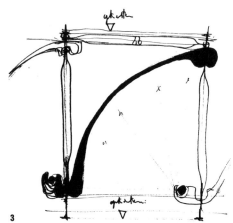

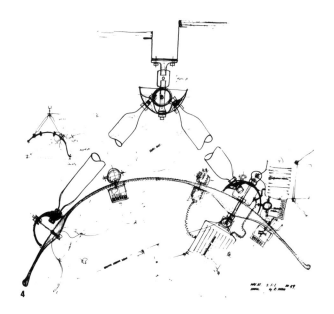

winter frost. Such pockets of plants shorten the promenade to provide an outlook that is a contrasting relief from the art; they provide a foreground view and some screening for privacy to the conservation rooms; and they form a suitably jungle backdrop to African and Oceanic sculptures. And, in a typical Piano device to emphasise entry, more planting (here unshaded by the canopy) flanks the route to the main entrance, which is set back into the building. Recessing the entrance also reinforces the cross axis (off centre, of course; symmetry denotes monumentality) defined by the entrance and the lobbies to which it leads. This intersects the similarly emphasised long axis of the promenade.

Although in the way it is done it seems utterly novel, the solution of the deep, oversailing roof on a space frame (or three-dimensional trusses) that accommodates services (and sometimes admits light) has ancestors in Piano's architecture and that of the USA. The B&B Italia Offices (1971–73) and Free-plan Houses (1972–74), both by Piano & Rogers, are examples. And Piano's own early Office Workshop in Genoa (1968–69) had a space-frame roof through which it was naturally lit. American precedent includes a corporate headquarters in Kalamazoo by Skidmore Owings & Merrill and, more to the point, the much-publicised prototype schools for southern California by Ezra Ehrenkrantz. What the Building Workshop, working closely with Peter Rice and Tom Barker of Ove Arup & Partners, added to this solution were the light-diffusing leaves.

In their usual quest to eliminate redundancy, Piano and Rice wanted the leaf to play a structural role as an integral part of the roof truss. For the 12-metre truss they chose to explore ductile iron, a material they had first encountered working on the Fiat VSS Experimental Car. Ductile iron, used for piano frames as well as parts of car chassis and suspensions, is formed by casting and so can take sculptural shapes, but unlike cast iron has considerable tensile strength. For the leaf, ferro-cement was chosen, a material with which Piano had recently designed and built himself a yacht. The original concept of the leaves was as very thin arcs of ferro-cement serving also as diagonal braces in the truss. But after extensive testing and development – using models and solar machines as well as computer modelling – so as to admit exactly the right amount of light of the desired quality, and also for structural reasons, the leaves became more substantial, considerably more complex and sculptural.

Besides controlling the amount of light and diffusing it, the leaves are shaped to help achieve stable temperatures in the galleries. Their horizontal tops reflect heat back through the glass and also hold a protective layer of hot air under it while minimising the downward radiation of heat. With air slowly fed in through the floor at close to room temperatures and collected at roof level, temperature and humidity are kept very stable. It was originally intended that the roof be made in Britain, where it could be closely checked by the engineers, and shipped to the USA. The leaves were made in Britain by a boat-builder after experiments to find a self-coloured finish of the right hue and reflectivity. Eventually a white marble powder was used

5

The Menil Collection

5 Renzo Piano and Peter Rice checking one of the final leaves.

6 Piano's sketch showing how the structural grid of the roof canopy was conceived of as a microcosm of the street grid.

7 A general view of the whole building. Because the simple low building is so distended, yet unarticulated at centre or corners, this is its least flattering aspect.

8 Location and site plan showing the concept of the 'village museum' with some functions dispersed in surrounding buildings. In the block to east is the Rothko Chapel and across the street from the south-east corner of the museum is the site of the Cy Twombly Pavilion, which is now under construction.

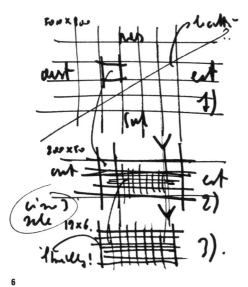

6

with white cement, and the surfaces when struck were polished with acid. But the ductile iron elements cast in Britain proved to have hairline cracks. They were eventually made in the USA by a subcontractor to the car industry.

The truss was cast as a series of individual triangular elements clamped together by bolted half-sleeves. The result is a truss that is as shapely as the leaf, its parts resembling bones and the whole truss closely resembling a much magnified section through a bone. Here is a good example of

how leading edge technology can emulate nature. Such emulation of nature was a nineteenth-century ideal, and the way it is achieved here is by updated versions of the nineteenth-century technique of casting. (The manufacture of the leaves was in fact a hybrid process of plastering into a mould, the top and back taking their form from the mould, the front and bottom being trowel-finished.) One of the major lessons Rice had learnt when designing the structure for the Pompidou was that it was through casting that he could reinvest in structures the character and sensual presence typical of nineteenth-century engineering but so lacking in the dry twentieth-century structures made of standard rolled sections.

The cast elements of the canopy and the qualities they project, together with the vegetal analogies of forest canopy and vine-covered pergola that they conjure, are a clear example of the strong affinities with the nineteenth century to be found in Piano's work. With top-light flooding down through cast and crafted organic forms, the Menil Collection is very close in spirit to, say, Deane & Woodward's Oxford Museum.

Until resurrected at the Pompidou, casting had been little used in twentieth-century

building, but was not uncommon in the manufacture of furniture. It is not surprising then that the exquisitely refined biomorphic shapes of the truss and leaf should seem to be exactly the sort of forms that Charles Eames might have created. Eames comes to mind because the building seems so American, having particular affinities with California of the 1950s and 1960s. If the canopy and joints of the trusses call to mind Ehrenkrantz, and these same joints and leaves evoke Eames, the white steel frame makes recognisable reference to Craig Ellwood, a mutual enthusiasm discussed by Piano and Walter Hopps, the then-curator of the collection. The clapboarding and steel frame also combines the two dominant American building traditions.

But the museum makes more immediate contextual connections. The steel frame resembles those of nearby Philip Johnson buildings, the auditorium and classroom building of St Thomas University done in his Miesian mode. And the colonnade evokes vague echoes of the verandahs of southern plantation houses. Yet it is also a stoa both for the public and for peripatetic scholars to ponder and converse in and so recalls the

147

7

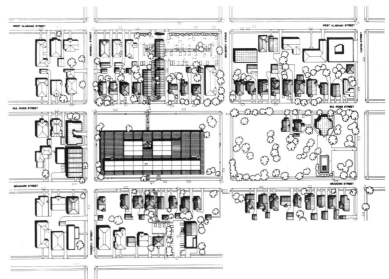

8

2

1

3

4

148 **The Menil Collection**

The museum was designed around an exceptional collection of 10 000 pieces, now kept in ideal conditions in the treasure house, **1**. The collection ranges from Cycladean idols, **2**, **11**, and Benin bronzes, **3**, to such Surrealist paintings as those by René Magritte, **4**, **7**, **9**, for which it is famous. Other modern artists represented include Giorgio de Chirico, **5**, Fernand Léger, **6**, George Segal, **8**, and Pablo Picasso, **10**.

5

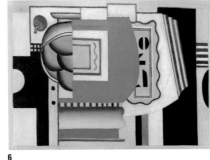

6

7

8

9

10

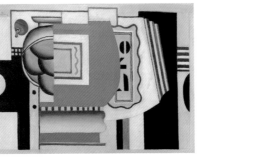

11

14

15

16

The Menil Collection

Further riches of the collection.

12 Antique works on short-term display in the public galleries.

13 Paintings stored in the treasure house, where they are readily available for study.

The collection includes Gothic carvings, **14**, paintings by Max Ernst, another well-represented Surrealist, **15**, **16**, Coptic portraits, **17**, African and Oceanic sculpture, **18–20,** and medieval icons, **22**, **23**.

12

13

17

18

20

19

22

23

21

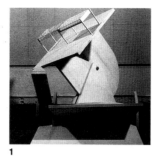

1

2

150   **The Menil Collection**

Perfecting the natural light by testing and refining the form of the leaf. What was sought is an even light that changes with that outside and is bright by normal museum standards because works are only displayed for short periods.

1, 2 Model of the canopy of leaves being tested in varying conditions to simulate those in Houston.

3 Part section through a gallery showing the final design of the leaves, which block out direct sun, and reflect and diffuse the light they admit. The leaves also trap an insulating layer of warm air above them. Their lower edge also supports the artificial lighting.

4 Model and test results used in checking the quality and intensity of internal lighting with variations outside.

5, 6 Models being tested on site in Houston.

Opposite page The eventual result. The serene spaces of the galleries and the art they show are brought alive by the suffused and ever-changing daylight admitted by the leaves. These do not overpower what is below them, but instead seem to float or even swim upwards in the light that floods down between them.

'*The daylight in the Menil is honest, pellucid and without additives. The quality of the light is like nothing else, anywhere, and may well set standards to make other architects lie awake at night.*' Reyner Banham

Greek Revival traditions of American civic architecture.

The building has other contextual resonances. Piano claims the main structural grid of the roof canopy was conceived as a microcosm of the grid of the neighbourhood. Like the grid of so many American towns and cities, this one is exactly oriented on the cardinal points. This could imply a cosmic connection to the north-facing leaves. (Actually there was no such conscious intention. The design of the Menil is typical of the way Piano looks for clues in the surroundings to provide formal and conceptual underpinnings for the elaboration of the design.) Yet just as the

biomorphic forms of the leaves seem to reach out past the building to suggest some connection to the spreading trees nearby, so in counter-thrust the abstract and cosmically oriented grid is brought down to earth by the pockets of planting that invade the ground floor.

But the neighbourhood grid is part of the surveyors' grid that reaches out to embrace most of America. Stretched out below its oversailing roof the Menil Collection projects some of that sense of reaching endlessly outwards that distinguishes much American architecture from the more rooted and contained closure of European architecture. It is in this spirit that the roof-canopy, with little relationship to the spatial subdivison below, was adopted, in preference to the use of monitors lighting each room or individual walls – a solution that would have been feasible with the scale of some of the rooms. Along with the light, one of the most affecting aspects of the Menil is the tension between the closed, squarish and rather centred rooms and the sense of endless space that the lines of leaves project.

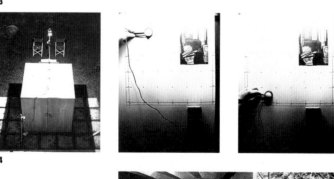

3

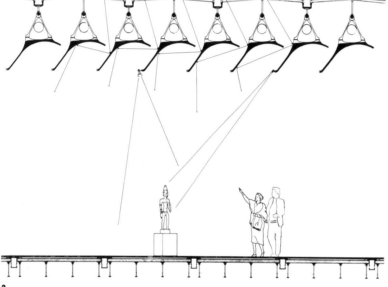

5

4

6

2

1

3

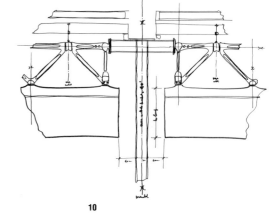

10

152 **The Menil Collection**

Manufacturing the pieces.

1–**4** Casting the ferro-cement leaves: **1**, the steel mould; **2**, positioning the steel fixings to which the ductile-iron elements will be attached; **3**, mesh reinforcement around fixing; **4**, polishing the front surface of the leaf with acid before it is struck from the mould.

5 Exploded and cutaway perspective of the piece shows how the ductile-iron elements of the truss and the ferro-cement leaf come together.

6, **7** Casting and checking a ductile-iron component in the factory.

8 Lifting and checking a leaf in the factory and,

9, test fixing the ductile-iron elements. The ferro-cement boats in the background are the factory's usual product.

10 Elevational sketch shows how the pieces are supported along the north colonnade.

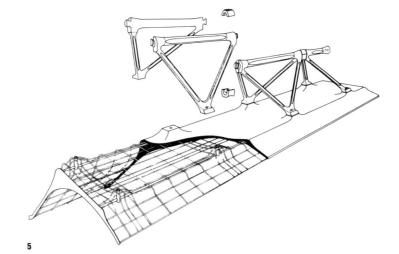

4

5

6

7

8

9

11

12

13

The Menil Collection

11, **12** Delivery of leaves.

13 Assembling ductile-iron trusses that connect
those that are integral with the leaves.

14, **16**, **17** The galleries under construction.

15 Shop drawing of typical ductile-iron element.

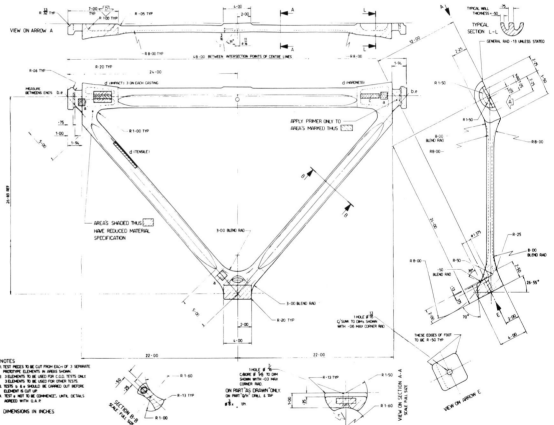

14

15

16

17

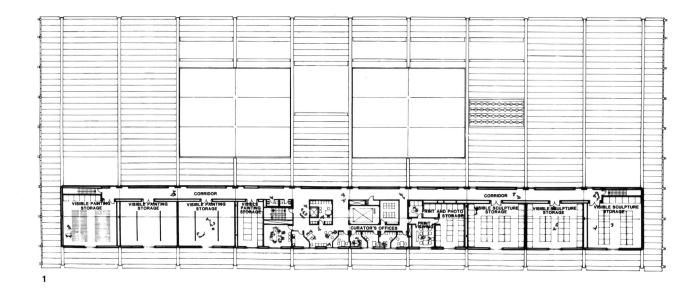

1

The Menil Collection

1 First-floor plan: the treasure house and curators' offices.

2 Ground-floor plan: galleries and back-up spaces.

3 Basement plan: plant, storage and workshops.

Opposite page The north-east corner of the colonnade that is a generously welcoming public space. The grey clapboarding and white steel connect visually with similar elements on the surrounding bungalows; and the projecting canopy of leaves, because it is sensually crafted rather than merely mechanical, suggests some organic connection with the surrounding trees.

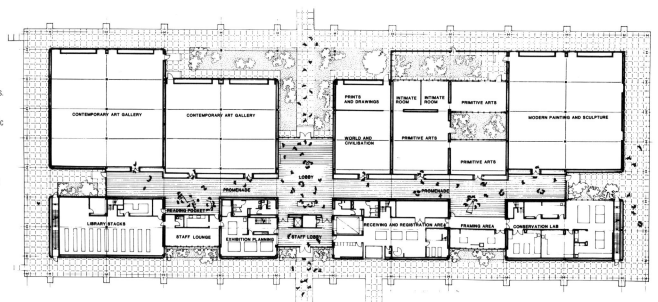

2

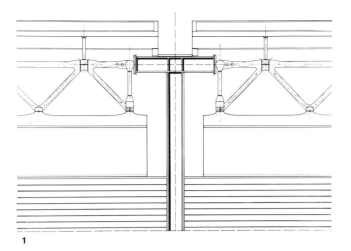

1

The Menil Collection

Views of the colonnade.

Opposite page Single bay of the east colonnade shows off the Craig Ellwood-influenced steel detailing. The bench gives an idea of the generous scale. To the left is a pocket of planting across which the public can glimpse the internal promenade and the conservation studio.

1 Elevational detail of top of the north colonnade showing connection of truss and leaf to column.

2 South-east corner of the museum, looking along the south colonnade.

3 Pocket of planting set back from the north colonnade beside open route, through which section below is drawn, to recessed public entrance doors.

4 Cross section through entrance lobby.

2

3

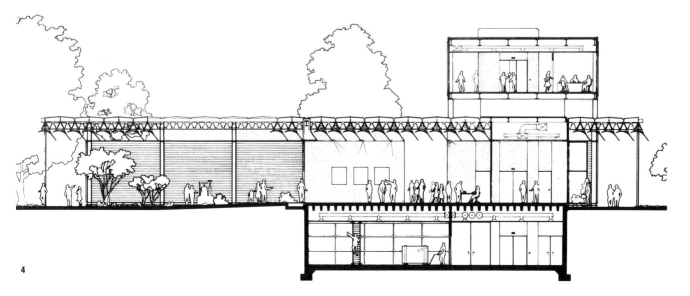

4

1

2

3

158 **The Menil Collection**

The ground floor spaces suffused with the ever-changing daylight that is admitted through the roof.

1–3 The galleries as subdivided for a particular show, and with visitors.

4, 5 The broad 'promenade' that leads to the galleries and off which open small intimate pockets seen to the right in **5**, and that usually display small works.

6 The entrance lobby with doors to the left of picture and promenade receding directly ahead.

Opposite page A gallery subdivided into smaller rooms by the introduction of partitions.

Following page Planted courtyards provide a suitable jungle backdrop to primitive art works as well as a sense of transparency and layering in the closed and introverted ground floor.

4

5

6

1

1 and opposite page Two views of the conservation studio that overlooks and receives ample north light from the pocket of planting between the end of the internal promenade and the colonnade. From the latter the public may glimpse this crucial museum function.
2 Exhibition planning room overlooked by curators' offices on the first floor so that staff also keep in touch with the museum's activities.
3 Staff lounge and reading room for the library seen through the opening on the right.
4 Making tests in the conservation laboratory.
5, 6 The framing studio is separated from the street-side southern colonnade only by a narrow pocket of planting so that its contents and activities are visible to passers by.

162 **The Menil Collection**

The rooms for the ancillary functions of the museum, where most of the specialist staff work, were considered as important as the public spaces and offer exceptional working conditions.

2

3

4

5

6

Client Menil Foundation: D de Menil (president); W Hopps (director); P Winkler (vice director)
Architect Piano & Fitzgerald
Design team R Piano, S Ishida (associate in charge), M Carroll, F Doria, M Downs, C Patel, B Plattner, C Susstrunk
Structural engineer Ove Arup & Partners (P Rice, N Nobel, J Thornton)

Services engineer Ove Arup & Partners (T Barker, A Guthrie)
Local structural engineer Haynes & Whaley Associates, Houston
Local services engineers Galewsky & Johnston, Beaumont
Fire prevention R Jensen, J Houston
Contractor E G Lowry, Houston

1

164

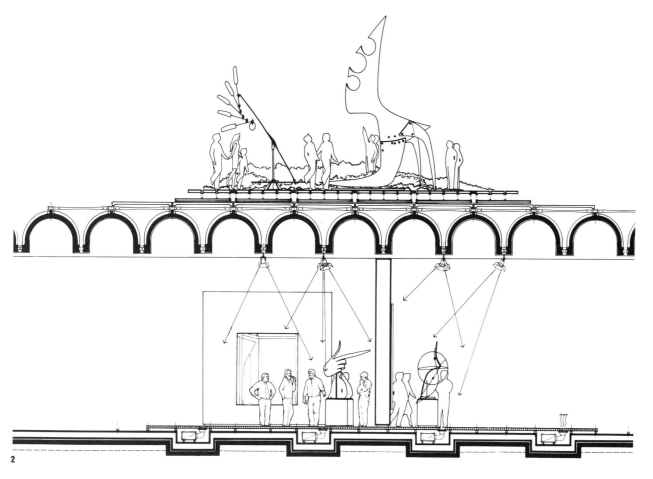

2

Contemporary Art Museum Newport Harbour, USA **Building Workshop, Italy** 1987–

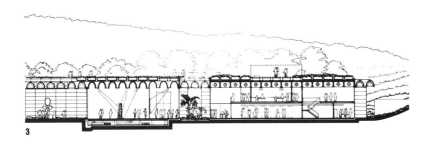

3

4

In 1987, the year after completing the Menil Collection, the Building Workshop was commissioned to design the Contemporary Art Museum for Newport Harbour, California. Sited at the bottom end of a long, narrow and sloping park, its cross walls would have echoed at larger scale the weirs that dam a gully along the side of the park. Again the galleries would have been lit through a glass roof, this time filtered through holes in the vaults that spanned between the cross walls to support the roof. In places they would also have supported earth where the park extended onto the roof before being connected by escalator down to the main entrance.

Apt to both its site and Californian tradition, the museum is a semi-landscape solution, with inside and outside interpenetrating. And like Genoa, there is a certain ambiguity about which level is ground level.

1 East elevation. The sloping park extends onto the roof.

2 Detail section. Pre-cast concrete vaults support a roof of glass, or paving and planting, and admits light through a pattern of holes.

3 Oblique section, which shows the interweaving of gallery and park.

4 Site plan. Cross walls echo the weirs in the gulley on the side of the park.

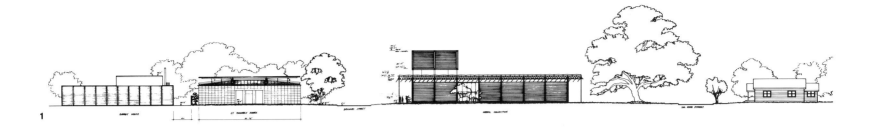

1

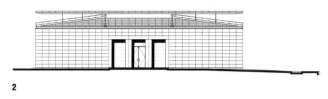

2

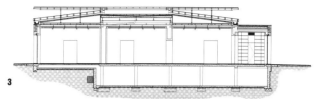

3

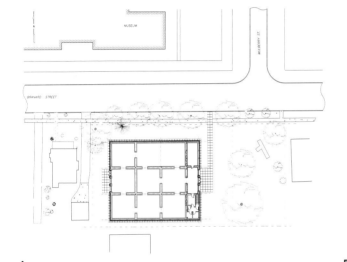

4

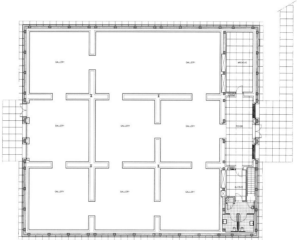

5

The Building Workshop is now constructing an annex to the Menil Collection, the Cy Twombly Pavilion, which will house works by the artist and stand among the surrounding bungalows. This is being treated as a simple independent pavilion, the galleries filling a square envelope. This will be rather deceptive in scale, as it will be considerably larger than than one would guess from the drawings.

Like the galleries of the Menil, the pavilion will be lit through the roof, though the solution is quite different. An external canopy of louvres will crown the building and shade the sloping and hipped glass roof. Below the glass, a fabric ceiling will diffuse the light. A central room holding a single large painting will be taller than the surrounding galleries and only artificially lit to create a contrasting and mysterious atmosphere. Unlike the Menil and the neighbouring bungalows, the pavilion will have concrete block walls, though of a colour similar to that of the clapboarding.

165

Cy Twombly Pavilion Houston, USA **Building Workshop, Italy** 1992–

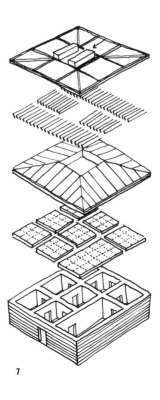

6

1 Elevation of the pavilion in context.

2 East elevation.

3 Section.

4 Site plan.

5 Plan.

6 Detail section of roof of several independent layers, which control light and heat.

7 Exploded diagram of main elements.

7

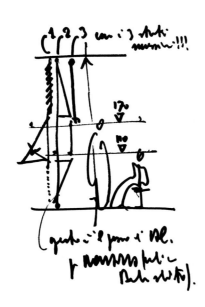

Aluminium Research Institute Novara, Italy **Building Workshop, France** 1985–87

The commission for this institute for research into new applications and treatments of aluminium grew out of an initial approach to design an aluminium curtain wall. The Building Workshop insisted that it preferred to design this in conjunction with a building on which it would be applied. The result is two systems of building components. The aluminium glazing system clads a slot-together structure of precast concrete components – the latter as heavy and robust as the former is light and delicate.

If the heavyweight concrete system seems atypical of the Building Workshop, then it is because the weight was required for technical reasons and because the building was designed and erected at considerable speed by Bernard Plattner of the Paris office with uncharacteristically little intervention from Piano. And yet the building has attributes readily associated with Piano himself – quite apart from having obviously been erected 'piece by piece'.

The precast structural system that makes special spaces for service runs recalls early influences, such as Louis Kahn's Richards Medical Research Centre with its served and servant distinctions, a building Piano knows well from when he taught on the same campus. Even more so, the Novara building recalls British architecture of the 1960s, in particular Arup Associates' Chemistry Laboratories at Birmingham University, the sort of building Piano got to know and became influenced by during his partnership with Richard Rogers. Yet it also has some affinity with a slot-together exhibition display system Franco Albini designed when Piano was working for him. Moreover, there is the usual inclusion of nature with plants intruding into the entrance hall and along the street edge of the ground floor rooms.

The institute consists of two buildings built at the same time. Edging the street is the three-storey laboratory and administration building already referred to. Across a court with

gravel and small trees that runs the length of this building is a single-storey workshop, the court face of which is clad in ribbed aluminium siding. Inside, it is a better than decent industrial building with a precast concrete structure and roof, with natural light admitted in strips between the beams, and around the tops of the walls. But it is on the front building that most of the attention has been lavished. This is straightforward in plan, with rooms along both sides of a central corridor from which extend the escape stairs. On the upper two levels are laboratories on the side facing away from the street, and on the street side are offices. On the ground floor are more offices (with a raised computer floor), a technical library, reception area and showroom. In the basement is a small auditorium.

As the structure was entirely prefabricated, it was erected in only three months. Its relative massiveness provides both stability for the trabeated dry-assembly structure and inertia against vibration from machines in the laboratories.

The primary structure consists of paired elements that create spaces for service runs. Along the corridor paired piers, at 8.4-metre centres and 1.2 metres between their outer faces (structure and glazing all conform to a 1.2-metre module), flank vertical ducts with access panels into the corridors. From these ducts, service connections run between the two beams that span from here to reach past and take bearing on the twin columns that articulate the facades. Secondary beams span between these paired beams and sit on nibs cast along their outer edge. Between the beams span slabs from which are hung suspended ceiling panels that are flush with the soffit of the secondary beams, into a channel in which are set the fluorescent light fixtures. Where a central service channel is required in the laboratories, this is included in a special element instead of the normal flat slab.

Heating and cooling is by air ducted along the top of the

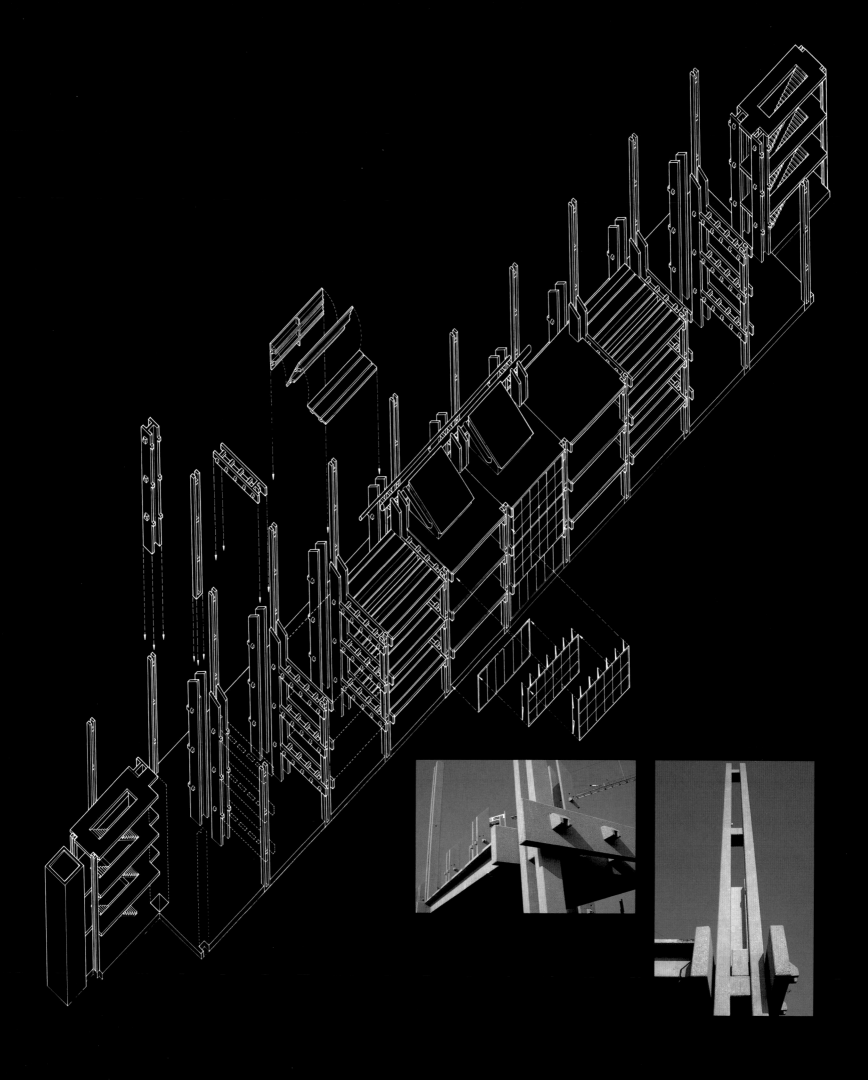

corridor and admitted into each primary bay through four controllable inlets. The air-handling plant is on the roof, through which the vertical ducts that flank the corridor project as twin rows of stacks.

Made of both extruded and cast aluminium elements, the curtain wall is of extreme delicacy. To keep the extruded mullions of minimal size, they are braced by elegant cast aluminium elements, which are set parallel to, and further in than, the mullions so that together they form a vertical truss. Then to hide these mullions and minimise the visible thickness of the frames, the glazing frames fold towards each other outside of the mullion, and the double glazing is silicon-bonded into them without any further restraining element to thicken the thin edge of the frame. Some of the glazing frames open as top hung windows. Fully assembled elements from the factory, 7.2 metres long by 3.6 metres high, are clipped to the concrete frame by aluminium elements developed as part of the system.

To secure other elements outside the facade, such as various forms of sun-shading, brackets are slid into a slot in the mullion to project out through the gap between the glazing frames. On the west-facing street elevation at Novara, such brackets secure fabric blinds that create a rather rumpled effect when pulled down, in contrast to the crisp and fine precision of the facade behind. When seen in actuality, this is a somewhat endearing touch that softens the otherwise mechanically systematic building – and besides, it could be seen as contextually appropriate too.

Although seemingly designed with attention given mainly to its components and their assembly, the building suits its context well. It is in a nondescript industrial area and opposite an open space

168 **Aluminium Research Institute**

Previous pages Construction photographs and exploded axonometric showing elements from which the office–laboratory block is assembled.
The office–laboratory block contrasts a heavy precast concrete structural system with a light and delicate glazing system.
1 Part of the street elevation with its floppy fabric blinds, seen through the trees of the park it overlooks.
2 The extruded and cast aluminium of the window system is utterly different from the chunky concrete of the structure.
3 Cross section.

1

2

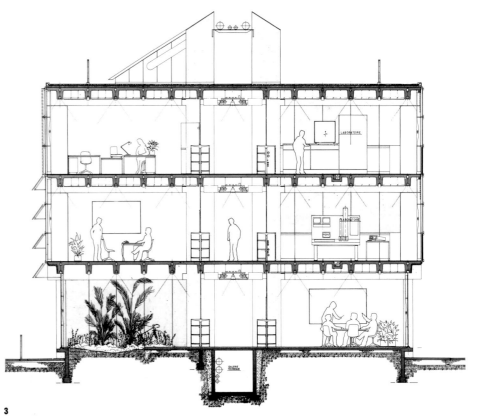

3

Aluminium Research Institute

Drawings of office–laboratory block.

4 Courtyard elevation.

5 First- and second-floor plan: **a** laboratory,
b office, **c** library, **d** reception, **e** show room,
f conference suite

6 Ground-floor plan.

7 Basement plan.

intended as a park, which though unkempt has fine trees. The projecting escape stairs, with their straight flights and landings filling a full structural bay, stretch the building to fill the street frontage. And the heavy concrete frame gives the building sufficient presence to assert itself over the big trucks that park along the road. Yet the vivid green window frames and floppy blinds in their contrasting, and somewhat vegetal, delicacy seem to signal some connection with the park across the road.

The connection with the park is made more literally on the ground floor where plants seem to have crossed the street to invade the stair and reception hall and, indeed, the whole street-side edge of the interior. Here the plants provide some screening and distancing from the street just outside the floor-to-ceiling glazing. Small parquet-like strips of wood flooring introduce another semi-natural element, which seems to have invaded the building, its jittery small scale quite a contrast to the big-boned concrete frame.

Inside, the feeling is of being in a heavy and tough frame that provides spatial articulation and a sense of shelter, but is only rendered usable and habitable by the insertion of the lightweight elements of services and fitments. Above work-top level, partitions along the corridor are glass, as are the doors. So even once partitioned there is a sense of transparency, and the order of the structural frame persists. As is to be expected for this client, various internal elements such as balustrade and handrails, and the supports for stair treads, are of cast or extruded aluminium. The last of these elements is a *tour de force* and used for external as well as internal stairs, cantilevering from a central concrete stringer to support a grc tread.

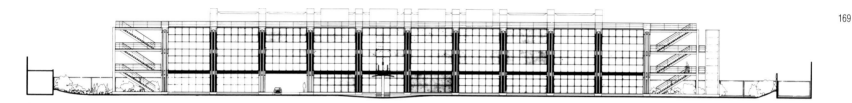

4

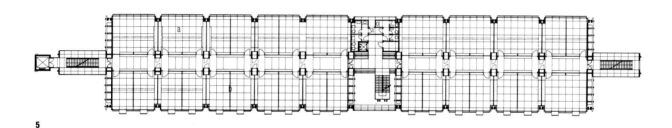

5

6

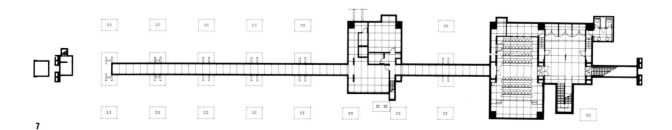

7

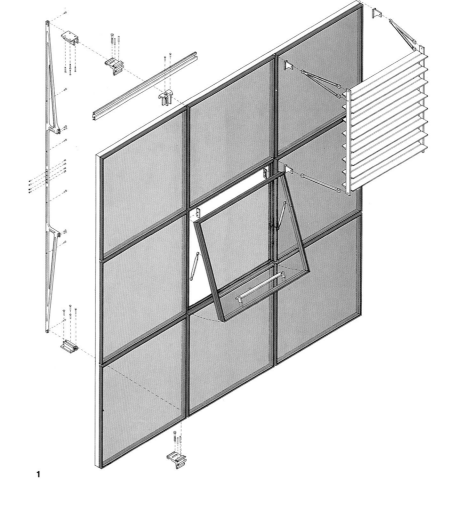

1

170   **Aluminium Research Institute**

The glazing system.

1 Exploded isometric of the glazing system components.

2 Oblique interior view shows how extruded frames and cast stiffeners come together to form a series of vertical trusses.

3–5, 8 Plan details show build-up of components of the glazing system. The shaded elements in **3–5** are extruded aluminium sections; **8** shows the addition of cast-aluminium stiffener. Components that are nowhere shaded are neoprene gaskets or the double glazing that is simply bonded into place with no further restraint, so that only a minimal amount of the frame shows on the outside.

2

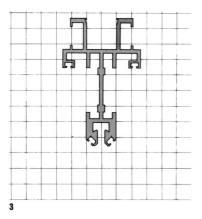

3

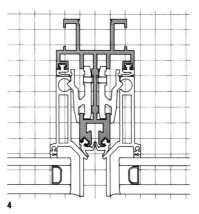

4

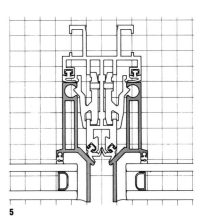

5

6

171

Aluminium Research Institute

6 The glazing already in place on the top two floors.

7 Pre-glazed frame filling whole structural bay secured to structure.

9 Section detail of head of glazing frame shows how it is secured by purpose-made elements.

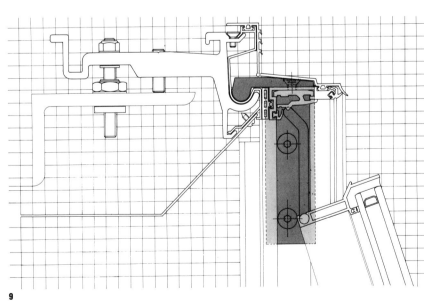

7

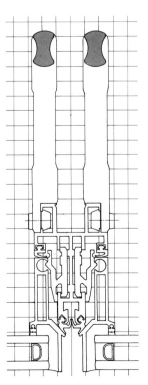

8

9

1

2

172 **Aluminium Research Institute**

Interior views, which show how the design plays lighter, more delicate elements against the heavy concrete frame. Besides the external glazing, the smalle- scale elements include the internal glazing frames and false ceiling panels, storage fitments and aluminium balustrades and tread supports, and the parquet flooring and plants. All of these break down the scale and temper the toughness of the concrete, while the transparency of the internal glazing allows the totality of the structural system still to be appreciated.

1 View from entrance hall across bottom of the stair hall, which is given vivacity by the internal planting along the street edge and the warmth and small scale of the parquet wood floor.

2 Sculptural stair and the glass-sided open well of the stair hall provide a focus that links the floors and puts the building's occupants on display.

3 View from stair hall through ground floor offices shows off the transparency of internal partitioning and how planting provides some screening from the street. Note also how ceilings and lighting are completely co-ordinated with the structure.

4 Small-scale aluminium components of the stair contrast with the heavy concrete components exposed in the stair hall, from where much of the building is visible.

5 Central corridor distributes conditioned air as well as people. It also shows the interplay of transparency and small human-scale elements against the solid and large-scale structural frame. Typically for a Building Workshop design, the kit of secondary elements and exposed ducts is colour coded.

3

4

5

6

Aluminium Research Institute

Exterior views again show the contrast between the heavy concrete frame and more intricate elements.

6 Northern end of the street facade seen from the park, which shows off the system-built character of the building. On the left is an external escape stair and service lift.

7 View from the park through the service stair, with its grc treads supported on cantilevering cast-aluminium supports, and across the courtyard to the workshop with its ribbed aluminium cladding.

8 Side (north) elevation showing workshop and office–laboratory block with separating courtyard and the park across the street to the west. The first-floor bridge across the court was not built.

Client Aluminia SpA
Architect Renzo Piano Building Workshop, Paris
Design team R Piano, B Plattner (associate in charge), R Self, R J van Santen, J Lelay, B Vaudeville, A Benzeno
Structural engineer M Mimram
Services engineer Sodeteg
Facade Italstudio
Local collaborating engineer Omega
Landscape architect M Desvignes
Contractors:
building contractor
Cattaneo, Bergamo;
facade subcontractor
Alucasa, Rho, Italy

173

7

8

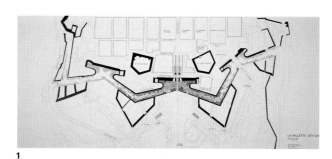

1

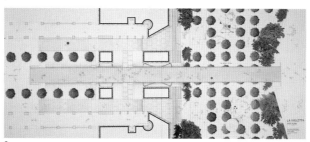

2

Historic restorations

The Building Workshop has been involved in a number of projects, most of them unrealised, involving interventions to restore, re-use and otherwise make the most of various historic structures and settings. In 1986 alone, proposals were prepared for the redevelopment of the moats and fortifications of the main cities of two different Mediterranean islands, Valletta on Malta and Rhodes on the Greek island of Rhodes, and for rehabilitating the famous basilica by Andrea Palladio in Vicenza. None of these projects was implemented and only that for Valletta was worked up in much detail.

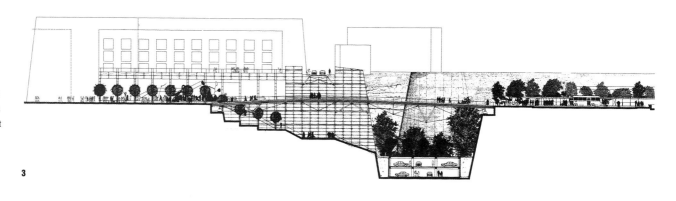

3

Valletta City Gate   Valletta, Malta   **Building Workshop, Italy and France**   1986

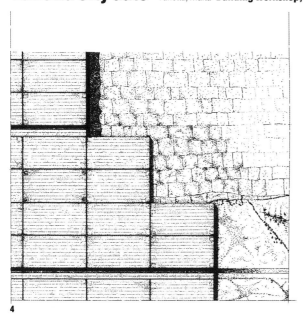

4

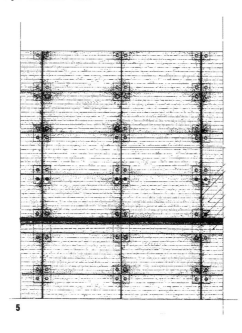

5

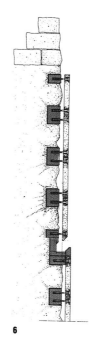

6

Client Malta Government
Architect Renzo Piano Building Workshop, Paris
Design team R Piano, B Plattner (associate in charge), A Chaaya
In collaboration with P Callegia, D Felice, K Zammit Endrich
Structural engineer M Mimram

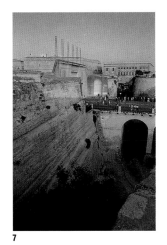

7

8

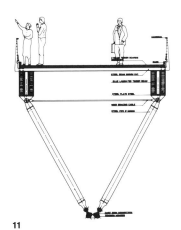

9

10

Set on a promontory, the sixteenth-century town of Valletta in Malta was defended from the rest of the island by fortifications, with the main access via the central City Gate that terminates the spinal axis of Republic Street. In modern times other routes into the city have been added. A planning study for the whole town was first undertaken by the Genoa workshop. It advised rebuilding on the sites vacated by war damage so that the old town would regain its sense of compact cohesion. The City Gate and the area around it were then the subject of a more detailed study by the Paris workshop.

Rebuilt several times through history, the present severe and bombastic City Gate dates from the 1950s. A broad bridge that almost conceals the moat below connects it to a large traffic roundabout that serves as a bus terminal. The proposal was to replace the gate with a simplified and somewhat narrower one, and the bridge with a narrow wooden pedestrian one. This bridge, with its bowed deck and steel props

and cable tension elements, was deliberately designed to have some of the temporary and tentative feeling of a drawbridge and to draw attention to the gardens in the shady bottom of the moat above two subterranean levels of parking. New stairs on both sides of the bridge and passing through arches below the gate would give access to these gardens, and prefabricated panels of new stonework would face the eroded walls of the moat as well as the new gate.

1 Site plan.
2 Plan of proposed new city gate, footbridge and steps down to the moat.
3 Section of proposed footbridge and stairs down to the moat, with parking garage and landscaping in the bottom.
4, 5 Elevations and, 6, section showing proposed use of large reconstituted stone panels held back to concrete fixings to stabilise the natural rock and old walls.
7, 9 The moat as it is now: 7, the existing vehicular bridge and city gate, which are due for demolition.
8 Valletta from the sea.
10 Aerial view showing City Gate and the moat in the context of the town.
11–14 Details of footbridge: 11, section; 12, part elevation; 13, connection of steel compression and tension elements; 14, part reflected plan.

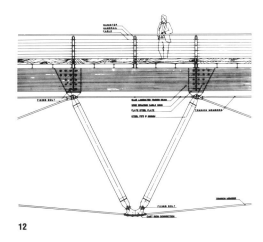

11

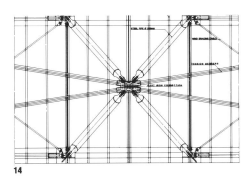

12

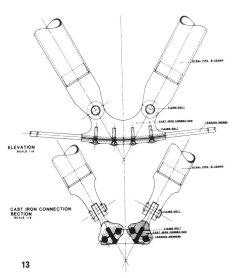

13

ELEVATION
SCALE 1/5

CAST IRON CONNECTION
SECTION
SCALE 1/5

14

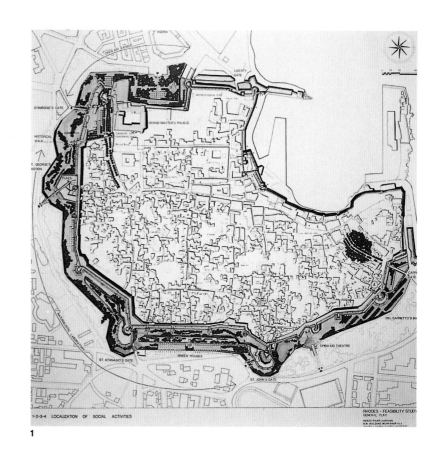

1

176   Before evacuating Rhodes and becoming the Knights of Malta, Christian knights had walled and moated the town of Rhodes to protect it from the Turks. A study undertaken by the Building Workshop for UNESCO and the Greek government proposed turning the moat into a linear garden to show off the diverse flora and fauna found on the island. Facilities for outdoor cultural and entertainment events were also to be included. Structures for some of these facilities, like all the staircases and elevated walkways that would lead people down to, over and through the moat, were to be made from timber baulks with simple metal joints in a way that would recall the siege towers and war machines that were once used to storm such walls.

Rhodes Moat Redevelopment   Rhodes, Greece **Building Workshop, Italy** 1986

1 Plan with proposed new landscaping, pedestrian paths and other public facilities.
2 Section through area exhibiting local flora and fauna, with a stair tower modelled on that of a medieval war machine.
3 Section showing proposed restoration and re-use of fortifications.

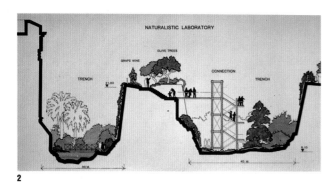

2

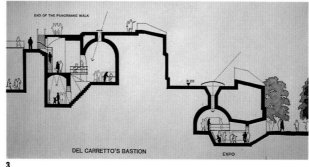

3

4 Cutaway wooden model of basilica.
5 Diagrams charting environmental conditions in the basilica.
6 Piano's sketch of a section of the basilica.

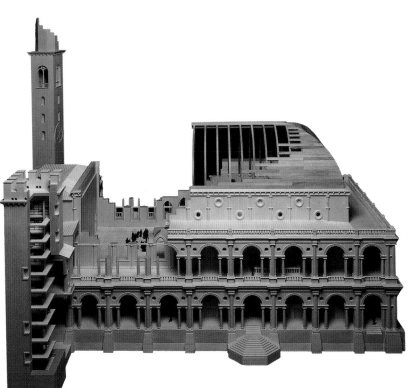

4

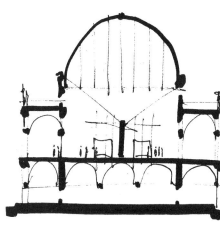

6

Palladio Basilica Rehabilitation Vicenza, Italy **Building Workshop, Italy** 1986

Client City of Vicenza

Architect Renzo Piano Building Workshop, Genoa

Design team R Piano, S Ishida (associate), G Grandi (architect in charge), G Bianchi, P Bodega, M Michelotti

Structural and services engineers
Ove Arup & Partners, M Milan, S Favero

Lighting Sivi Illuminazione

Cost control S Baldelli, A Grasso

Modelmaker G Sacchi

5

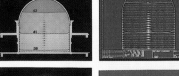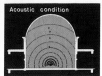

A secular civic structure, the basilica in Vicenza was originally a medieval hall, the surrounding double-level colonnade of which was remodelled by Palladio. The roof was rebuilt after being destroyed by a fire caused by a bomb in the Second World War.

The Building Workshop's proposals, requested after an exhibition of its work had been held there, mainly involved patterns of re-use and environmental control with minimal physical intervention. With Ove Arup & Partners, the architects plotted air movements and temperature gradients at different times of the year in the tall volume of the hall, measured the hall's acoustic properties (showing it to be ideal for Renaissance music) and proposed lighting that would best show off the magnificent space without causing further degradation. Functionally, it was proposed that the basilica and the buildings linked to it, which were to be the main subject of the rehabilitation, should serve a combination of civic and contemporary cultural uses. But despite the extreme tact of the proposals, local academics opposed Piano's involvement on the grounds that he was unsuitable because of his associations with architecture that exploited and exposed high technology.

177

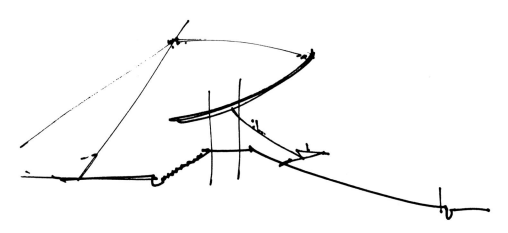

San Nicola Stadium Bari, Italy **Building Workshop, Italy** 1987–90

Some of the Building Workshop's architecture is simultaneously contextualist and alien, responsive to setting, yet also strange and intrusive. A number of its works display this tension in some, often very small, degree. But the most extreme examples of this tendency are two buildings designed and built virtually simultaneously, one by the Paris office, the other by the Genoa office. These are the Bercy-Charenton Shopping Centre (see volume two) on the outskirts of Paris and the San Nicola Stadium for soccer and athletics outside Bari in southern Italy. Although the shopping centre takes its curves directly from the adjacent motorway interchange, and the stadium opens up hospitably to the Apulian landscape, both look like huge and only momentarily settled spacecraft. In part the product of the quest for lightness, such imagery emphasises the strangeness that is probably the inescapable consequence of innovative work.

This tension between contextuality and incongruity is just one of a number of opposing tendencies that the San Nicola Stadium brings into poised equilibrium. What is seen from the distance is only part of the stadium, a raised superstructure of upper tiers and semi-translucent roof. Concealed by a gently mounded crater is the lower tier of seats, with a large amount of submerged ancillary spaces below them, and the playing field that is two metres below natural ground level. Just as the hovering upper tier contrasts and yet comes together, without any uneasy clash, with the earthbound lower tier, so too is the intense inward focus of the whole structure on the playing field counterbalanced by its extraordinary openness and extroversion. And though the upper tier is clearly assembled from huge and heavy precast elements, the double curves of the undersides of these make them seem as soft and light as suspended fabric.

The form of the stadium, with the upper tier separated by slots into petal-like banks that float and project outwards above the planted slopes around the bowl of the lower tier, is Piano's response to the local landscape, married of course to his perennial quests for lightness and transparency (or as here, openness). Typically, the olive- and orchard-covered Apulian plain is interrupted only by gently swelling slopes, the conical bumps of *trulli* (the traditional stone shelters) and the defensively walled *maseria* (the larger farmsteads).

Into this setting the most memorable intrusion is the Castel del Monte, the thirteenth-century hunting lodge of Federico II, which looks as though it has been extruded up from its dominant hill-top. This was a prime inspiration for the stadium, which is another geometrically closed form generated by optimal sight-lines. But instead of growing from the ground, the stadium's upper tier floats above the crater it crowns and to which it is connected only by stairs that seem dropped down like drawbridges from the slots between the banks of seating.

Another major consideration of the design, which was built for the 1990 World Cup and in anticipation of the hooliganism such events bring, was security and crowd control. The same devices that give the structure its sense of openness and lightness, the vertical dissociation of upper and lower tiers and the slots between the banks of seating, also segregate the fans into groups of controllable size. Thus devices that may seem to serve obsessional aesthetic concerns also deal unobtrusively with one of the most problematic issues in stadium design. There is, for instance, none of the usual fencing that is too often seen by fans as a provocative challenge to be breached. Ringed by car parking, there is no single dominant gate into the stadium. Instead there is one on each of the 26 paths that lead up towards the respective stairs to the upper tiers. So the stadium can be quickly evacuated with the landscaped slopes serving as a refuge in any emergency.

CLUB BIANCO ROSSO
Gatto & Volpe
BARI CLUB
CASAMASSIMA
würstel
Wüber
FRATTINI
CROCE ROSSA
ITALIANA

1

180 **San Nicola Stadium**

The stadium and the context that inspired its design.

1, 2 The upper tier of the stadium looms out over the slopes that it crowns in a manner inspired by the Castel del Monte, **2**, which commands the top of the highest hill that rises from the Apulian plain.

3–5 Also important as an inspiration were the typical structures that punctuate the vineyards and orchards of the Apulian plain. Like the Castel del Monte, the conical roofed *trulli*, **3** and **5**, and the defensive farmhouses known as *maseria*, **4**, are made of a single unadorned material, stone, so influencing the decision to build the stadium in plain concrete.

6 Cross section of early design with busy clutter of dog-leg stairs and raised service capsules distracting from the purity of form of the floating upper tier. The rake of the upper tier is less steep than in the final design and its section is tapered towards the top in a manner quite unlike the built scheme.

7 Section of press and VIP block with the elevation of two 'petals' of the upper tier behind.

8 Early study of the structure and geometry of the upper tier.

There is, though, a separate VIP and press entrance that leads to special facilities for them in a block against the arena and straddling its projected cross-axis. From here can also be reached the glassed-in press and VIP box that projects over the top of the upper tier as a rather too-stylised period piece, a momentary lapse in the Building Workshop's studied avoidance of the merely fashionable.

Facilities for local teams and visiting players – such as changing and medical rooms, laundry and offices for administration and specialist staff – are all submerged below the lower tier of seating. They are served by a subterranean ring-road to which there are vehicular entrances at either end of the long axis of the arena. Down here too are wcs for spectators, which are reached by stairs down from a broad promenade that rings the top of the crater, behind the lower tier of seating.

The promenade is the key unifying element of the design, from which the poised equilibrium that it resolves between conflicting forces is most exhilaratingly experienced – yet it is difficult to appreciate just how fine the promenade is from drawings and photographs. It connects all spectator circulation: the radial routes to and from parking, the aisles of the lower tier and the stairs to the upper tier as well as down to the lavatories. During matches, stalls for drink and food are set up on its broad curving expanse, the views along which are closed by the free-flying stairs to the upper tier. Underneath this is not the usual clutter of muscular structure supporting obviously heavy loads, but only the columns that line both sides of the promenade and the clean graceful curves of the underbelly of the upper tier, which seem to hang in satin-soft pleats. To those on the promenade, the

simple curves of path and tier above also offer at their most intense the two primary and contrasting experiences the stadium affords, a compressed view in and down on the playing field, and an almost explosive sense of expansive openness outwards and up to the countryside and sky.

The San Nicola Stadium is, then, quite unlike stadia of the dominant Mediterranean tradition that originated with Roman arenas like the Colosseum and spread to include the Iberian bull-ring. These are closed and introverted structures. Instead, the Bari stadium reaches further back to the tradition of the Greek theatre, which was built into the earth as the lower tier is here, and where action was played out against the backdrop of the landscape. This openness to nature, which is such an evident recurrent theme in the Building Workshop's designs, confirms how un-Italian is Piano's approach.

The initial design, for football only, would have meant a more intense relationship between spectator and playing field. But later, the client decided to include an athletics track (as is usual with Italian stadia). This considerably altered the plan geometry to a configuration that approximates an ellipse and distances the spectators so leading to some inevitable loss of emotional

2

3

4

5

6

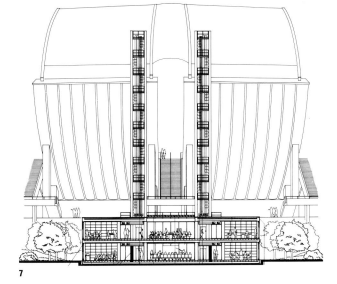

intensity during matches. The free-flying stairs, that are so exactly right that it is difficult now to imagine that any other sort were considered, in fact found their form very late. With their simple concrete flights and balustrades they are robust and straightforward, in a way that is uncharacteristic for the Building Workshop, as are the handrails on the balustrades and elsewhere in the stadium – all of which are perfect for a building of this type and size.

Atypically for the Building Workshop, the stadium is mostly made of a single material, concrete. The steel and fabric canopy is only a partial lid to the dominant structure below. Besides providing shade and some shelter from the rain it also helps to protect the playing area from turbulent winds. The concepts for the whole structure and the details of geometry and sight-lines were worked out in conjunction with Ove Arup &

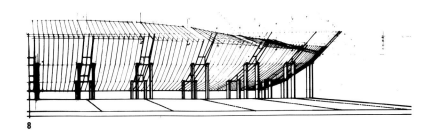

Partners under Peter Rice. But the final calculations and supervision of the concrete structure were done by the Bari engineers, Studio Vitone & Associates. Arup's though remained entirely responsible for the steel and Teflon canopy.

The characteristic repetitive structural 'pieces' of the stadium are the 310 banana-shaped, and inverted T-sectioned, precast concrete beams that support the upper tiers, and the 26 huge petal-like stands they form. Together, stands separated by slots and the double curved lower flanges of the beams clearly reveal the modularity of the structure. The slanting tops of the beams support the stepped seating at three slightly different angles that increase in steepness with height, for the best combination of sight-lines and overall compactness.

Other aspects of the shape of the beams fulfil aesthetic rather than functional or structural purposes. Thus the curve of the underneath of each beam, that is tighter in radius towards the bottom, is perfectly judged for the impression it gives from the crater-top promenade. The secondary curve of the lower flange of each beam hides inconsistencies in the staining of the concrete and inaccuracies of assembly. And the outward projection at the top of the beam

is only a cornice, but the shadow line it creates is aesthetically crucial. These huge beams were precast in three parts near the site and lifted onto the in-situ columns, only four of which support each petal-like bank.

Stretched over a steel structure cantilevered from the head of the stands, is the Teflon canopy that reasserts the unity of the whole above the slots that separate each petal to give to these upper levels their striking sense of openness. The inner edge of the canopy carries the floodlighting, making unnecessary the usual independent masts. Indeed, with the underside of this upper tier floodlit and the roof brightly translucent, the stadium resembles a spaceship or gigantic exotic bloom, so that it seems to be about the only stadium designed for both night use and immediate recognition by an international television audience such as that which watched the 1990 World Cup.

181

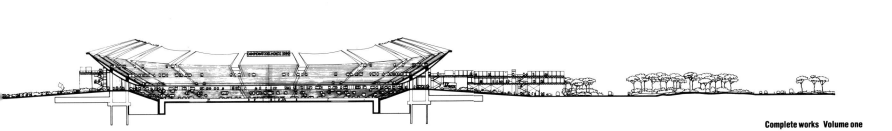

1

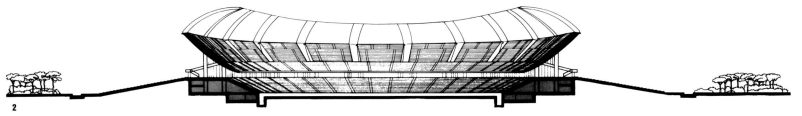

2

San Nicola Stadium

1 View from the lower tier down the long axis of the stadium shows how it counterposes an inward focus with a sense of openness. The latter is gained from the horizontal gap of the promenade between lower and upper tiers and by the vertical slots between the petal-like stands of the upper tier.

2 Cross section of final design with simple flying stairs to the upper tier. It shows how the unified bowl of the stadium is made of an upper tier that floats above the open promenade, in contrast to the lower tier set into the mounded crater. Hidden below the promenade is a service ring-road flanked with facilities for players and clubs, and wcs for spectators.

184 **San Nicola Stadium**

Approaching the stadium.

1 From a distance the stadium seems to hover over the plain, almost like a gigantic space ship. Yet the upper tier is also seen to be made up of petal-like units separated by slots that can be seen through. The greater height of the sides compared to the ends is apparent too, adding a subtle complexity to the curves of the roof and the top of the upper tier.

2 Coming closer and climbing the slope the upper tier and stairs project outwards in dramatic gestures of welcome , and the petal-like banks of the upper tier are seen to be made of huge beams.

1

2

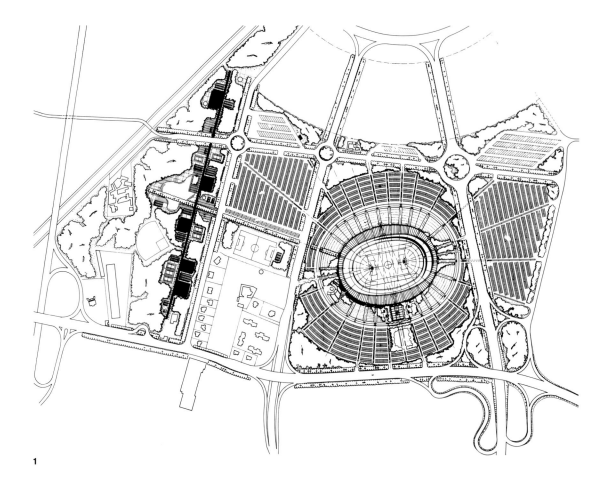

186 **San Nicola Stadium**

Plans.

1 Site plan shows the stadium ringed by planted slopes of the crater with radial paths from surrrounding parking that has good motorway access. To the left is a straight spine of further sports facilities, an unrealised part of the original proposals.

2 Diagram of some of the setting-out geometry of the stadium and mounded crater.

3 Plan at level mid-way up the lower tier.

4 Plan at playing field and service road level.

a service road and parking, **b** club and players' facilities, **c** press and vip centre, **d** spectators' wcs

1

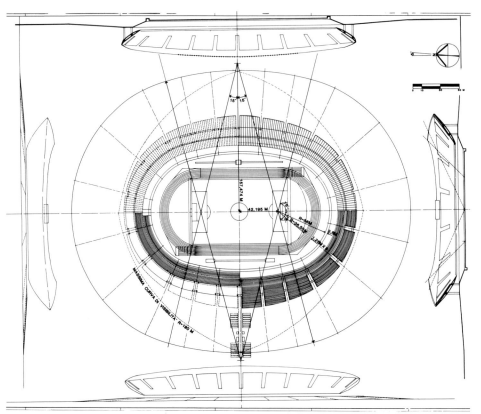

2

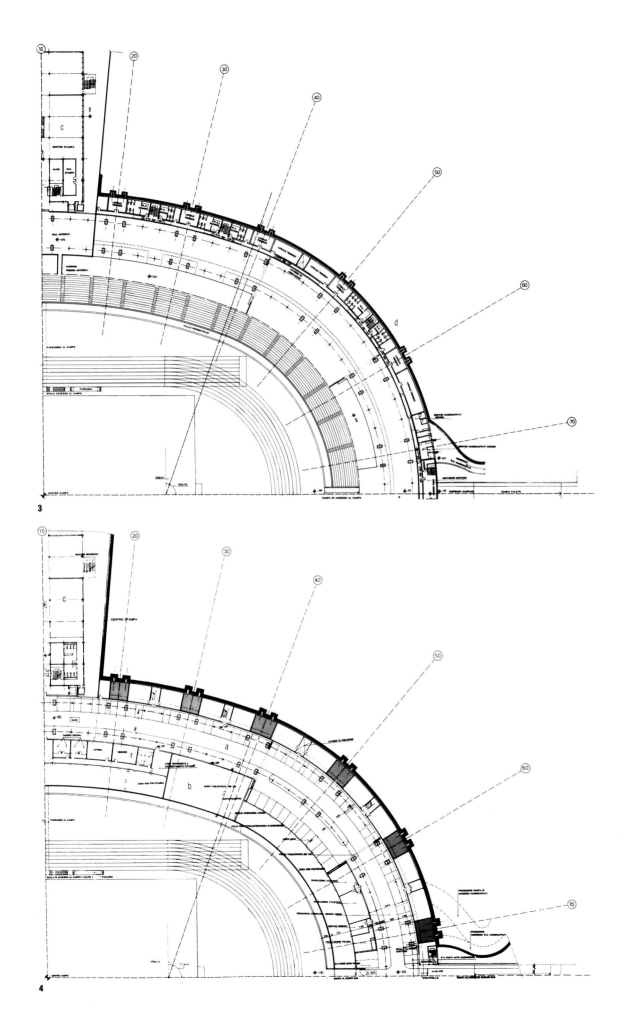

3

4

188 **San Nicola Stadium**

Approach and promenade.

1 The stairs to the upper tier create portals over the stepped ramps that climb the mounded slope to the promenade that rings the top of the lower tier. Some upper tier seating on the far side is visible beyond the people on the promenade.

2 The promenade with its contrasting views: that to the left is focused downwards onto the playing field; that to the right explodes outwards and upwards to the countryside and sky.

3 The main elements of the design are brought together in a single dramatic view from the press and vip block. Above are the soft sagging curves of the upper tier and, visible through the slot up to which the stair climbs between flanking columns, is the fabric roof. Straight ahead is the promenade, visible also on the far side between parts of the upper and lower tiers.

1

2

3

190 **San Nicola Stadium**

Upper level plans.

1 Plan at level mid-way up the upper tier.

2 Plan at promenade level.

3 Roof plan.

4 Plan at top of upper tier.

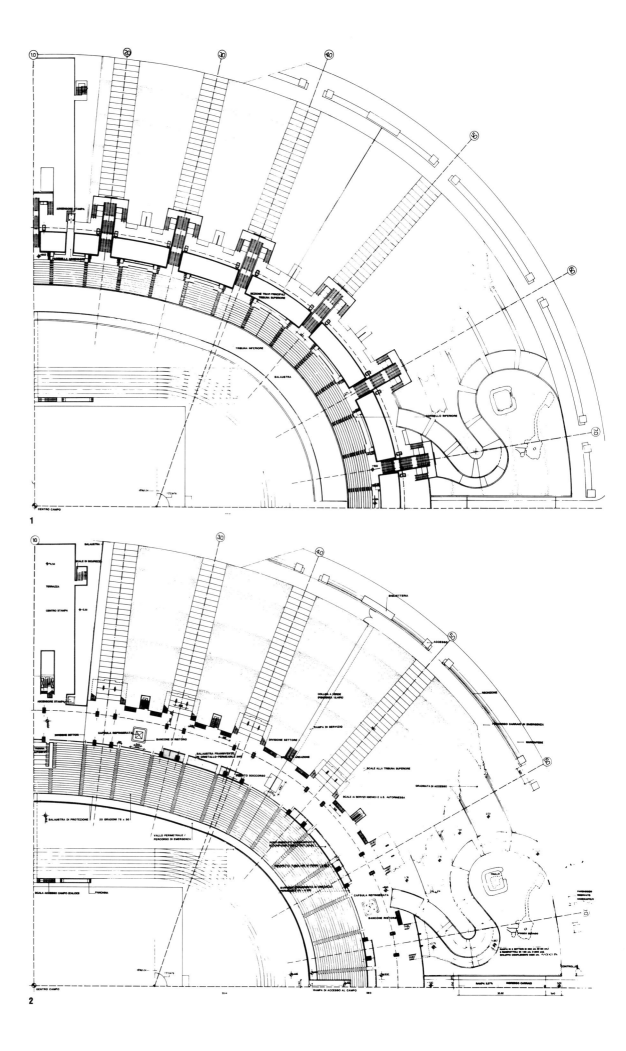

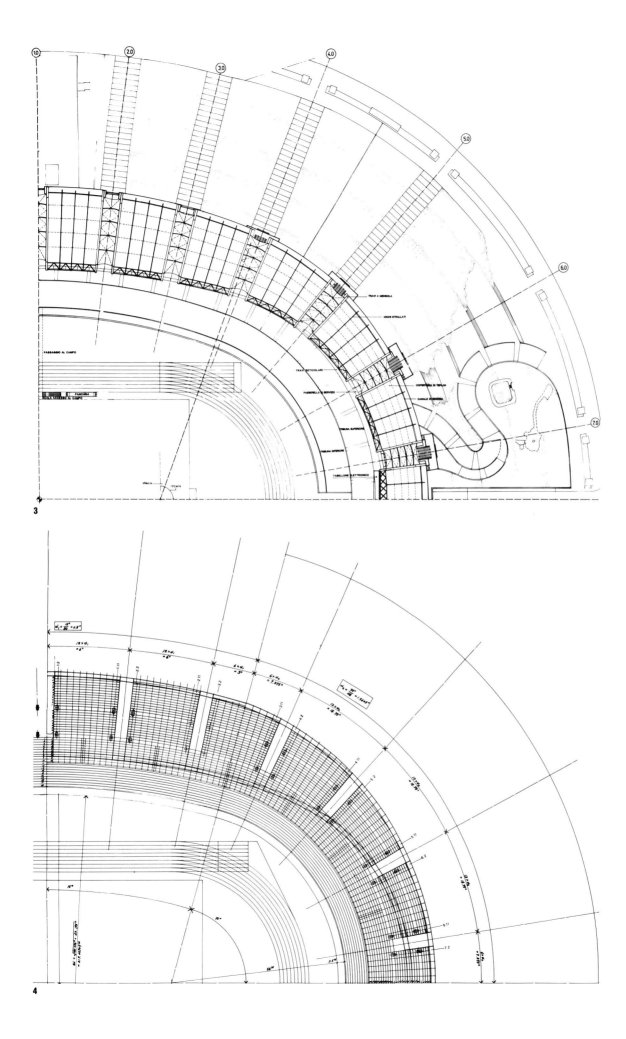

3

4

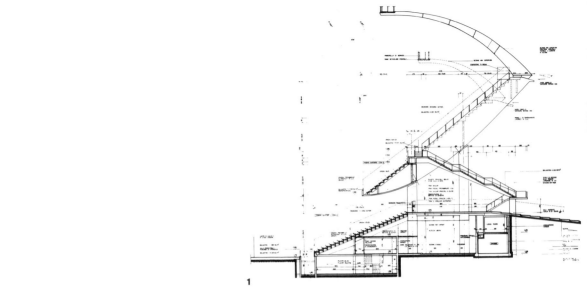

1

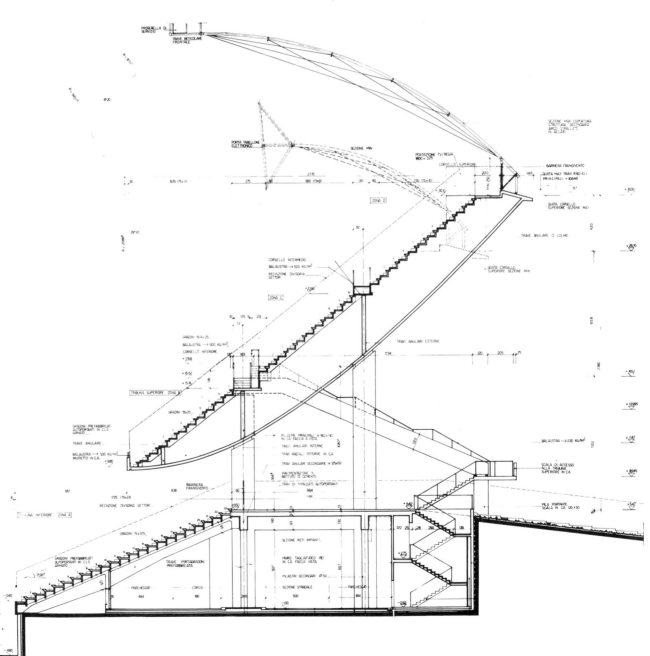

192 **San Nicola Stadium**

Construction drawings.

1 Section through slot to upper tier.

2 Section through side of stadium (dotted line shows top of the upper tier and roof at the ends of the stadium). Note that the underside of the upper tier is not a constant curve but is shaped for aesthetic effect, not structural reasons alone.

Opposite page View from the lower tier emphasises separation of lower and upper tier. It also shows the contrasting cantilevered steel elements that support the fabric roof: one a heavy tapering arm and the other a light tube with tension stays. The sections on this page each show a different one of these conditions. Visible around the top of the roof is the continuous catwalk that gives service access to the floodlights.

2

1

San Nicola Stadium

Stadium in use.

Opposite page A normal weekend match with fans on the lower tier sheltering from showers below the overhang of the upper tier. As well as sheltering the upper tier from sun and rain, the roof was shaped in a wind tunnel to prevent gusting on the playing field.

1–6 Views of the 1990 World Cup matches, for which the stadium was originally built.

1, **5**, **6** Views in the setting sun emphasise the diaphanous nature of the roof and show how the slots that provide the extraordinary sense of openness also segregate the fans into groups of manageable size, an essential safety precaution for such events.

2, **4** A match at night, floodlit from the inner perimeter of the roof.

3 The graceful interplay between the curves of plan and section emphasise both the inward focus and the contrasting openness to outside.

2

4

5

6

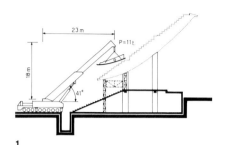

1

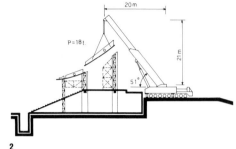

2

196

5

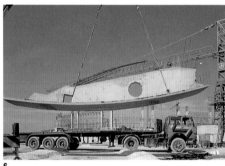

6

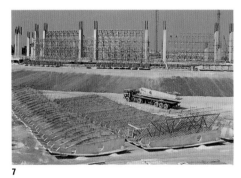

7

8

San Nicola Stadium

Construction views.

1–4 Sequence shows erection of the upper tier:
1–3, the bottom of the segmental beam that constitutes the primary piece of the design is made up of three precast elements (of 11, 18 and 25 tonnes respectively) that were lifted into place by crane; **4**, the beam was then completed with in-situ concrete before the precast seating elements were lifted into place.

5–7 The precast parts of the segmental beams were cast in a field near the site, **7**, before being lifted onto trucks, **6**, and delivered to the site again, **7**, where they were neatly arranged ready for erection, **5**.

8 Aerial view shows different parts of the stadium in different stages of construction.

9 Exploded diagram of the major repetitive elements.

10 The nature of the construction and the mix of precast and in-situ concrete components is clear in this view of the upper tier under construction above the promenade. The upper precast part of the beam in the foreground is yet to be positioned while in the background the lower tier is being built.

11 Precast seating elements of the lower tier being placed in position.

12 Upper tier with some precast seating elements in position over the segmental beams, and the heavier of the two kinds of steel cantilevers for the roof in place.

13 Concrete parts nearing completion, but still awaiting roof and landscaping.

14 Section through part of the upper tier showing inverted-T segmental beams.

15 Section through a segmental beam showing distribution of steel reinforcing bars.

Following page Floodlit in the evening and at night, the stadium resembles some gigantic exotic bloom giving it a distinctive and memorable image on the world's television screens.

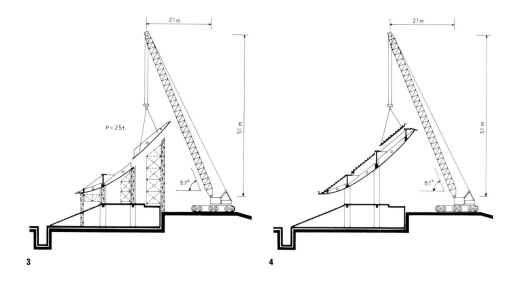

3

4

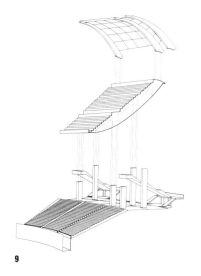

9

Client City of Bari

Architect Renzo Piano Building Workshop, Italy

Design team R Piano, S Ishida, F Marano
(associates), O Di Blasi (architect in charge),
L Pellini

Modelmakers D Cavagna, G Sacchi

Landscape architect M Desvigne

Structural engineer Ove Arup & Partners
(P Rice, T Carfrae, A Lenczer), M Milan-Venice

**Executive engineers for reinforced
concrete** Studio Vitone, V Gianuzzi, L Maggi,
N Cardascia, F Bonaduce

Supervision of prefabricated elements
N Andidero

Site co-ordination J Zucker, M Belviso

Contractor Bari 90 Srl

10

11

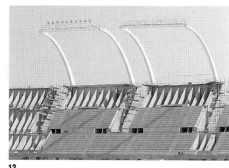

12

13

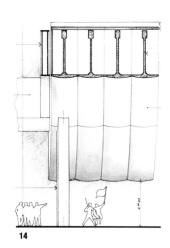

14

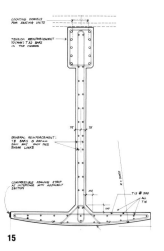

15

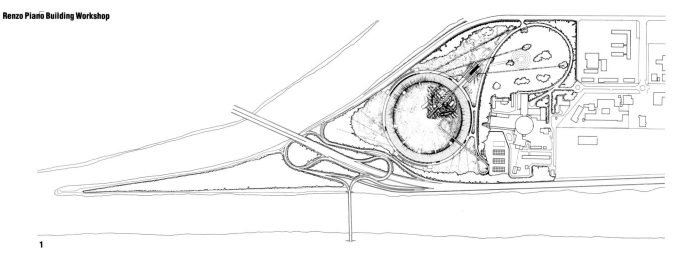

1

200

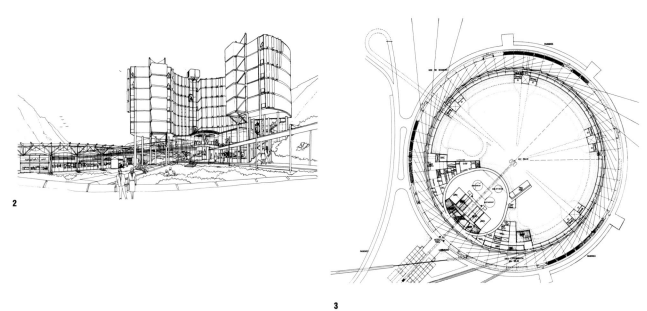

2

3

The research facility was to be set in the narrow angle between the junction of two rivers outside the city of Grenoble with its backdrop of the Alps. The 300-metre diameter ring of the synchrotron was to accelerate atomic particles, the high-energy X-ray emissions from which would have been bent by magnet along 60 tangents to create that number of research areas.

The circular building to house the accelerator ring formed the extrovert rim of a landscaped crater, from which nearby buildings and motorway would be screened to leave visible only the magnificence of the mountains. Within this ring places were designed where researchers could meet: the library, conference room and cafeteria, as well as the control rooms and computer centre.

Outside the ring and connected to these facilities by a pedestrian bridge, an administration block was planned, itself forming a partial ring.

Client ESRF, European Synchrotron Radiation Facility

Architect Renzo Piano Building Workshop, Paris

Design team R Piano, N Okabe (associate in charge), P Vincent, J Leleay, M O'Carroll, P Merz, J L Chassis, C Morandi.

Structural engineer Ove Arup & Partners (P Rice)

Environmental control Ove Arup & Partners (T Barker)

Lighting Ansaldo

Fire prevention Initec

Landscaping M Corajoud

Planning Seri, Renault, BET (Bureau étude technique), Novatome, France, Interatom-RFA USSI, France

1 Site and location plan of synchrotron.
2 Perspective of the administration block with the synchrotron behind and to the left.
3 Plan.
4 Concept sketch of plan and section, which shows the dished bowl in centre of the synchrotron ring.

European Synchrotron Radiation Facility Grenoble, France **Building Workshop, France** 1987

Topographic projects

Two projects involving large curving forms set in the landscape to become almost part of the topography itself, and so demonstrating another dimension to the Building Workshop's quest to integrate its works with nature, foundered for the most frustrating of reasons. A competition-winning design by the Paris workshop, the European Synchrotron Radiation Facility for a science park near Grenoble was developed in some detail. But then, in a typical bureaucratic fudge, it was decided to parcel the scheme out between architects from the countries contributing to its cost in portion proportional to that

contribution. The Sistiana Tourist Resort was for two adjacent bays, one natural and the other existing but man-made, near Trieste. But though great care was taken to impinge minimally and only enhance the topography, the development was halted by pressure from local environmentalists.

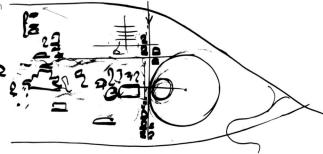

4

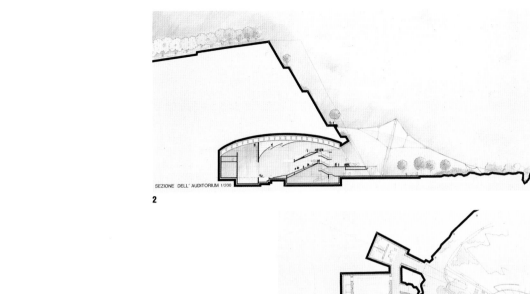

2

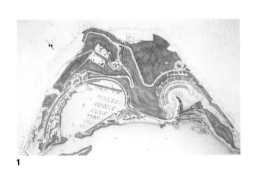

1

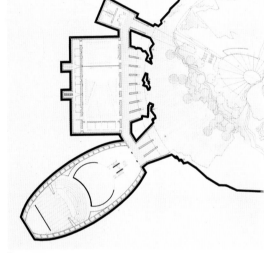

3

Sistiana Tourist Resort Trieste, Italy **Building Workshop, Italy** 1987

The unexecuted scheme for the Sistiana Tourist Resort, focused on a 60-hectare site consisting of the natural bay of the port of Sistiana, with its steep well-wooded slopes, and the adjacent smaller man-made bay of a steeper-sided quarry.

Larger facilities, such as an auditorium and congress hall, were to be concealed by being excavated into the sides of this quarry. Housing in both bays was to be kept to three stories maximum, in terraced strips along the contour and screened by tree planting. The water surface of the natural bay was to be enlarged to increase its capacity as a marina, and the entry to it from the sea screened by islands landscaped to match local topography and vegetation.

201

Client Finsepol SpA, Trieste
Architect Renzo Piano Building Workshop, Paris
Design team R Piano, B Plattner (associate in charge), L Couton, A Chaaya, R Self, O Lidon, P L Coppat, E Agazzi, F Joubert, G Torre
Modelmakers O Doizy, A Schultz
Structural engineers Ove Arup & Partners, M Milan, Studio Boghetto
Services engineers Manes Intertecnica SRL
Landscaping M Desvigne, C Dalnoky, Tecnoforest
Local architects G Furlan, G Galli, G Pauletto

1 Site plan showing natural bay and old quarry.
2, 3 Plan and section of the proposed leisure and cultural facilites built into the face of an old quarry.
4 Section showing large-scale facilities, hidden under earth and planting, edged by tourist rooms and restaurants overlooking the sea.

4

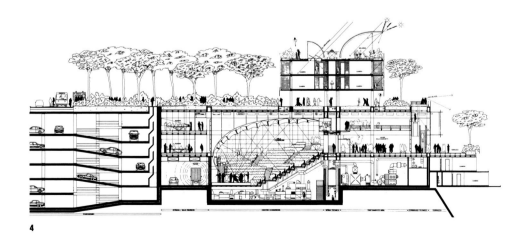

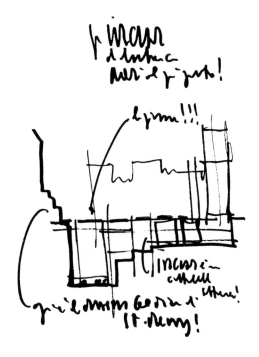

IRCAM Extension Paris, France **Building Workshop, France** 1988–89

The corner tower of the extension to the earlier subterranean building for the Institute for Research and Co-ordination of Acoustics and Music (IRCAM) was the first obviously urban and contextual building by the Building Workshop. Yet the contextual problems were more than how to fit in with and turn the corner between the old buildings that flank both its faces. The tower also has to face up to and address the great work of Piano's youth, the Pompidou Centre. This is a challenge Piano & Rogers ducked with the original IRCAM, which is as mutely shy and secretive as the Pompidou is garrulously and indiscreetly self-revealing.

To fulfil this dual contextual role, the tower marries contemporary technology with an updated use of a traditional material, terracotta. This is, however, the same strategy as used at the Menil Collection where the clapboarding reconciles it with its suburban setting. Yet despite the use of terracotta and the prominently pivotal location, the tower achieves an even greater sense of lightness than the Menil, which might be a problem as much as an achievement.

Shaped only by the demands of acoustic isolation and adjustability, the original IRCAM building is the ultimate functionalist machine, almost totally devoid of formal flourishes except those at the service of its own and its occupants' performance. Devised by science to be at the service of music, it is a centrally located yet secret bunker in which scientists and musicians collaborate on a goal close to Piano's heart: to abolish the boundary between art and science, research and creation. It was designed and built, on its site adjacent to the Pompidou Centre and as part of the total cultural complex, while the Pompidou was being built.

Both for acoustic reasons and to return to view the choir and transept of a large Gothic church, it was built below what is now the place Igor Stravinsky. Even here, though, the rooms for performance and research had to be isolated on flexible mountings to avoid being disturbed by vibrations from underground trains and overhead traffic. These rooms are designed so that their acoustics can be adjusted through a very wide range of characteristics. But with the largest, even its volume and shape can be adjusted by movable floor, ceiling and wall panels.

Yet no matter how well it suits these specialist rooms to be underground, it is not very pleasant for offices. And besides, IRCAM had only the most minimal and enigmatic of exterior presences. Some ventilators and, over a circulation well below, a glass roof of compound rooflets (that might be mistaken for some modern sculptor's representation of a pond, a response to the nearby one full of Tinguely sculptures) were all that hinted at the secret realm below. Now though, in what was a small corner lot, the underground bunker has sprouted a conning tower that gives it an above ground presence and entrance as well as a small stack of offices.

The tower has two staircases: the larger descends three levels into the ground to reach all levels of the original bunker; the smaller stair winds five levels up to give access to the offices and the two old buildings adjacent to the tower. One of these has been converted into a library, the other into meeting rooms. A glazed lift that climbs a slot in the facade also reaches all these levels.

In its internal provisions the tower is very modest, little more than a circulation core. But because of its prominent position as a pivot, not only between the old buildings, but also between the squares in front of and to the side of the Pompidou (the place Georges Pompidou and place Igor Stravinsky), as well as between the buildings and the Pompidou, much care and expense has been lavished on the exterior.

To emphasise this pivotal role the extension is massed as a tower. Hence it is taller than the adjoining buildings, and its

1

204 **IRCAM Extension**

1 Place Igor Stravinsky with the ventilators of the
hidden IRCAM and the site of its extension as a
vacant corner on the right.
2 Circulation well of the subterranean IRCAM
with the Pompidou Centre visible through its
glass roof.
3 Excavation for the original IRCAM.

presence and verticality are
reinforced by the opaque corner,
the windows stacked in slots and
the transparency of the link to the
building facing place Igor
Stravinsky. Stepping forward
from its neighbours edging the
plateau Beaubourg, not only
emphasises its pivotal presence
but also picks up the street
alignment further west towards
Les Halles. Yet in projecting
above and forward from its
neighbours, it also seems to step
upwards and out towards the
Pompidou. Further connection is
implied by the steel structural
frame exposed at the top and to
one side of the lift core, and by
the crisp gridding of the
aluminium frames of glazing and
cladding. These relate the
buildings in time and spirit, even
though the IRCAM tower is
deferential and delicate in a way
that the Pompidou Centre
emphatically is not.

The way the terracotta
elements are held in aluminium
frames derives from that early
icon of High-Tech and prime
inspiration of the Pompidou, the
Maison de Verre, where steps
and other elements are made in a
very similar manner. At IRCAM
though the terracotta elements
that fill the aluminium frames
relate the tower to the converted
brick buildings that it connects.
These immaculately made
elements not only resemble the
brick in material and colour, but
are horizontally grooved to
match the bricks in scale too.
They are held against hidden rails
by plastic clips slid into extruded
holes in the terracotta, and
spaced by small aluminium
cruciform elements that are
visible close up.

Everything about the exterior
is very finely proportioned, both
in the size and shape of the panels
and the elements within them as
well as the hierarchy of larger
units the panels form collectively,
and in the sizing of all the gaps so
as to induce a lively visual
vibration to offset any merely
mechanical quality. These panels
relate in size to the glazing, the
details of which are very fine.

However, the way the
structure is hidden, except
towards the top of the lift core,
by the cladding panels that
project forward from it and that
do not even meet to close the
corner properly, is somewhat
disturbing. No matter how
considerable the virtues of the
design, the result seems rather
flimsy and insubstantial,

especially beside the Pompidou.
Perhaps Piano's quest for
lightness has gone too far here so
that the cladding seems close to
being blatantly decorative,
almost like applied packaging.
This of course is to overstate the
case against a material that will
weather well and, if the
supporting elements give no
trouble, should be virtually
maintenance free. Unfortunately,
a sealant used on lower panels
within reach of graffiti vandals
has darkened the terracotta
around the base. (This problem
was avoided with similar
cladding units used for the
Columbus International
Exposition by filling the bottom
panels with stone.)

The other detail that niggles at
the IRCAM Extension is the
entrance bridge across the glass
roof of the circulation slot of
the original building. Its
humpbacked symmetry, that
makes it part of the piazza and
almost like a garden element,
seems a slightly silly joke. It
might have been better if it had
been treated as an element
reaching out from the tower,
perhaps as a drawbridge, to put
its foot in the piazza and better
link the two.

3

2

4

7

8

IRCAM Extension

4 Steel frame under erection viewed from the Pompidou Centre.

5, **6** Rooms in the original IRCAM: **5**, highly sound absorbent room used for experiments; **6,** view over engineer's mixing console into recording studio.

7, **8** Interiors of main performance space in original IRCAM: **7**, perspectival section showing how it adjusts in section as well as acoustics; and, **8**, as set up for a performance.

9 Cladding components on site awaiting erection.

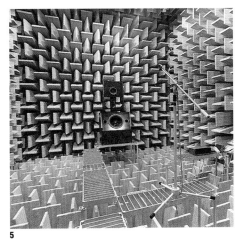

5

9

6

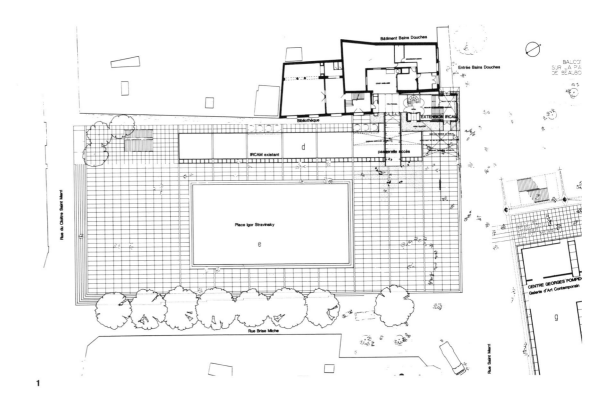

IRCAM Extension

1 Site and ground floor plan.
a new tower extension, **b** existing building converted into meeting rooms, **c** existing building converted into library, **d** glass roof over well of original IRCAM, **e** place Igor Stravinsky, **f** place Georges Pompidou, **g** Pompidou Centre
2 Long section of the original IRCAM with the east elevation of the tower extension and building refurbished as a library.

1

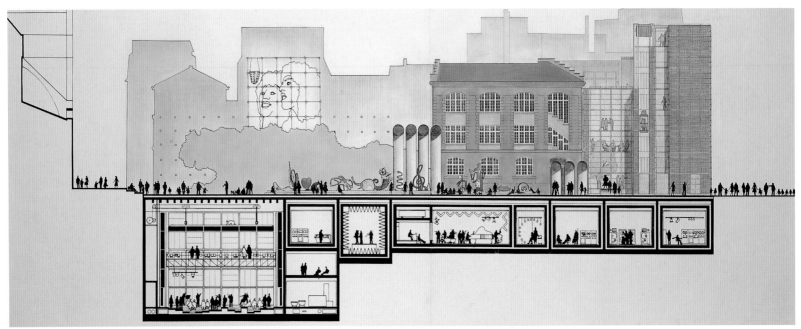

2

3

IRCAM Extension

The tower serves as a townscape pivot, its terracotta cladding linking it with adjacent buildings, its tower-like form punctuating the corner between the two squares and suggesting a relationship with the Pompidou Centre.

3 View from place Igor Stravinsky, which shows the tower stepping up and revealing some of its structure to emphasise the connection with the Pompidou Centre, the huge scale of which makes it seem closer than the tower, although it is actually further away.

4 View from place Georges Pompidou of the tower and the building that now contains meeting rooms.

4

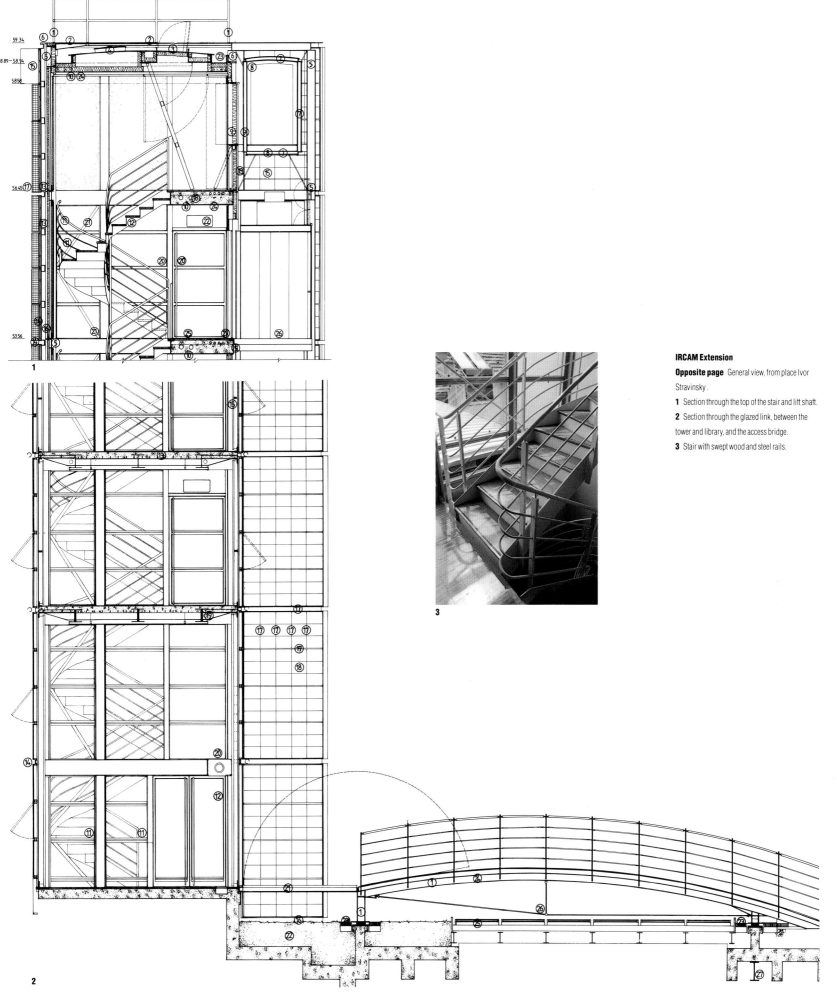

1

2

3

IRCAM Extension

Opposite page General view, from place Ivor
Stravinsky .

1 Section through the top of the stair and lift shaft.

2 Section through the glazed link, between the
tower and library, and the access bridge.

3 Stair with swept wood and steel rails.

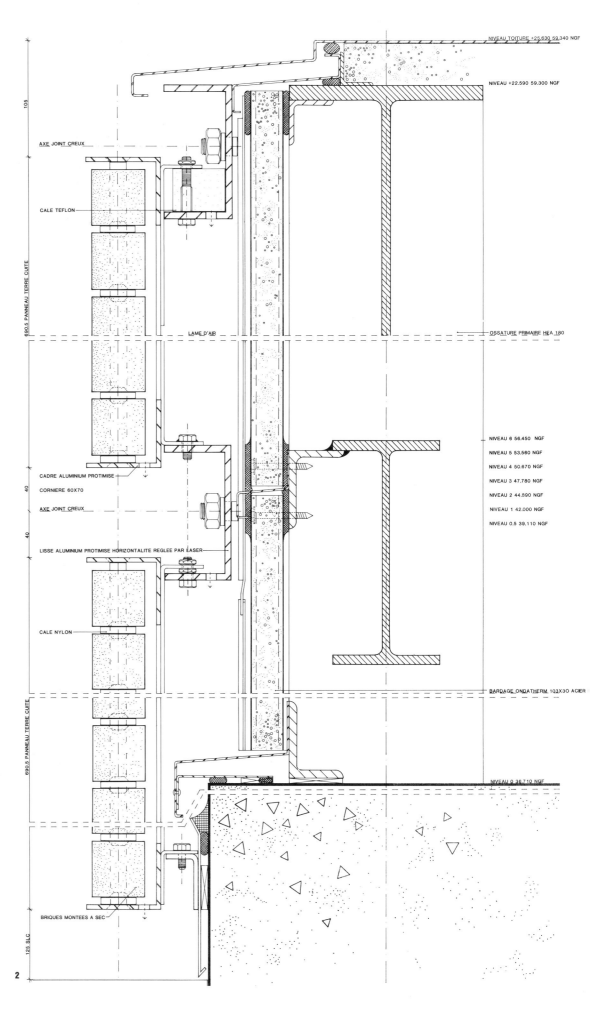

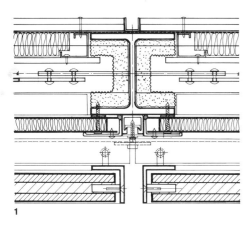

210 **IRCAM Extension**

Cladding details.

1 Detail plan showing, from bottom (exterior) to top: cladding panels; outer layer of insulation; fire-proofed I-beam and rivetted flange of horizontal I-beam; inner layer of insulation with vapour barrier and plasterboard.

2 Detail section of the top and bottom cladding panels and of the large gap between groups of panels.

1

2

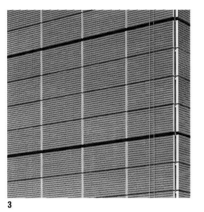

3

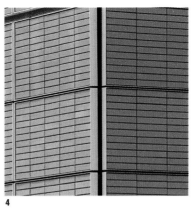

4

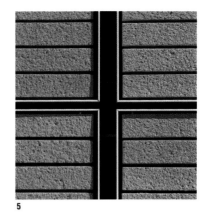

5

IRCAM Extension

3–5 Sequence of progressively closer views of cladding: **3**, at the corners, cladding is clearly expressed as non-structural and non-weather-excluding; **4**, immense care has gone into the proportions and spacings and their subtle hierarchies; **5**, close-up view of the corners of four aluminium-framed panels of terracotta, which shows the crispness of manufacture and fine textured surface.

6 Exploded isometrics of component parts, connections and assembly of cladding panels.

211

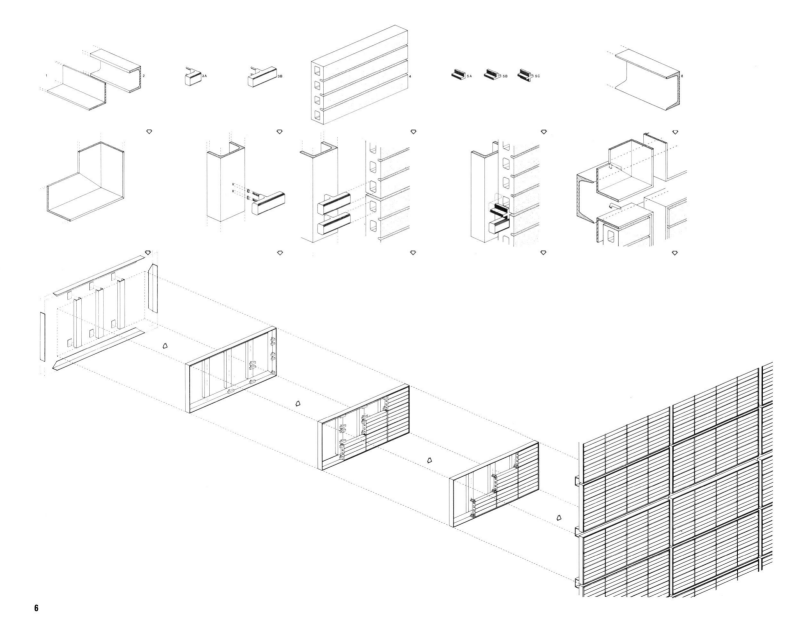

6

1

Clients Ministry of Cultural Affairs, Centre Georges Pompidou
Architect Renzo Piano Building Workshop, Paris
Design team R Piano, N Okabe, P Vincent (associates in charge), J Lelay (architect in charge), F Canal
In collaboration with J L Chassais, A O'Carroll, N Prouvé
Structural and services engineers AXE IB, GEC Ingenèrie
Cost control AIF Services
Project management GEMO

212 **IRCAM Extension**

1 Detail of east elevation, which shows the terracotta units abutting the brick of the building they extend. It also shows that the detailing of the glazing is as refined as that of the cladding. Double glazing is held by the visible clips as well as by glueing to the frame. The yellow elements are external blinds.

2 Close-up view of the head of the tower and lift.

3 Close-up view of the base of the tower and entrance bridge.

4 Plan detail of glazing with opening section to the right.

Opposite page An uncompromisingly contemporary building that fits seamlessly into its urban setting, proving even to the previously sceptical that Piano can make convincing urban architecture.

2

3

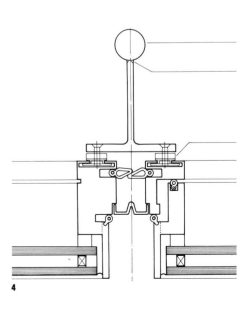

4

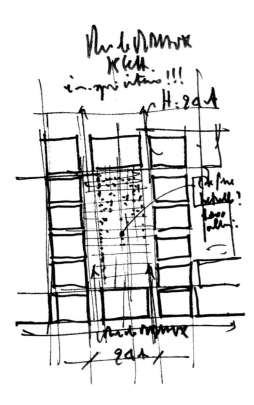

Of all the works by the Building Workshop, the Rue de Meaux Housing represents the most conventional commission. Low-cost housing for a municipal client on a city-centre site, it is the sort of highly circumscribed project that most other European architects have to struggle with and survive on. Yet it also marks a significant milestone in the Building Workshop's oeuvre. Its most conspicuous aspect, the cladding, is a development from that of the slightly earlier tower extension to IRCAM, which on a prominent, pivotal site, explores city-centre contextualism with a cladding of terracotta elements. Together, the IRCAM Extension and Rue de Meaux Housing were important in demonstrating to sceptics that the Building Workshop could produce convincing urban architecture.

But the buildings and their use of terracotta are very different. The IRCAM Extension took its cue from the Menil Collection, which is clad in the same weather-boarding as the surrounding bungalows so as to settle into its suburban setting. The terracotta elements of IRCAM were devised to connect the smallish tower with the brick of the two adjoining buildings, while the steel frames they are set in make some connection with the neighbouring Pompidou Centre. At the very much larger rue de Meaux scheme, the terracotta cladding tile is not only four times the area of a standard brick face, but neighbouring buildings are stuccoed. So the terracotta achieves not contextual continuities, which are here achieved more by site planning and massing, but a fineness of scale and a warm-coloured finish that will weather well. (There are in the general neighbourhood, however, brick buildings with stone or stucco string courses and other details with which the finishes of the Rue de Meaux Housing have some affinity.)

Also, at IRCAM the aluminium frames that secure the terracotta elements are set forward from the concealed structure, creating an effect so light and delicate as to verge on the prissy. At rue de Meaux the tiles face grc panels and the effect, despite the crisp faceting and the extraordinary thinness of horizontal louvres, is much more robust. This difference reflects accurately those of location, size and programme – but also perhaps the contrasting characters of the two associates who ran the Paris office and were responsible with Piano for the design, Noriake Okabe (succeeded by Paul

Rue de Meaux Housing Paris, France **Building Workshop France** 1988–91

Vincent) for the IRCAM tower, and Bernard Plattner for the Rue de Meaux Housing.

The rue de Meaux scheme is one of a number of new housing projects in what is a slightly seedy and densely populated neighbourhood in the north of Paris. It is in the 19th arrondissement, between the Buttes-Chaumont and the place Stalingrad. Local planners had wanted a public route across the deep site, flanked by fingers of housing leaving only small pockets of open space. But the Building Workshop argued for and adopted instead an enclosed rectangular garden that would have most impact as a verdant outdoor room. Overlooked by most of the 220 apartments, the garden is planted with tall slender birches and ground cover that, besides making a striking visual impression, inhibit such noisy uses as gatherings and games.

In contrast to the utopian aspirations of the Modern Movement and many of the housing projects still being built in northern Europe, the Rue de Meaux Housing is not an attempt to create an intensely active social machine that provokes community-forging encounters. Instead it is almost the antithesis of this, a quiet refuge in which both the green oasis of the central garden and the facades that frame it are largely devised to protect anonymity rather than stir social interaction and personal display. Indeed the impression these and the absence of any community forging programmatic intentions give is that this is not low-cost housing, but a retreat for the well-off. The measure of such an achievement was immediately recognised, not just in awards accrued, but in a critic and photographer, both very prominent in architectural circles, taking up residence there.

Those who gave the awards no doubt recognised that in the simple massing and flat facades of this scheme there is both a restraint and a richness that is an immense relief after the silly sculptural posturings of so much current French public housing. But, though site organisation is efficient and effective, and apartment planning clean and competent, neither are particularly innovative. It is the facades that are. Instead of being the focus of a superficial quest for identity and inventive expression in gratuitous gymnastics, they explore both the potential of a new material, grc, and its combination with a traditional one, terracotta. Together the materials produce a facade of a delicate crispness not usually possible in cheap construction, yet one that will age gracefully as it softens with patination.

Such a conjunction of a new material and an old one used in a new way is typical of the Building Workshop. So too is the way new technology, the cold grey grc, is brought together with and tempered by nature, which here is manifested in the warmth and weathering of the 'natural' terracotta as well as in the plants

of the garden. Yet something natural is also implied in the vivacity of the facades that are proportioned to induce a slight optical flicker that animates some affinity with the fluttering leaves to which they are a backdrop.

Except where set back at upper levels to comply with light angle ordinances, the housing is kept to pure rectangular blocks around the garden – though some minor arms bridge over service lanes to meet neighbouring buildings and retain the contiguous urban grain of the area. Two slots off the street offer tantalising glimpses of, and controlled access to, the central garden off which all apartments are reached. Both the sliver of garden seen from the street, and the full view on entering it, gain immeasurably from the upward tilt of the garden that displays it most effectively. The slots through from the street also break up what would otherwise be a long facade into three blocks of similar scale to the old buildings that line the street.

At the bottom levels of these new street-side blocks are some shops, and passing under the extreme ends of the two outer blocks are access routes for service vehicles. That on the north-east corner of the site is an entrance to a large depot for municipal vehicles, some of which park under the new housing block that flanks it (a small compensation for giving up the rue de Meaux site, that had all been part of this depot). In the south-west corner is an entrance for garbage trucks and fire engines servicing the housing, and beside this an entrance to the subterranean parking garage that stretches under all the new blocks.

Within the single volume of the blocks is quite a range of apartment sizes. The generic apartment type, that fills the

216 **Rue de Meaux Housing**

1 Location plan: **a** rue de Meaux, **b** central garden, **c** municipal depot
2 Detail of elevation of QB Housing, Genoa, the facades of which are forerunners of those at rue de Meaux.
3 Oblique view of the rue de Meaux facade in its context.

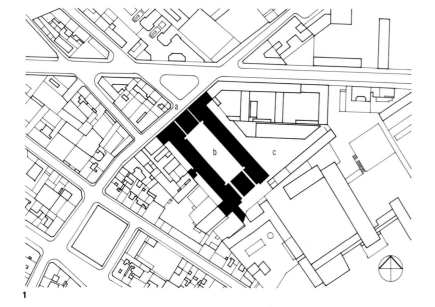

1

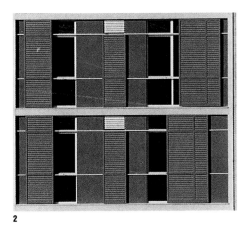

2

3

middle levels of the blocks that flank the long sides of the garden, is dual aspect with a main room that looks in on the communal garden and out to the neighbourhood. Both sides have balconies, those overlooking the garden partially screened for privacy by the grc louvres. On the lower levels of these blocks, apartments face the garden with double-height, studio living rooms. At upper levels where light angles necessitate set-backs are roof terraces, some of them to duplex apartments. These terraces are shaded by horizontal louvres on steel frames that follow the 45-degree light angles, and the recessed facades of these terraces are faced in enamelled steel panels.

Just as the apartment plans are generally conventional, so too is the concrete cross-wall construction. Formal emphasis is not dissipated on complex structure, massing or plans, but focused on the faceting and proportions of the grc and terracotta elements, and on the way these are composed as facades. These form autonomous gridded planes, behind which even balconies remain that mediate between inside and out. These facades are as much part of the external realm they edge as the interiors they front.

Although there are differences between them, all facades are faced with the same materials and module. The grc cladding panels are modulated on a 90 by 90cm grid and are always three such modules high by three or four wide. The grid that marks the modules projects slightly to create a flush frame around the panels of terracotta tiles. The 42 by 20cm tiles are clipped very simply to nibs on the very thin (12mm) grc, behind which is the insulation. The intention was that all these elements be assembled together in the

factory and delivered to site as a complete unit. The contractor however, unused to such methods, chose to assemble everything in situ.

On the facades facing the narrow ends of the garden and those facing adjacent properties, these panels are fairly flat. But on the long elevations of the garden and the street facade, the modulating grid is bracketed outwards, creating a deeper more articulated facade. Set against the back of the cladding panel behind open modules, across which some grid rails extend for protection, are white-framed French windows, in front of which are the yellow frames of pull-down blinds. On the long garden facades, these blinds also shade the more open parts of balconies. Elsewhere the balconies, like the stairs immediately behind the facades, are shaded by thin horizontal louvres that are tapered to look so fine as to raise doubts, perhaps misplaced, about their robustness.

The major grid of the panels themselves, and the modular grid that subdivides them, together with the insistent horizontal hatching of the louvres, give an abstractness to these facades that largely suppresses the identity of apartments, stairs and balconies. Yet these same elements, with their precisely judged proportions and spacings, and with the stepped pyramidal placing of the screens of louvres, give to these facades their jittery vitality, a quality that would be tiresome if applied throughout the scheme rather than restricted only to these facades, which are the compositional climax.

To bring light into the double-height studio living rooms at the bottom of these facades, their fronts are entirely glazed. But the panes are etched with the pattern of the terracotta tiles above, to maintain the fine scale and some continuity with them, as well as to ensure privacy.

On the street facade the bottom two levels are glazed with shop-fronts. But here the modular grid from the cladding panels above extends in front of

the first-floor glazing, to give it a scale similar to the rest of the facade and to soften the transition between it and the tenant's shop-front. (The same device might have worked well across the top half of the studio windows in the garden facades.) On the upper levels of the street facade, the windows are simply stacked in vertical rows to give it a similar rhythm and stable order as the older facades in the street. There is then a nicely judged hierarchy in the relative animation of the various facades. They are quietly understated on the sides facing other properties, and liveliest around the garden, with the street facades somewhere in between.

Yet the street facades falter in one crucial way. The problem is not the introduction of new materials. Rather it is that despite the facades' continuation of the cornice line of an adjacent building, they themselves lack a cornice to cap them properly and suggest closure to the space of the street. What would have worked well here is a detached and projecting flat cornice like those so popular in modern Swiss architecture. These are recommended and functionally legitimised because of the air turbulence they provoke that dries out the vulnerable top of the facade.

217

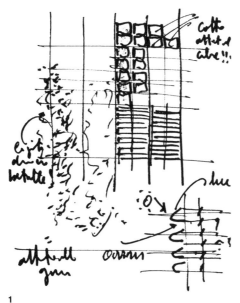

1

2

218 **Rue de Meaux Housing**

Much of the design effort went into proportioning and sizing the elements, the gaps between them and the degree of relief, to achieve an effect that though restrained and disciplined is also rich and vibrant.

1 Piano's sketch of how the play of repetitive gridded elements might achieve a similar vibrancy of effect as the fluttering leaves in front of them.

2 Detail of street facade, which shows the crisp modelling achieved by bracketing out panels. Lower panels are open grids that maintain some discipline to the upper level of shops yet to be fitted out by tenants.

3 Elevation facing the central garden shows the richness that can be achieved by the proportioning and placing of a few repetitve elements.

Opposite page A close-up view of the elements of the facade.

3

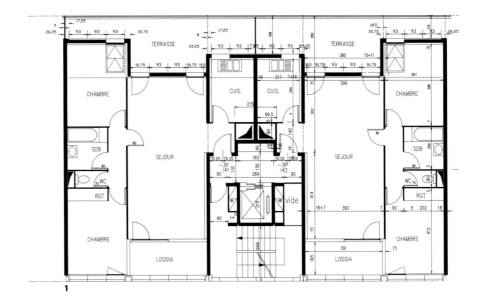

1

Rue de Meaux Housing

1 Plan of a pair of typical two-bedroom apartments with double orientation living–dining room on either side of a vertical circulation core.

2 Typical (second and third) floor plan.

3 Site and roof plan.

4 Service and fire access lane on the eastern edge of the site. Note how the building reaches across the lane to connect to a neighbouring building and continue the urban grain of the area; and also the restraint and flatness of these side facades compared to those of street and central garden where each panel brackets outwards.

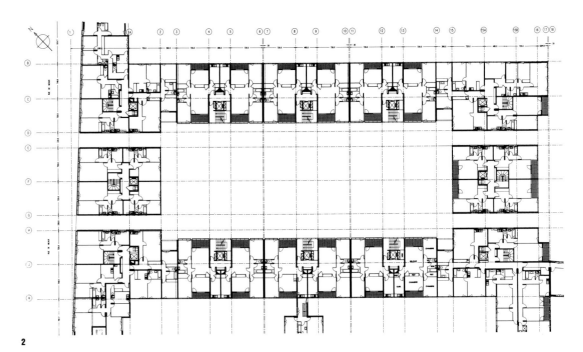

2

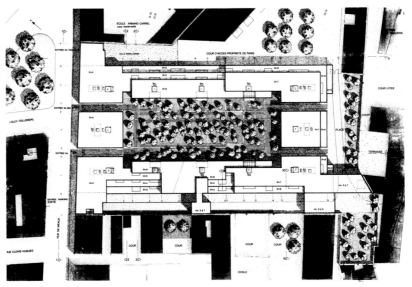

3

1

2

Opposite page The block that closes the southern end of the central garden, screened by a spinney of slender silver birch trees.

1 Elevation to rue de Meaux.

2 Cross section through central garden.

3 Longitudinal section through central garden showing the elevation that overlooks it.

4 Section along service lane on eastern edge of the site, which shows the elevation facing neighbouring properties.

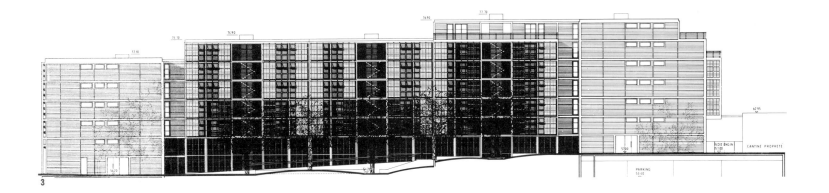

3

4

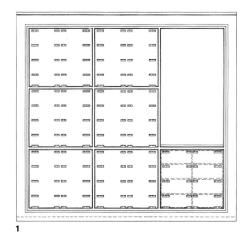

1

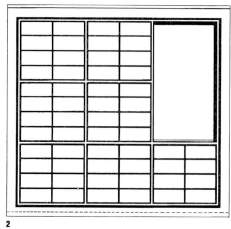

2

224 **Rue de Meaux Housing**

Construction views and cladding details.

1, **2** Views of grc facades prior to fixing of terracotta tiles.

3, **4** Typical flat cladding panel used on elevations facing neighbouring properties before, **3**, and after, **4**, fixing the terracotta tiles.

5–10 Detail sections of side elevation cladding panels: **5**, grc panel alone; **6**, with nibs attached to secure tiles; **7**, in position against slab and insulated behind with some tiles in place; **8**, grc panel with window opening; **9**, with nibs and window; **10**, in position with insulation.

11, **12** Typical cladding panels on garden elevation before, **11**, and after, **12**, fixing terracotta tiles.

13–17 Detail sections of openings in garden elevation cladding panels: **13** and **14**, for window; **15–17** balcony front with horizontal louvres.

18 Construction view with the first panels of terracotta tile fixed to nibs visible on the bare grc panels.

3

4

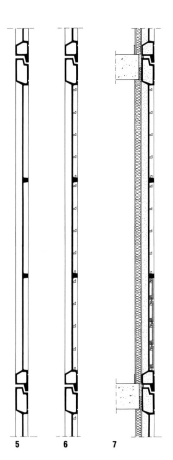

5   6   7

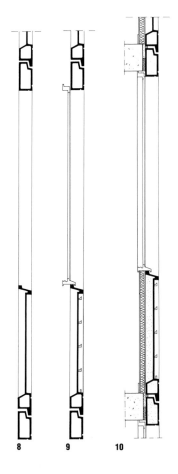

8   9   10

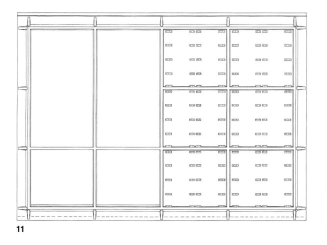

11

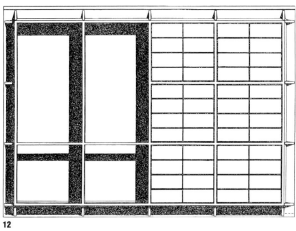

12

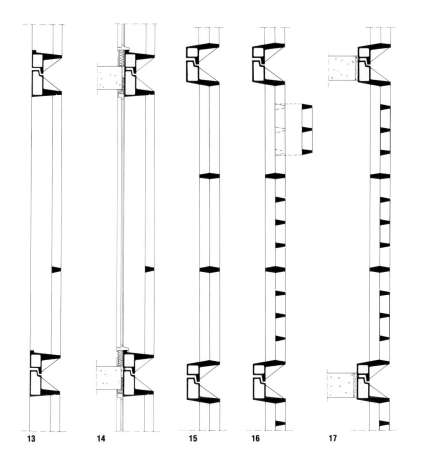

13   14   15   16   17

18

1

2

226 **Rue de Meaux Housing**

Views of the central garden, a verdant outdoor room, more like a refuge for the well-to-do than part of low-cost state housing:

1 Balcony, as seen from living room, with facade on far side of garden in background.

2 Looking along the western edge of a garden to a gap that leads to the street.

3 Entrance to apartments off the central garden.

4 Horizontal louvres shading balconies and staircase.

5–8 Views showing the treatment of paving and planting in winter, **5** and **6**, and summer, **7** and **8**.

Opposite page Autumnal view of the central garden seen from gap leading into its south-east corner. This view contrasts with that from the street approach, from where the garden slopes up so that the landscaping makes greater impact.

3

5

6

4

7

8

Client RIVP Les Mutuelles du Mans
Architect RenzoPiano Building Workshop, Paris
Design team R Piano, B Plattner (associate in charge), F Canal, C Clarisse, T Hartman, U Hautsch, J Lhose, R J van Santen, J F Schmit
Structural and services engineer
GEC Ingenière
Landscaping M Desvigne, C Dalnoky, P Conversey
Contractor Dumez

Biographical notes

For all its collaborative ways of working, there is an inevitable hierarchy in the Renzo Piano Building Workshop. For the most part this is based on how long members have worked for it, especially in direct collaboration with Piano himself, developing designs and being responsible for projects. On the following pages, arranged to reflect this hierarchy, are brief biographies of Piano and the most significant of his current design collaborators. Last, but far from least in importance, are listed two co-ordinators, both of whom represented major clients before joining the Building Workshop, and the two consultants who have collaborated on all the major works.

Right: the Genoa team in the Vesima Laboratory-Workshop

Renzo Piano

Flavio Marano, Renzo Venanzio Truffelli, Shunji Ishida, Mark Carroll (clockwise from top left)

230   **Renzo Piano AIA, RIBA, BDA**

Born in Genoa on 14 September 1937, he studied architecture at the University of Florence and Milan Polytechnic, graduating from the latter in 1964. Subsequently he worked with Franco Albini, and then, with the support of his father, a builder, started experimenting with and building lightweight structures. During this period, in which his practice was known as Studio Piano, he also collaborated for short periods with Z S Makowski in London, Marco Zanuso in Milan and Louis Kahn in Philadelphia. But his main mentor, then and later, was Jean Prouvé.

Between 1971 and 1978 he was in partnership with Richard Rogers (Piano & Rogers), and between 1978 and 1980 with the late engineer, Peter Rice (Piano & Rice Associates). In 1981 he formed the Renzo Piano Building Workshop with offices in Genoa, Paris and, since 1989, in Osaka.

Piano has been visiting professor at important universities around the world, including Columbia University in New York, University of Pennsylvania in Philadelphia, Oslo School of Architecture, Central London Polytechnic and the Architectural Association in London, and the universities of Stuttgart, Tokyo and Delft. Exhibitions of his work have been held in many cities worldwide, including Paris, London, Berlin, Naples, Vicenza, São Paolo, New York, Houston, Los Angeles, Philadelphia, Toronto, Boston, Sydney, Tokyo, Osaka, Nagoya and Sapporo.

In 1978 he received an award from the Union of International Architects in Mexico City and in 1981 the Compasso d'Oro in Italy and an AIA honorary fellowship in the USA. In 1984 he was awarded Commandeur des Arts et des Lettres in France and in 1985 the Legion d'Honneur. In 1986 he was awarded an RIBA honorary fellowship in London and in 1989 the Royal Gold Medal of the RIBA and the Cavalieri di Gran Croce in Italy. In 1990 he received an honorary doctorship from Stuttgart University and was awarded the Inamori Foundation Prize in Kyoto. In 1991 he was awarded the Richard Neutra Prize in Pomona, California, and in 1992 was given an honorary doctorship from Delft University.

Noriaki Okabe

Bernard Plattner

Founding associates of the Renzo Piano Building Workshop

Shunji Ishida   *associate architect*
Born in Shizuoka, Japan, in 1944, he graduated in architecture from the Hokkaido University in 1968. Then, after studying with Professor Seike at the Tokyo Institute of Technology, he worked for Arup Associates in London from 1969–70. From 1971–77 he worked for Piano & Rogers in Paris. In 1978 he became an associate architect in the Building Workshop and has worked in the Genoa office ever since.

Flavio Marano   *associate engineer*
Born in 1933, he graduated in civil engineering from Genoa University. After extensive experience in construction engineering, he started working with Renzo Piano in 1968 and was the engineer for the structures by Studio Piano. In 1987 he became associate engineer but, from a long time before that, he has been managing all contracts and administration in Genoa.

Noriaki Okabe   *associate architect*
Born in 1947, he studied architecture at the Waseda University in Tokyo. In 1974 he joined Piano & Rogers and worked on the Pompidou Centre and IRCAM. After collaborating with Piano in Genoa, he became an associate in 1978 and then chief architect (with Bernard Plattner) in the Paris office in 1981. Since the Building Workshop won the 1988 international competition for the Kansai International Airport Terminal, he has represented the practice in Osaka. He was also associate-in-charge of the Schlumberger Renovation (with Bernard Plattner) and the Bercy-Charenton Shopping Centre.

Bernard Plattner   *associate architect*
Born in 1946, he studied architecture at Zurich Polytechnic (ETH). In 1973 he started working with Piano & Rogers on the Pompidou Centre. Since then he has continued to work with Renzo Piano and became an associate in the Paris office in 1978. He now runs the Paris office with Paul Vincent. Among the projects he has worked on with Piano as associate-in-charge are parts of the Schlumberger Renovation, the Aluminium Research Institute in Novara, detailed studies for the Valletta City Gate on Malta and Rue de Meaux Housing in Paris. Now he is playing a similar role on the Potsdamerstrasse project for Berlin.

Paul Vincent

Paris office: the previous premises

Alberto Giordano

Peter Rice

Osaka office

Other associates

Paul Vincent *associate architect*
Born in 1955, he graduated from the architectural section of the École des Beaux-Arts in Paris where he studied structures, mathematics, morphology and typology. He joined the Paris office in 1983 and became an associate in 1989. He took over responsibility for the IRCAM Extension (from Noriaki Okabe) and is working on the project for the J M Tjibau Cultural Centre in New Caledonia and the Cité International for Lyon.

Mark Carroll *associate architect*
Born in Hartford, Connecticut, in 1956, he studied architecture at Clemson University, South Carolina. He joined the Renzo Piano Building Workshop in 1981 and has worked on a variety of projects including the Menil Collection. In 1985 he became a registered architect in Italy and, in 1992, became an associate architect.

R Venanzio Truffelli *associate architect*
Born in Parma, Italy, in 1957, he graduated in architecture from Genoa University in 1981. He joined the Renzo Piano Building Workshop in 1983 and became an associate architect in 1992. He has been responsible for part of the rehabilitation of Genoa harbour for the 1992 Columbus Exposition and is currently working on projects for railway stations in Italy.

Recently appointed project architects working in direct collaboration with Piano

Emanuela Baglietto
Born in Genoa in 1960. She is project architect for the Mercedes Benz complex in Stuttgart, Germany.

Giorgio Bianchi
Born in Genoa in 1957. He was responsible for the rehabilitation of a part of Genoa harbour for the 1992 Columbus Exposition and is working on the Potsdamerstrasse project for Berlin, Germany.

Giorgio Grandi
Born in Genoa in 1957. He is project architect for the Banca Popolare di Lodi and the Padre Pio Pilgrimage Church in Foggia. He previously worked on the rehabilitation of Genoa harbour for the 1992 Columbus Exposition.

Donald L Hart
Born in Nousser, Morocco, in 1954. He is project architect for a second series of metro stations for Genoa and was responsible for the realisation of the Congress Centre, part of the 1992 Columbus Exposition project.

Claudio Manfreddo
Born in Buenos Aires, Argentina, in 1956. He was responsible for the realisation of the Habour office, part of the 1992 Columbus Exposition project. He is project architect for the Ravenna Sports Hall.

Maurizo Varratta
Born in Genoa in 1955. He is project architect for the rehabilitation of the FIAT Lingotto Factory in Turin and previously worked on the first group of metro stations for Genoa.

Olaf de Nooyer
Born in Schiedam, the Netherlands, in 1960. He is the architect in charge of the Museum of Science and Technology, Amsterdam and was responsible for the realisation of the 'crane', part of the rehabilitation for the 1992 Columbus Exposition.

Kenneth Fraser
Born in Greenock, Scotland, in 1964. He is responsible for the design development of the Padre Pio Pilgrimage Church in Foggia, Italy.

Co-ordinators

Alain Vincent
He was the client's representative for the Schlumberger Renovation. Since 1986 he has worked for the Renzo Piano Building Workshop as admininistrative co-ordinator of the Genoa, Paris and Osaka offices.

Alberto Giordano
He was chairman of the board for the ongoing Fiat Lingotto Factory rehabilitation. Now he works for the Renzo Piano Building Workshop as team and general co-ordinator.

Consultants

Of the many consultants who have worked with the Renzo Piano Building Workshop, the immense contributions of two in partiuclar stand out. Both first worked with Piano, as engineers with Ove Arup & Partners in London, on the Pompidou Centre and have collaborated on all his major works since then.

Tom Barker
Born in 1936, he joined Ove Arup & Partners in 1971 as a mechanical engineer. He is now a director of Ove Arup & Partners and continues to collaborate on Renzo Piano Building Workshop's major projects.

Peter Rice

Born in Ireland in 1935, he studied civil and structural engineering at Queen's University, Belfast, and Imperial College, London. He joined Ove Arup & Partners in 1956 and became a director in 1978. Between 1977 and 1979 he was a partner in Piano & Rice Associates. In 1984 he became a director of Rice Francis Ritchie in Paris and a director of the Ove Arup Partnership in London.

Besides being the structural engineer and a major collaborator on the designs of all Piano's major works since the Pompidou Centre, and having worked on the Sydney Opera House, Rice was the structural engineer for many of the distinguished buildings of our time. These include Lloyd's of London and P. A. Technology, Princeton by Richard Rogers + Partners and the Mound Stand at Lord's Cricket Ground in London by Michael Hopkins and Partners. He was also the structural engineer for many special parts of buildings such as the conservatories at the Museum of Science and Industry, La Villette , and the 'Clouds' at the Grande Arch, La Défense, both in Paris.

In 1992 Rice received the Royal Gold Medal of the Royal Institute of British Architects. He died later the same year. The last building for which he was completely responsible for the structural engineering is the Kansai International Airport Terminal, although he was also involved in the Padre Pio Pilgrimage Church.

Renzo Piano Buiding Workshop

Genoa, Paris, Osaka

Associates

Mark G Carroll *associate architect*
Shunji Ishida *associate architect*
Flavio Marano *associate engineer*
Noriaki Okabe *associate architect*
Bernard Plattner *associate architect*
Renzo Venanzio Truffelli *associate architect*
Paul Vincent, *associate architect*

Project architects

Emanuela Baglietto
Giorgio Bianchi
Antoine Chaaya
Loïc Couton
Olaf de Nooyer
Kenneth Fraser
Giorgio Grandi
Donald L Hart
Akira Ikegami
Tetsuya Kimura
Claudio Manfreddo
Maria Salerno
Ronnie Self
Taichi Tomuro
Maurizio Varratta
Hiroshi Yamaguchi

Design team

Alessandra Alborghetti
Roger Baumgarten
Eva Belik
Jan Berger
Maria Cattaneo
Dante Cavagna
Patrick Charles
Geoffrey Cohen
Ivan Corte
Stefano D'Atri
Paul Darmer
Vittorio Di Turi
Ahmed El Jerari
Allison Ewing
Ruben Fernandez Prado
Junya Fujita
Alain Galissian
Andrea Gallo
Domenico Guerrisi
Christopher Hays
Giovanna Langasco
Paola Maggiora
Domenico Magnano
Joost Moolhuijzen
Jean-Bernard Mothes
Hanne Nagel
Michael Palmore
Filippo Pagliani
Lionel Penisson
Ronan Phelan

Daniele Piano
Fabrizio Pierandrei
Dominique Rat
Milly Rossato
Susanna Scarabicchi
Stefan Schäfer
Kelly Shannon
Anne-Hélène Temenides
Vittorio Tolu
Bruno Tonfoni
Yoshiko Ueno
William Vassal
Florian Wenz
Hiroshi Yamaguchi

Co-ordination

Alberto Giordano

Education and publicity

François Bertolero
Daniela Capuzzo
Isabella Carpiceci
Carla Garbato
Noriko Takiguchi

Administration

Kathy Bassiere
Gianfranco Biggi
Philippe Goubet
Sonia Oldani
Michele Ras
Angela Sacco
Hélène Teboul
Alain Vincent

Secretaries

Rosella Biondo
Andrea Bosch
Stefania Canta
Sylvie Milanesi
Hiroko Nishikawa

232

Acknowledgements

The development of the Building Workshop since its birth nearly 30 years ago is due to the efforts of those listed below; a list that includes those who have either worked with us or with whom we have had a close association. The list does not include the many more people who have contributed in some other way to our efforts over the years. We take this opportunity to express our gratitude to all. Renzo Piano

Laurie Abbot
Maria Accardi
Peter Ackermann
Naderi Kamran Afshar
Emilia Agazzi
Alessandra Alborghetti
Michael Allevi
Michel Alluyn
Arianna Andidero
Sally Appleby
Andrea Arancio
Catherine Ardilley
Magda Arduino
P Audran
Veronique Auger
Frank August
Alexandre Autin
Carmela Avagliano
Patrizio Avellino
Rita Avvenente
Carlo Bachschmidt
Alessandro Badi
Emanuela Baglietto
Antonello Balassone
Nicolo Baldassini
François Barat
Henry Bardsley
Giulia Barone
Sonia Barone
Fabrizio Bartolomeo
Christopher Bartz
Bruno Bassetti
Kathy Bassiere
Sandro Battini
Roger Baumgarten
Paolo Beccio
Eva Belik
Annie Benzeno
Jan Berger
François Bertolero
Alessandro Bianchi
Giorgio G Bianchi
Gianfranco Biggi
Gregoire Bignier
Germana Binelli
Judy Bing
Rosella Biondo
Jean François Blassel
A Blassone
William Blurock
Paolo Bodega
Marko Bojovic
Sara Bonati
Manuela Bonino
Gilles Bontemps
Andrea Bosch
Pierre Botschi
Sandrine Boulay
Ross Brennan
Gaelle Breton
Maria Cristina Brizzolara
Cuno Brullmann
Michael Burckhardt
Hans-Peter Bysaeth

Alessandro Calafati
Patrick Callegia
Maurizio Calosso
Michele Calvi
Nunzio Camerada
Daniele Campo
Florence Canal
Andrea Canepa
Stefania Canta
Daniela Capuzzo
Alessandro Carisetto
Monica Carletti
Elena Carmignani
Isabella Carpiceci
Emanuele Carreri
Mark Carroll
Elena Casali
Marta Castagna
Cristiana Catino
Maria Cattaneo
Enrica Causa
Dante Cavagna
Simone Cecchi
Giorgio Celadon
Ottaviano Celadon
Alessandro Cereda
Antoine Chaaya
Patricia Chappell
Patrick Charles
Jean Luc Chassais
Hubert Chatenay
Pierre Chatelain
Ariel Chavela
Laura Cherchi
Raimondo Chessa
Christophe Chevalier
Catherine Clarisse
Geoffrey Cohen
Franc Collect
Daniel Collin
Giulio Contardo
Philippe Convercey
Pier Luigi Copat
Colman Corish
Monica Corsilia
Ivan Corte
Giacomo Costa
Raffaela Costa
Loïc Couton
Paolo Crema
Raffaella Belmondi Croce
A Croxato
Mario Cucinella
Irene Cuppone
Catherine Cussoneau
Lorenzo Custer
Stefano D'Atri
Catherine D'Ovidio
Isabelle Da Costa
Paul Darmer
Lorenzo Dasso
Mike Davies
Silvia De Leo
Simona De Mattei

Olaf de Nooyer
Daniela Defilla
S Degli Innocenti
Alessio Demontis
Julien Descombes
Michel Desvigne
Carmelo Di Bartolo
Ottavio Di Blasi
Brian Ditchburn
Maddalena Di Sopra
Vittorio Di Turi
Helene Diebold
John Doggart
Olivier Doizy
Eugenio Donato
François Doria
Michael Dowd
Mike Downs
Klaus Dreissigacker
Klaus Drouin
Frank Dubbers
Susan Dunne
Philippe Dupont
Susanne Durr
John Dutton
Mick Eekhout
Ahmed El Jerary
Alison Ewing
Roberta Fambri
Roberto Faravelli
Giorgio Fascioli
Maxwell Fawcett
David Felice
Alfonso Femia
Jacques Fendard
Agostino Ferrari
Maurizio Filocca
Laurent Marc Fischer
Richard Fitgerald
Eileen Fitzgerald
Peter Flack
Renato Foni
M Fordam
Gilles Fourel
Gianfranco Franchini
Kenneth Fraser
Nina Freedman
Marian Frezza
Enrico Frigerio
Junya Fujita
Rinaldo Gaggero
Alain Gallissian
Andrea Gallo
Carla Garbato
Robert Garlipp
G Gasbarri
Angelo Ghiotto
M Giacomelli
Davide Gibelli
Alain Gillette
Sonia Giordani
Alberto Giordano
Antonella Giovannoni
Marion Goerdt

Marco Goldschmied
Enrico Gollo
Anahita Golzari
Philippe Goubet
Francoise Gouinguenet
Robert Grace
Giorgio Grandi
Cecil Granger
Don Gray
Nigel Greenhill
Magali Grenier
Paolo Guerrini
Domenico Guerrisi
Alain Gueze
Barnaby Gunning
Greg Hall
Donald Hart
Thomas Hartman
Gunther Hastrich
Ulrike Hautsch
Christopher Hays
Eva Hegerl
Pierre Henneguier
Maìre Henry
Gabriel Hernandez
Caroline Herrin
Kohji Hirano
Harry Hirsch
Andrew Holmes
Eric Holt
Abigail Hopkins
Masahiro Horie
Helene Houizot
Jean Huc
Ed Huckabi
Frank Hughes
Filippo Icardi
Frediano Iezzi
Akira Ikegami
Djenina Illoul
Paolo Insogna
Shunji Ishida
Robert Jan van Santen
Angela Jackson
Tobias Jaklin
Amanda Johnson
Frederic Joubert
Jan Kaplicky
Elena Karitakis
Robert Keiser
Christopher Kelly
Paul Kelly
Werner Kestel
Irini Kilaiditi
Tetsuya Kimura
Laurent Koenig
Tomoko Komatsubara
Akira Komiyama
Betina Kurtz
Frank La Riviere
Jean Baptiste Lacoudre
Antonio Lagorio
Giovanna Langasco
Stig Larsen

Denis La Ville
François La Ville
Laurent Le Voyer
Jean Lelay
Renata Lello
Olivier Lidon
Bill Logan
Johanna Lohse
Federica Lombardo
François Lombardo
Steve Lopez
Riccardo Luccardini
Simonetta Lucci
Rolf Robert Ludwig
Claudine Luneberg
Massimiliano Lusetti
Paola Maggiora
Domenico Magnano
Nicholas Malby
Milena Mallamaci
Natalie Mallat
Claudio Manfreddo
Flavio Marano
Andrea Marasso
Francesco Marconi
Massimo Mariani
Alberto Marre Brunenghi
Cristina Martinelli
Daniele Mastragostino
Manuela Mattei
Marie Helene Maurette
Ken McBryde
Grainne McMahon
Simone Medio
Barbara Mehren
Roberto Melai
Mario Menzio
Eveline Mercier
Benny Merello
Peter Metz
Marcella Michelotti
Paolo Migone
Sylvie Milanesi
Emanuela Minetti
Edoardo Miola
Takeshi Miyazaki
Sandro Montaldo
Elisa Monti
Joost Moolhuijzen
Denise Morando Nascimento
Gerard Mormina
Ingrid Morris
Jean Bernard Mothes
Farshid Moussavi
Mariette Muller
Philip Murphy
Andrea Musso
Hanne Nagel
Shinichi Nakaya
Hiroshi Naruse
Roberto Navarra
Pascale Negre
Andrew Nichols
Hiroko Nishikama

Susanne Lore Nobis
David Nock
Marco Nouvion
Anna O'Carrol
Tim O'Sullivan
Alphons Oberhoffer
Stefan Oehler
Noriaki Okabe
Antonella Oldani
Sonia Oldani
Patrizia Orcamo
Stefania Orcamo
Roy Orengo
Carlos Osrej
Piero Ottaggio
Nedo Ottonello
Antonella Paci
Filippo Pagliani
Michael Palmore
Giorgia Paraluppi
Chandra Patel
Pietro Pedrini
Luigi Pellini
Danilo Peluffo
Gianluca Peluffo
Lionel Penisson
Mauro Penna
Patrizia Persia
Gil Petit
Ronan Phelan
Paul Phillips
Alberto Piancastelli
Carlo Piano
Daniele Piano
Lia Piano
Matteo Piano
Enrico Piazze
Gennaro Picardi
Alessandro Pierandrei
Fabrizio Pierandrei
Fabrizio Pietrasanta
Sandra Planchez
Bernard Plattner
Monica Poggi
Andrea Polleri
Roberta Possanzini
Fabio Postani
Nicolas Prouvé
Costanza Puglisi
Gianfranco Queirolo
Michele Ras
Maria Cristina Rasero
Dominique Rat
Neil Rawson
Judith Raymond
Antonella Recagno
Luis Renau
Tom Reynolds
Elena Ricciardi
Kieran Rice
Nemone Rice
Peter Rice
Jean Yves Richard
Gianni Robotti

Giuseppe Rocco
Richard Rogers
Renaud Rolland
Emilia Rossato
Bernard Rouyer
Lucio Ruocco
Ken Rupard
Antonella Sacchi
Angela Sacco
Saint Jean Gerard
Riccardo Sala
Maria Salerno
Maurizio Santini
Francesca Santolini
Paulo Sanza
Paul Satchell
Alessandro Savioli
Susanna Scarabicchi
Maria Grazia Scavo
Stefan Schafer
Helga Schlegel
Giuseppina Schmid
Jean Francois Schmit
Maren Schuessler
Andrea Schultz
Ronnie Self
Barbara-Petra Sellwig
Mario Semino
Patrik Senne
Anna Serra
Kelly Shannon
Randy Shields
Madoka Shimizu
Cecile Simon
Thibaud Simonin
Alessandro Sinagra
Luca Siracusa
Jan Sircus
Alan Smith
Stephanie Smith
Richard Soundy
Claudette Spielmann
Adrian Stadlmayer
Alan Stanton
David Summerfield
David Susstrunk
Jose Luis Taborda Barrientos
Hiroyuki Takahashi
Norio Takata
Noriko Takiguchi
Helene Teboul
Anne Helene Temenides
Carlo Teoldi
Peter Terbuchte
G L Terragna
David Thom
John Thornhill
Cinzia Tiberti
Luigi Tirelli
Elisabeth Tisseur
Vittorio Tolu
Taichi Tomuro
Bruno Tonfonni
Graciella Torre

Laura Torre
Olivier Touraine
Alessandro Traldi
Renata Trapani
Renzo Venanzio Truffelli
Leland Turner
Mark Turpin
Yoshiko Ueno
Kiyomi Uezono
Peter Ullathorne
Colette Valensi
Maurizio Vallino
Antonia Van Oosten
Michael Vaniscott
Maurizio Varratta
Paolo Varratta
Claudio Vaselli
William Vassal
Francesca Vattuone
Bernard Vaudeville
Martin Veith
Reiner Verbizh
Laura Vercelli
Maria Carla Verdona
Silvia Vignale
Antonella Vignoli
Mark Viktov
Alain Vincent
Paul Vincent
Patrick Virly
Marco Visconti
Louis Waddell
Jean Marc Weill
Florian Wenz
Nicolas Westphal
Chris Wilkinson
Neil Winder
Martin Wollensak
George Xydis
Masami Yamada
Sugako Yamada
Hiroshi Yamaguchi
Tatsuya Yamaguchi
Emi Yoshimura
John Young
Gianpaolo Zaccaria
Kenneth Endrich Zammit
Lorenzo Zamperetti
Antonio Zanuso
Martina Zappettini
Walter Zbinden
Maurizio Zepponi
Massimo Zero

233

234 **Select bibliography**

Books

Piano, R, Arduino, M, Fazio, M
Antico è Bello, Rome/Bari, Laterza, 1980

Donin, G *Renzo Piano, Piece by Piece,*
Rome, Casa del Libro Editrice, 1982

Dini, M *Renzo Piano, Projects and
Buildings 1964–1983,* London,
Electa/Architectural Press, 1984

Nono, L *Verso Prometeo,* Venice, La
Biennale/Ricordi Editori, 1984

Piano, R *Chantier Ouvert au Public,*
Paris, Arthaud Editeur, 1985

Piano, R *Dialoghi di Cantiere,* Bari,
Laterza Editrice, 1986

Piano, R and Rogers, R *Du Plateau
Beaubourg au Centre Georges Pompidou,*
Paris, Editions du Centre Georges
Pompidou, 1987

Renzo Piano, Il Nuovo Stadio di Bari
Milan, Edizione l'Archivolto, 1990

**Renzo Piano, Buildings and Projects
1971–89** New York, Rizzoli, 1990

**Exhibit Design: Renzo Piano Building
Workshop** Milan, Libra Immagine, 1992

Exhibition catalogues

**Renzo Piano: the process of
architecture** London, 9H Gallery, 1987

Renzo Piano Paris, Editions du Centre
Georges Pompidou, 1987

Renzo Piano Tokyo, Editions Delphi
Research, 1989

**Renzo Piano Building Workshop:
selected projects** P Buchanan, New
York, the Architectural League of New
York, 1992

Monographic issues of journals

AD Profiles No 2, 1977: *Centre Georges
Pompidou*

AA February 1982: *Renzo Piano
Monografia*

A+U No 3, 1989: *Renzo Piano Building
Workshop: 1964–1988* (includes article by
R Banham, 'Making architecture: the high
craft of Renzo Piano')

A&V No 23, 1990: *Renzo Piano Building
Workshop: 1980–1990* (includes the
following articles: 'The most beautiful craft
in the world: Renzo Piano and the passion
for building' by J Sainz; 'Between design
and engineering: technology at the service
of man' by P Buchanan; 'Desires and
prejudices: the frugality of an industrial
craftsman' by R Banham)

GB Progetti August–November 1990:
Crown Princess

GB Progetti May/June 1991: *Columbus
International Exposition*

Process Architecture January 1992:
*Renzo Piano Building Workshop:
1964–1991, in search of a balance*

Articles

1966
Arts and Architecture August 1966,
pp20–30: 'Structural plastics in Europe'
by Z S Makowski

1967
Domus March 1967, pp8–22: 'Ricerca
sulle strutture in lamiera e in poliestere
rinforzato'

1968
Domus November 1968, p6: 'Nuove
tecniche e nuove strutture per l'edilizia'

1969
Systems Buildings and Design
February 1969, pp37–54: 'Plastic
structures of Renzo Piano' by
Z S Makowski

Techniques et Architecture May
1969, pp96–100: 'Italie recherche de
structure' by R Piano

Domus October 1969, pp10–14:
'Uno studio–laboratorio'

1970

Architectural Design March 1970, pp140–145: 'Renzo Piano'

Architectural Forum March 1970, pp64–69: 'Rigging a roof'

Bauen + Wohnen April 1970, pp112–121: 'Structuren aus Kunstoff von Renzo Piano' by Z S Makowski

AA Quarterly July 1970, pp32–43: 'Architecture and technology' by R Piano

1971

Domus February 1971, pp12–15: 'Renzo Piano, per un'edilizia industrializzata'

Domus October 1971, pp1–7: 'Piano e Rogers: Beaubourg'

Industrial Design October 1971, pp40–45: 'Grand Piano'

AMC November 1971, pp8–9: 'Councours Beaubourg, "Est-ce un signe de notre temps?"' by M Cornu

1972

Techniques et Architecture February 1972, pp48–55: 'Projets des lauréats'

Casabella March 1972, pp00: 'Padiglione dell'industria Italiana all'Expo 70 di Osaka'

Domus June 1972, pp9–12: 'A Parigi, per i Parigini l'evoluzione del progetto Piano + Rogers per il Centre Beaubourg'

Deutsche Bauzeitung September 1972, p974–976: 'Paris Centre Beaubourg'

1973

Architecture d'Aujourd'hui July/August 1973, pp34–43: 'Centre Culturel du Plateau Beaubourg'

Domus August 1973: 'Centre Plateau Beaubourg'

Architecture d'Aujourd'hui November/December 1973, pp46–58: 'Piano + Rogers'

1974

Domus January 1974, pp31–36: 'Edifici per gli uffici B&B a Novedrate'

Architectural Design April 1974, pp245–246: 'B&B Italia factory'

Architecture Intérieure June/July 1974, pp72–77: 'Architecture et transparence'

Zodiac No22, pp126–147: 'Piano'

Architectural Review December 1974, pp338–345: 'Factory, Tadworth, Surrey'

1975

Domus April 1975, pp9–12: 'A Parigi musica underground'

Architectural Design May 1975, pp75–311: 'Piano + Rogers'

Acier. Stahl. Steel September 1975, pp297–309: 'Main structural framework of the Beaubourg Centre, Paris' by Peter Rice

Construction September 1975, pp5–30: 'Le Centre Georges Pompidou' by R Bordaz

1976

RIBA Journal February 1976, pp61–69: 'IRCAM design process'

A+U June 1976, pp63–122: 'Piano + Rogers: architectural method'

Architectural Design July 1976, 442–443: 'Beaubourg furniture internal system catalogue' by Piano & Rogers

1977

Domus January 1977, pp5–37: 'Centre National d'Art et de Culture Georges Pompidou'

RIBA Journal January 1977, pp11–16: 'Piano + Rogers'

Architecture d'Aujourd'hui February 1977, pp40–81: 'Le défi de Beaubourg'

Bauwelt March 1977, pp 316–334: 'Frankreichs Centre National d'Art et de Culture Georges Pompidou'

Bauen + Wohnen April 1977, pp132–139: 'Centre National d'Art et de Culture G Pompidou ein arbeitsbericht von zwei architekturestudenten' by J Bub and W Messing

Architectural Review May 1977, pp270–294: 'The pompidolium'

Domus May 1977, pp17–24: 'Piano & Rogers, 4 progetti'

GA No44, 1977, pp1–40: 'Centre Beaubourg: Piano + Rogers' by Y Futugawa

Domus October 1977, pp1–11: 'Parigi: l'oggetto funzional' by P Restany, C Casati

Werk–Archithese November/December 1977, pp22–29: 'Eiffel vs Beaubourg' by C Mitsia, M Zakazian and C Jacopin

Techniques et Architecture
December 1977, pp64–66: 'Ce diable Beaubourg' by M Cornu

1978

Domus June 1978, pp12–13: 'Tipologie evolutive'

Casabella September 1978, pp42–51: 'Esperienze di cantiere tre domande a R Piano'

AA October 1978, pp52–63: 'IRCAM'

1979

Abitare January/February 1979, pp2–21: 'Da uno spazio uguale due cose diversissime'

Architectural Review August 1979, pp120–123: 'Heimatlandschaft' by L Wright

Bauen + Wohnen September 1979, pp330–332: 'Mobiles-quartier laboratorium'

Abitare October 1979, pp86–93: 'Per il recupero dei centri storici. Una proposta: il laboratorio mobile di quartiere'

Spazio e Società December 1979, pp27–42: 'Piano Rice Associates il laboratorio di quartiere' by L Rossi

236

1980

Toshi Jutaku February 1980, pp14–23: 'Free–plan four house group' by Toshi Jutaku

Architects' Journal 30 April 1980, pp852–53: 'Technology, tools and tradition' by Peter Buchanan

Design July 1980, pp58: 'Fiat's magic carpet ride'

AA December 1980, pp51–54: 'La technolgia n'est pas toujours industrielle'

1981

AA February 1981, pp92–95: 'C G Pompidou'

Domus May 1981, pp27–29: 'Sul mestiere dell'architetto

Ottagono June 1981, pp20–27: 'Colloquio con R Piano' by P Santini

Building Design 31 July 1981 pp11–14: 'Pianoforte'

Architettura November 1981, pp614–662: 'Renzo Piano itineraio e un primo bilancio' by R Pedio

Casabella November/December 1981, pp95–96: 'Renzo Piano Genova'

1982

Abitare March 1982, pp8–9: ' Fiat vettura sperimentale e sottosistemi'

Cite August 1982, pp5–7: 'A clapboard treasure house' by S Fox

Building Design 20 August 1982, pp10–11: 'Renzo Piano: still in tune'

Architectural Review October 1982, pp57–61: 'Renzo Piano'

Casabella October 1982, pp14–23: 'Abitacolo e abitazione'

1983

Casabella April 1983 pp18–19: 'Parigi 1989' by P A Croset

Domus April 1983, pp10–15: 'La macchiina climatizzata'

Modulo June 1983, pp20–33: 'Taller de Barrio: colloqio con Renzo Piano y Gianfranco Dioguardi'

Techniques et Architecture June/July 1983, pp51–61: 'Des technologies nouvelles pour l'habitat ancien'

Architectural Review August 1983, pp26–31: 'Piano machine'

Archi–Crée September 1983, pp118–123: 'Schlumberger à Montrouge'

Casabella September 1983, pp34–36: 'L'allestimento di Renzo Piano per la mostra di Calder' by M Brandli

Moniteur September 1983, pp60–67: 'Un chantier experimental à Mountrouge' by J P Robert

Spazio e Società September 1983, pp50–62: 'La cultura del fare' by L Rossi

Building Design 23 September 1983, pp32–34: 'Piano's progress' by Martin Pawley

Architectural Review November 1983, pp68–73: 'Piano rehab'

Domus November 1983, pp56–59: 'Calder a Torino'

Techniques et Architecture November/December 1983, pp121–138: 'Artisan du futur' by R Piano

Architettura December 1983, pp888–894: 'Retrospettiva di Calder a Torino' by R Pedio

1984

Omni January 1984, pp112–115: 'R Piano: sub–systems automobile' by G R Palffy

Spazio e Società March 1984, pp66–69: 'R Piano: sub–systems automobile' by M Fazio

Building Design 18 May 1984, pp26–28: 'Lingotto Piano/Schein'

Architecture d'Aujourd'hui June 1984, pp14–23: 'Renovation du site industriel Schlumberger, Montrouge' by Y Pontoizeau

Abitare September 1984, pp4–6: 'Una mostra itinerante per far conoscere il computer'

Architecture d'Aujourd'hui October 1984, pp59–64: 'Projets & realisations' by Y Pontoizeau

Architectural Review November 1984, pp70–75: 'Arcadian machine'

Architettura November 1984, pp818–824: 'Exhibit IBM, padiglione itinerante di tecnologia informatica' by R Pedio

GA Document November 1984: 'L'expo IBM'

Architectural Review December 1984, pp53–57: 'Piano + Nono'

1985

SD January 1985, pp47–67: 'Renzo Piano and his methods'

Modulo March 1985, pp164–170: 'La grande nave lignea' by G Simonelli

Architectural Review May 1985, pp58–63: 'Piano pieces' by J Glancey

Techniques et Architecture May 1985, pp42–53: Restructuration d'un site industriel à Montrouge'

Forum No 29, 1985, pp138–144: 'The traps of technology' by P Buchanan

A+U June 1985, pp67–74: 'Music space for the opera "Prometeo" by L Nono' by R Piano, S Ishida

Archi–Crée August/September 1985, pp64–69: 'Natura, la revanche' by O Fillion

Casabella October 1985, pp26–29: La Schlumberger a Montrouge di Renzo Piano' by J P Robert

Techniques et Architecture October 1985, pp101–111: 'Entretiens avec Renzo Piano' by A Pelissier

Werk, Bauen + Wohnen November 1985, pp23–28: 'Kunstliches und Naturliches' by E Hubeli

Architecture d'Aujourd'hui December 1985, pp12–15: 'Des chantiers permanents'

GA December 1985, p84–99: 'Urban conversion of the Schlumberger factories' by N Okabe

1986

Architettura April 1986, pp246–253: 'Reazione spaziale di Renzo Piano negli uffici Lowara a Vicenza'

Werk, Bauen + Wohnen April 1986, pp4–9: 'Eine mobile oper und ein "quartierlabobor"'

Architecture d'Aujourd'hui September 1986, pp1–37: 'Piano de A à W' by D Mangin

Domus September 1986, pp29–37: 'Renzo Piano, progetto Lingotto a Torino' by M Pruisicki

Abitare October 1986, pp28–31: 'Progetto bambù' by F Zagari

Arca December 1986, pp28–35: 'Il museo de Menil a Houston' by O Boissiere

Progressive Architecture December 1986, pp25–33: 'Piano and Palladio, virtuoso duet' by D Smetana

1987

Moniteur January 1987, pp58–59: 'Le Synchrotron de Grenoble'

Architects' Journal 21 January 1987, pp20–21: 'Piano lessons'

Building Design 23 January 1987, pp14–15: 'Piano solo'

Architectural Review March 1987, pp32–59: 'Piano practice' by E M Farrelly

Architecture May 1987, pp84–91: 'Simplicity of form, ingenuity in the use of daylight'

Progressive Architecture May 1987, pp87–97: 'The responsive box' by P Papadanmetriou

Texas Architecture May/June 1987, pp40–47: 'Pianissimo, the very quiet Menil Collection' by R Ingersoll

Art in America June 1987, pp124–129: 'In the neighborhood of art', Reyner Banham (reprinted in *A+U*, November 1987)

Casabella June 1987, pp54–63: Renzo Piano, lo stadio di Bari e il Sincrotone di Grenoble'

Domus July/August 1987, pp32–43: 'Renzo Piano, Museo Menil, Houston' by E Ranzani

Architectural Review September 1987, pp70–80: 'The quiet game'

Ottagono September 1987, pp48–53: 'Piano: la basilica Palladiana non si tocca' by G K Koenig

Techniques et Architecture October/November 1987, pp146–165: 'Renzo Piano: la métamorphose de la technologie' by J F Pousse

A+U November 1987, pp39–122: 'Renzo Piano', Reyner Banham and Shunji Ishida

Domus November 1987, pp17–24: 'Renzo Piano: sovversione, silenzio e normalita' by V M Lampungani and E Ranzani

RIBA Journal November 1987, pp28–35: 'Piano's entente cordiale' by S Heck

SD November 1987, pp48–50: 'The Menil Art Museum' by Shunji Ishida

Baumeister December 1987, pp36–41: 'Sammlung in Houston'

Werk, Bauen + Wohnen December 1987, pp30–39: 'Konstructinen für das Licht'

1988

Abitare January 1988, pp192–197: 'Destinazione museo' by F Irace

Detail May/June 1988, pp285–290: 'Menil Collection Museum in Houston, Texas'

1989

Spazio e Società January–March 1989, pp104–106: 'Quale Piano e per chi?' by R Radicioni

Building Design 20 January 1989, pp26–28: 'Flying high' by G Picardi

Architecture d'Aujourd'hui February 1989, pp42–53: 'L'Aéroport du Kansai à Osaka' by M Champenois

Techniques et Architecture February 1989, pp65–68: 'Kansai: le course contre le temps' by A Pelissier

Architectural Review March 1989, pp4–9: 'Piano's Lingotto' by Peter Davey

Architectural Design March/April 1989, pp52–61: 'Kansai International Airport'

Architectural Review April 1989, pp84–88: 'Piano quays, Osaka airport' by D Ghirardo

Architecture d'Aujourd'hui April 1989, pp50–54: 'Musée d'art moderne à Newport' and 'Ensemble touristique dans la baie de Sistiana' by M Desvigne

Blueprint April 1989, pp52–54: 'Italy's Brunel' by A Nahum

World Architecture April 1989, pp72–77: 'Piano plays nature's theme'

Domus May 1989, pp34–39: 'Il concorso per l'aeroporto internazionale di Kansai' by V Magnano Lampugnani

238 **Building Design** 22 September 1989, pp20–21: 'A gate for Malta'

Architectural Review October 1989, pp60–75: 'Piano quartet' by Colin Davies

Techniques et Architecture
October/November 1989, pp114–119 and pp120–123: 'Raison de forme centre commercial de Bercy 2 à Charenton–le–Pont, and extension de l' IRCAM, Paris' by J F Pousse

Domus December 1989, pp14–16: 'Renzo Piano: allestimento al Lingotto' by E Ranzani

1990
Domus January 1990, pp76–79: 'Renzo Piano: libreria, Teso, Fontana Arte' by O di Blasi

Domus February 1990, pp38–47: 'Ampliamento dell' IRCAM a Parigi' by E Ranzani

Moniteur February 1990, pp76–79: 'Une usine modulaire en forêt'

Domus May 1990, pp33–39: 'Renzo Piano, stadio di calcio e atletica leggera, Bari' by E Ranzani

Moniteur June 1990, pp32–39: 'Le Stade de Bari'

Architectural Review September 1990, pp71–73: 'Soft shore'

Werk, Bauen + Wohnen September 1990, pp22–29: 'Ort und stadium'

Arup Journal Autumn 1990, pp3–8: 'The San Nicola stadium'

Techniques et Architecture
December 1990/January 1991, pp44–49: 'Le Grande souffle: stade de carbonara, Bari, Italie'

1991
GA Document March 1991, pp60–95: 'Renzo Piano Building Workshop' by S Ishida and N Okabe

Architectural Review May 1991, pp83–90: 'Eastern promise'

Moniteur June 1990, pp51–61: 'Détail: Renzo Piano facades en briques et composite'

Domus May 1991, pp44–71: 'La transformazione delle città: Genova' by E Ranzani

Architectural Review July 1991, pp59–63: 'French connection'

Techniques et Architecture July 1991, pp38–47: 'Côte jardin'

Domus July/August 1991, pp27–39: 'Complesso residenziale a Parigi'

1992
Architectural Review January 1992, pp56–57: 'Piano's magic carpet' by P Buchanan

Abitare March 1992, pp229–234: 'Renzo Piano, aeroporto Kansai'

De Architect March 1992, pp60–65: 'Kansai International Airport'

Progressive Architecture April 1992, pp94–95: 'The place of sports'

A+U July 1992, pp70–114: 'Renzo Piano Building Workshop: shopping centre Bercy; Bari soccer stadium; subway station, Genoa' by R Ingersoll and S Ishida

Architecture d'Aujourd'hui October 1992, pp92–97: 'Deux étoiles Italiennes' by J C Garcias

Recent articles relating to work that will be published in succeeding volumes are generally omitted from this bibliography. They will appear in the bibliographies of the relevant future volumes.

239

240 **Photographic credits**

Archive Centre Pompidou
Archive Schlumberger Montrouge
Graziano Arici
Patrick Astier
Richard Bryant/Arcaid
Peter Buchanan
Martin Charles
Peter Cook/Arcaid
David Crossley
Michel Denancé
Fiat Archive
Gianno Berengo Gardin
Stefano Goldberg
Paul Hester
Alaistair Hunter
Shunji Ishida
Robert Jan van Santen
Philippe Migeat
Emanuela Minetti
Publifoto
Danielle Quesney
Marc Riboud
Hickey Robertson
Fulvio Roiter
Deidi von Schaewen
Chicco Trivellato
GL Trivellato
Mauro Vallinotto
Bernard Vincent

The drawings of the IBM Travelling Pavilion
shown on pages 118–9 are by Kurt Ackermann
and were first published in *Tragwerke in der
Konstrucktiven Architekture*

The publisher and Renzo Piano Building
Workshop wish to thank the Menil Collection for
permission to illustrate the gallery's exhibits